To Fire Committed

The History of Fire Fighting in Kent

For the successful performance of his duty a fireman must value his profession greater than glory, and have a devotion that rises above material reward. In not underrating the power and danger of fire he must face it with courage.

Above all he must encourage and practise that spirit of good comradeship based on mutual trust and understanding which binds men of his calling the world over and to whom this book is dedicated.

To Fire Committed

The History of Fire Fighting in Kent

by

Harry Klopper

Published in 1984 by
The Kent Council of the Fire Services National Benevolent Fund
© Harry Klopper 1984
Hardback ISBN 0 9509816 05
Softback ISBN 0 9509816 13

By the same author
The Fight against Fire
First Signatures

Printed by The Whitefriars Press Limited, Tonbridge, Kent.

Foreword

For over 30 years now it has been my privilege to work in close co-operation with the fire services of this country and especially with officers and men of the Kent County Fire Brigade, the protectors of the County in which I have lived for so many years. I have met them at work, at huge fires, at disasters and at rescue operations; I have met them on or off duty, in their stations and homes; I have watched them train and I have taken part in their social activities.

Always I had to admire their courage and endurance, their helpfulness and good comradeship, and their unlimited cheerfulness in the face of great hazards and strains. I therefore find it a great satisfaction to have been entrusted with the recording of the history of fire-fighting in Kent – a story full of valour and service to the community, spanning more than 13 centuries.

It would have been impossible for me to do so without the generous help I have received from so many people – so many that it would be quite impossible to mention them all individually.

I am most grateful to Mr R. D. H. Doyle C.B.E., until June of this year Chief Fire Officer of the Kent Brigade, and to Major J. L. Thomas, Chairman of the Kent Fire and Public Protection Committee, for making the publication of this book possible at all; to Chief Officer Gary Whitworth, who took over command of the Brigade from Mr Doyle; to the senior officers and secretarial staff at Brigade headquarters for their unfailing co-operation and technical advice and for looking after the 1,001 administrative details which would have confounded me, and to all those who had to shoulder a lot of extra work on my behalf.

I am especially grateful to the memory of Mr Jimmy Clifton, who sadly died last year, shortly before I started writing this book. Jimmy, as he was affectionately known, transferred as an administrative officer on the formation of the Brigade in 1948, and during that time he developed the Kent Fire Brigade Museum from small beginnings into one of the finest in the country. The items and documents Jimmy Clifton had collected, mostly in his spare time, from every corner of Kent, and indeed from the rest of the country, enabled me to write this book.

Let me thank Jill Levick, my personal assistant during the whole period of writing this book without whose unfailing patience, humour and hard work, it would have been impossible for me to complete this task successfully.

My thanks are also due to Mr Howard Crawley who read and corrected my manuscript and without whose advice, this book would have been the poorer. Last, but by no means least, my thanks go to the many ex-firemen and fire-women, as well as private citizens who responded to my appeal for material; and to my many friends in the County's fire stations who have for so long responded patiently to my many requests.

Harry Klopper.

Kent Fire Brigade Headquarters,
June, 1984.

Contents

PART I Early Days 600–1800

PART II Insurance Brigades and Volunteers 1801–1935

PART III The War, AFS and NFS 1936–1947

PART IV Kent County Fire Brigade 1948 to the present

Mr Reginald Doyle, C.B.E., Chief Fire Officer, Kent Fire Brigade 1977–1984.

Chief Fire Officer Gary Whitworth, F.I.Fire E., Kent Fire Brigade 1984–.

Major J. L. Thomas is Chairman of the Kent County Council Fire and Public Protection Committee, to which he was elected in 1979. Commissioned from the Royal Military Academy Sandhurst in 1952, Major Thomas saw service in many parts of the world including active service in the Far East.

Introduction

From the day in our earliest history, when man learned to strike two stones together and produce a spark, fires must have occurred. Even earlier, lightning struck the impenetrable forests that covered much of Britain and especially Kent; trees were set on fire and vast tracts were consumed by the unstoppable flames. Only gradually did man learn to tame fire for his own uses; but still at times fearing it as his worst enemy, while worshipping it as his God. Fire was the very essence of life and yet its destroyer. Man learned to make simple tools and weapons but for centuries he found no answer to the flames which destroyed his simple dwellings, his fields and forests, and his very life.

Long after man had mastered the various arts that made life more pleasant, even safer, long after he had begun to weave intricate cloths, build fine houses, print books, find some answers to diseases, he was still helpless in the face of fire which, in a few short hours, destroyed what it had taken years to create. Quick to organise for war and destruction, clever in the forging of weapons, man's only defences against fire were a few buckets of water, a pole with an iron hook on the top and headlong flight.

Kent was the first County to be surveyed for the Domesday Book which recorded 500 manors and churches within its boundaries. Her coast line was open to raids by the Danes and there is a recording in Bede's of a disastrous fire at Canterbury in the early 7th century which was stopped – miraculously – by Archbishop Mellittus. Unfortunately miracle workers were not always at hand, and with houses and other buildings mainly constructed of wood and thatch, with narrow streets, and the extensive use of naked flame for lighting, heating and cooking, fire risk to life and property was terrific. Once a fire started it got quickly out of hand, flying brands setting alight roofs and beams, and flames from burning buildings often joining up to form conflagrations which consumed whole streets, villages and towns.

Many lives were lost, cattle were burned to death, crops lost, and thousands of pounds worth of damage – an enormous amount in those days – was done to property. Until the beginning of the 16th century there was very little indeed that could be put into the path of the roaring flames. 'Leathorn buckets', hooks, wooden hand squirts and syringes, and in conflagrations, kegs of powder to blow up buildings and create fire breaks were the only help at hand. It is interesting to note that one of the first ordinances of William the Conqueror was a law requiring all house fires to be extinguished at night-fall, the origin of curfew. In those days, Kent, the principal gateway to England, with its vast forests, its coal, its agriculture and famous ports and towns, was as unprotected from fire as was the rest of the country – which had forgotten the quite effective fire protection which existed in the County in Roman times, with water pumps, fire-watchers (vigilantes), and strict fire laws.

It was not until the first half of the 17th century that the first primitive fire engines, made of wood and operated by four or five men, appeared. At about the same time, wooden water mains made from hollowed-out elm trees were laid in some towns.

While the country, and with it Kent, made very little progress in the fight against fire, an event occurred which forced new efforts on Government and citizens alike. The Great Fire of London in 1666 – incidentally not the biggest, although the most famous, there having been at least two others in previous centuries – brought about a flurry of activities resulting in new inventions, new organisations and new laws. In the 1670's sewn-leather fire-hose was invented; the wooden manual engines were improved; and in 1690 the first Fire Insurance Company was started in London. However, it took more than a century before the Kent Fire Insurance was started in 1802 in Maidstone. In the same year the Hythe Volunteer Fire Brigade was formed – the oldest in the County – and in 1824 the Ashford Fire Engine Association was incorporated.

The insurance brigades provided fire cover for many years to come, but more and more local volunteer brigades sprung up all over Kent, in towns and villages alike. Their equipment was often basic, their enthusiasm great and their courage beyond question. Many a volunteer died or was maimed in the service of the community. By 1829 the first steam fire engine had been built in London; a year later a practical breathing apparatus was invented in France; by the 1850's canvas hose had started to supersede the heavy and cumbersome leather hose, and in 1895 the first petrol motor fire pump, a Daimler, was demonstrated at Tunbridge Wells. By 1902 the first turntable ladder had been built in Germany and a new era of municipal, volunteer and parish fire brigades began in Kent. These lasted until the beginning of the war, the setting up of the Auxiliary Fire Service and the nationalisation of the Service in 1941. With the end of the National Fire Service in 1948 came the creation of the Kent Fire Brigade as we know it today – a Service of men and women, full-time and part-time who, like their predecessors in the old volunteer associations, and like those who fought and died in the Blitz, are always ready to help, to save lives and property, and to risk life and injury in the service of the people of Kent. They are TO FIRE COMMITTED.

But now let us again begin at the beginning . . .

Part I

Early Days 600–1800

Fig. 1. Hose cart, circa 1600, from Canterbury Cathedral.

Fig. 2. Four-man manual fire engine, early 1700s, from Lullingstone Castle.

Fig. 3. Manual fire engine, 1773, from town of Sandwich.

Fig. 4. Horse-drawn fire engine, 1890, Lydd Fire Brigade.

The ancient city of Canterbury, famous throughout the world, was the scene of the earliest recorded urban fire in Kent. In the early 7th century the population, mainly living in hutments and hovels made from and containing highly flammable materials, were not only defenceless against the ravages of fires, but were also often the victims of fire raids by the Danes. Gradually Christianity spread its influence and people began to turn to their local churches in times of disaster. Miracles were expected and sometimes seemed to occur but the churches' usual fire-fighting operations were restricted to carrying relics and bones of saints around the burning buildings and to ringing the church bells. The bell ringing had at least a practical effect because it warned people that fire had broken out, and they would run to the scene to see what they could do to help.

As already mentioned, it was in 624 that Archbishop Mellitus appeared to have had some success in saving most of Canterbury from destruction. In his history, Bede gives a graphic description of that fire. "The great fire reached the church of the Four Crowned Martyrs, the casting of water would not stop it and it came rushing towards the Cathedral. Archbishop Mellitus, suffering from gout, had himself carried there, and flaming with divine love and sanctity, prayed, whereupon the wind miraculously changed and blew the fire away". Little had been recorded about fires in the City for the next 500 years, but outbreaks must have been frequent and destructive in the narrow, congested streets with their closely-packed thatched shops and dwellings. It was in 1174 that fire spread from such a house to the nearby Canterbury Cathedral, destroying the whole of its choir and damaging much of the rest. Appalled by the disaster, the monks decided to remove all the shops near the Cathedral and offered the owners new premises at a safe distance. This action may well have saved the Cathedral which was untouched when a disastrous fire devastated most of the town in 1198.

At a time when fire-fighting relied on the most primitive tools of water buckets and long-handled hooks, the little port of Sandwich seems to have been one of the first in the County to try to organise a more rational way of dealing with fire. In the 'Customal of Sandwich', published in 1301, there is a reference to fire protection. "Also in dry weather, the Common Sargeant should see that every person has a tub of water at his front door for fear of fire. And if any person refuses to place one there, or being warned by the Sargeant shall neglect to appear at the nightly watch by himself, or a substitute, the Sargeant shall take a distress to the value of one and twenty pence, and carry the same to the Mayor, there to be detained till the money be paid, unless the Corporation pleases to favour the delinquent. He is also to take care that no boats lie in the creeks leading from the gates of the town to the haven longer than one complete tide, in order that there may be ready access to the water in case of fire".

Nearly 300 years later, the first organised fire precautions in Maidstone could be found in the Borough Burghmote Book. This laid down in 1591 that "all inhabitants were to be assessed for the buying of chains, buckets and hooks for the better defence of the town against any sudden fire".

Fire-fighting in the County, such as it was, was organised by a parochial body known as the Vestry, which appointed Parish Overseers whose duties included the care of the aged and poor, and the fighting of fires. One of the earliest recorded appointments of Overseers was in the parish of Cranbrook in 1601. One year later in 1602, the Mayor and Corporation of the town and port of Faversham recorded in their Wardmote Book an Act for leathern buckets and latchers that "forasmuch as diverse houses of late days situate within the liberty of the town have been blasted with fire and burned down to the impoverishment of the inhabitant tenants and their landlords and to the endangering of the houses and household stuff of their neighbours and no sufficient provision within the same town in such cases to be used heretofore . . . therefore for the common good of each inhabitant within the liberty of the same town in such dangerous times, be it enacted, established and provided that the Mayor and Jurats now being shall provide and but 2 leathern buckets, containing 2 gallons at least apiece, and that every Commoner and every other inhabitant being thought a person of ability shall likewise provide and have 1 leathern bucket containing 2 gallons at least, and the same leathern bucket shall cause to be hanged in some place of their dwelling houses where they may be best found and readily set in time of such necessity. Every man shall have his proper name or mark painted upon the same bucket for the better knowing and finding of them after the fire quenched, and that the Common Crier of the town immediately after the fire quenched, shall upon pain and forfeiture of his office and imprisonment, seek out and gather together all the buckets of the inhabitants that shall be used in and about the quenching of the fire, so that everyone may come by his own again. Such person or persons that do not provide such buckets of leather contrary to this Order shall forfeit to the Mayor, Jurats and Commonealty of Faversham the sum of 6 shillings and 8 pence for every bucket so lacking, and that every person not paying the forfeitures shall be committed to prison until they have paid the forfeiture and provided a bucket according to the Order. The said forfeitures of 6 shillings and 8 pence to be employed towards the buying and providing of leathern buckets and other provisions for fire within the foresaid town. It is further enacted that the Chamberlains of the town from time to time shall at the common charge buy and provide 2 great broad long latchers of fir poles with hooks, chains and ringles of iron such as are the cities of London and Canterbury, and in the town of Maidstone to be used in time of distresses of fire, and shall be hanged in the Market House under the Court Hall, there to be in readiness when any need shall happen in suchlike cases".

For many years the buckets, hooks and latchers (ladders) were the only defence the people of Kent could throw against the flames that devoured their homes and farms. Gradually during the 1670's crude wooden manual fire engines were introduced, but they were badly housed, had untrained handlers and very poor pumping power with a pulsating flow of water. Each time a fire occurred, these manual pumps had to be dragged there by volunteers over 'foul and dangerous' roads, and in wet weather the pumps often got stuck in the mud and ruts. No escapes for saving lives existed and anyone trapped by fire had to rely on rescue attempts by courageous neighbours or jump to safety from the windows or roofs. This situation makes a striking contrast with present day practice when the first and foremost duty of the Brigade is to save lives.

The Great Fire of London in 1666 provided the impetus throughout the nation to think again seriously about fire precautions and fire-fighting. Not only in Britain, but also in Europe (where similar conflagrations practically destroyed whole cities), the authorities and inventors got to work to try to minimise these tragedies. For a time Holland was in the forefront; and in 1670 a Dutchman invented a wooden manual fire engine with flexible hose and to complement this, another Dutchman invented a sewn-leather hose to replace the old, copper-riveted one. In 1690, a Dr Nicholas Barbon started the first fire insurance company – the Phoenix – in London, and opened the way for the start of the fire insurance brigades which became such an important feature of the fight against fire for over a century.

Gradually fire precautions, still crude and basic, began to improve. In 1700 a fire-engine was presented to the town of Dover by the then Mayor and was used for the first time in August of the same year to extinguish a conflagration. This engine survived until 1751 and a man was paid 10 shillings a year for 'oiling' its pipes. In 1715, the corporation of Dover made a ruling, charging that "all persons admitted as freemen should in future provide a bucket to be put in the Court Hall for the Corporations use in case of fire".

Rochester too, seems to have realised the need for adequate fire protection, for already in 1709 their records show that the Corporation "ordered their two sargeants at Mace to be principal Mace to the two fire engines of the City and that each be paid 20 shillings a year for which they shall manage and play the said engines upon all accidents of fire". By 1735, Rochester seemed to have had already three pumps, and one Edmund Greer agreed with the Mayor and citizens to keep them in "good and sufficient repair and to play the engines belonging to the City four times a year at least and keep them in order for £3 a year". In 1741, another fire engine was presented to Rochester by its Mayor. This gift

5

seems to have been mainly for the private protection of His Worship, because he stipulated that "the fire engine shall stand in such places of the City as Mr Mayor and his family shall from time to time direct". A step forward in the large, ineffective manual pumps came in 1721, when Richard Newsham patented a fire engine incorporating an air vessel in its mechanism which enabled it to throw a constant uninterrupted jet of water.

In the early part of the 18th century, Gravesend, a pleasant and picturesque little port and watering-place, was devastated by a conflagration which almost put an end to the town as a habitable place. Nor was it the only disaster for the town – on at least three other occasions during the next 100 years, Gravesend was again almost razed to the ground and its history of serious fires continued almost to the present day. The first 'Great Fire of Gravesend' broke out at 11 o'clock on the night of August 24th 1727, in a barnyard adjoining the churchyard. When it finally had burnt itself out, 120 houses, besides stables, shops, pubs, out-houses and barns, had been destroyed (a letter to a London newspaper claimed at least 250 buildings destroyed); and the damage was unofficially estimated at £200,000, an amount that would nowadays be reckoned in hundreds of millions of pounds. The people of Gravesend were ill provided for such a visitation by fire. The only engine in the town was unfit for service having not even been played in practice for three years. Nor would a single manual pump have made the slightest impact on such a conflagration.

At the time of the fire a Dr Thorpe, an eminent antiquary and author, was visiting the town and gave this eye-witness account of the disaster. "The fire's destructive progress burnt down all the houses on Gravesend side from Mr Bishop's adjoining the Katherine Wheel; all the houses in the High Street to the Chequer's Corner and thence on both sides of the way in the West Street, from the Christopher Corner to the Red Lion Brew House and was then stopped by blowing up the Unicorn. The Parish Church was also entirely destroyed and on Milton side it burnt the prison adjoining the market, all the inns and houses in the High Street to the Town Quay and thence on both sides of the way in East Street to the Brigantine and was stopped there by blowing up the Rose". More major fires, but not as destructive as the outbreak in 1727, happened in Gravesend in 1731, 1748, 1779 and 1801. The first mention of a fire-fighting appliance in Dartford was in 1740 when a manual, similar in design to that invented by Robert Newsham, was in use in the town. The cost of cleaning and maintaining this engine was the responsibility of the church-wardens.

When the parishioners of Sittingbourne lost their beloved church in a disastrous fire in July 1762, they decided to petition the King and the Lord High Chancellor to help them to collect the then enormous sum of £2,250 to rebuild their church. Their petition, which is in the County Archives, is here reproduced in full.

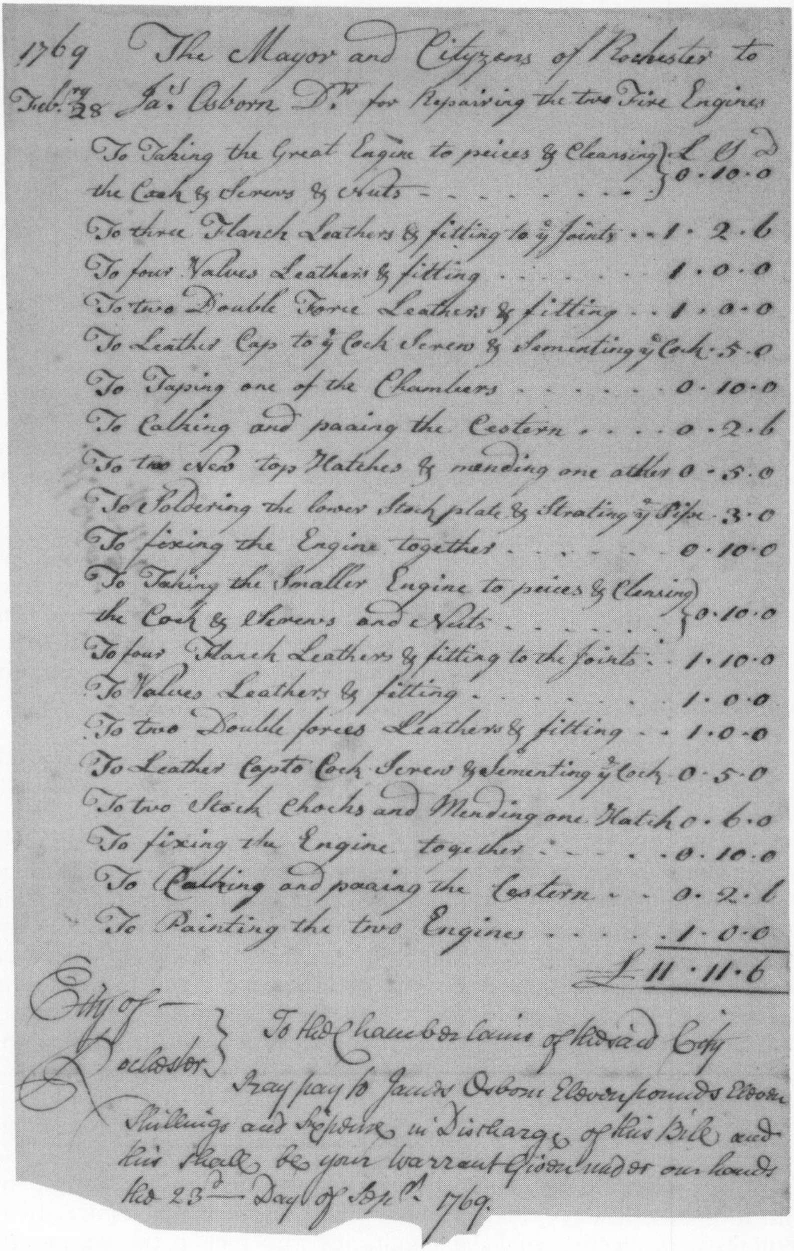

1769   The Mayor and Cityzens of Rochester to
Feb.ry 28   Jas Osborn Dr for Repairing the two Fire Engines

	£	s	d
To Taking the Great Engine to peices & Cleansing the Cock & Screws & Nuts — . . . . }	0	10	0
To three Flanch Leathers & fitting to ye joints . .	1	2	6
To four Valves Leathers & fitting	1	0	0
To two Double Force Leathers & fitting . .	1	0	0
To Leather Caps to ye Cock Screw & Cementing ye Cock		5	0
To Tapping one of the Chambers	0	10	0
To Calking and paaing the Cestern . . .	0	2	6
To two New tops Hatches & mending one other	0	5	0
To Soldering the lower Stank plate & Strating ye Pipe		3	0
To fixing the Engine together	0	10	0
To Taking the Smaller Engine to peices & Cleansing the Cock & Screws and Nuts . . . . . . }	0	10	0
To four Flanch Leathers & fitting to the joints .	1	10	0
To Valves Leathers & fitting	1	0	0
To two Double forces Leathers & fitting . .	1	0	0
To Leather Caps to Cock Screw & Cementing ye Cock	0	5	0
To two Stank chocks and Mending one Hatch	0	6	0
To fixing the Engine together	0	10	0
To Calking and paaing the Cestern . .	0	2	6
To Painting the two Engines	1	0	0
	£ 11	11	6

City of
Rochester }   To the Chamberlains of the said City

Pray pay to James Osborn Eleven pounds Eleven Shillings and Sixpence in Discharge of this Bill and this shall be your warrant Given under our hands the 23d Day of Septr 1769.

Fig. 5. A bill for £11.11.6 for the repair to two Rochester fire engines, dated Sept. 1769.

7

"11 January 1763.

The humble petition of the Minister, Churchwardens and principal inhabitants of the town and parish of Sittingbourne in the said County whose names are hereunto subscribed.

SHEWETH that on Saturday, the Seventeenth day of July last between the hours of twelve and one of the clock of the same day a most sudden and dreadful fire happened in the said church through the carelessness of plumbers employed in repairing the lead work thereon which raged so furiously that in the space of two hours or a little more entirely burnt down and consumed the same with the various ornaments therein, together with the Church Chest wherein were deposited the Ancient Rate Books, Wills of Benefaction and other records and all the Paupers Certificates, nothing being left standing of that spacious building but the steeple tower (which with the bells were with the utmost difficulty preserved) and some of the outside walls, so that the numerous inhabitants are not destitute of a place in which to meet for the public worship of Almighty God.

THAT the charges of rebuilding the same (exclusive of the Parsonage Chancel) and defraying all incidental expenses occasioned by such fire, together with the necessary repairs of to the said church steeple and walls, after deducting £6.10s. for damaged timber sold, upon a very modest computation and estimate amounts to the sum of £2,250 which your Petitioners are now to your Worships on the offers of several able and experienced surveyors who have carefully examined and estimated the same.

THAT your Petitioners being burdened by numerous poor and the annual charges to maintain them being very great they are not of themselves capable of raising such sum to rebuild their said Church.

YOUR PETITIONERS therefore humbly prayeth that your Worships will please to certify to the Right Honourable the Lord High Chancellor of Great Britain the condition of your Petitioners and other inhabitants of the said Parish thereby recommending them to His Lordship's consideration that his Lordship will be pleased to grant them His Majesty's most gracious Letters Patent under the Great Seal of Great Britain to authorise them to ask and receive charitable contributions of all his loving subjects towards enabling them to rebuild there said Parish Church.

AND your Petitioners shall ever pray etc.

Thomas Bland, Vicar"

In 1769, when Bexley Heath was still mainly inhabited by highwaymen and footpads, Bexley Village already had a kind of fire service. In the minutes of a meeting of local dignitaries who met in the vestry of St Mary's Church is an item referring to the purchase of two fire hooks and a ladder of 36 rungs; and a leather helmet inscribed 1769 is still in the possession of the local council. Responsible for this equipment was the parish beadle, who drew a quarterly wage of £3 15s, a very high remuneration for those days, and further proof of how keen the citizens of Bexley were on their fire protection. In 1776 they added one of the new Newsham manual pumps to their arsenal.

The early history of fire-fighting in Tunbridge Wells is shrouded in mist, but although by the middle of the 19th century the town had a volunteer brigade and, most unusual for the times, a Salvage Corps, there must already have been great consciousness of what fire could do to life and property in the 1790's. A stone plaque was dug up in 1898 on the land of the Marquis of Abergavenny and when cleaned, showed the words, partly engraved in old English letters: "By subscription by inhabitants of Tunbridge Wells. Fire Engine 1794". This plaque was first attached to the old Tunbridge Wells Fire Station in Calverley Street and was later incorporated in the wall of the present station in Grove Hill Road.

The new century brought disaster to Chatham. The first great fire of the town happened in June 1800. It destroyed nearly 100 dwellings, 13 warehouses, the famous Chatham House and Best's Brewery. Several lives were lost in the inferno, many townspeople were injured and damage caused was over £30,000. Immediately following the disaster, a Committee was set up by the Gentlemen of the town to "collect moneys for the relief of the sufferers" and in 1801, an account of the fire and the subscription was published by William Jefferys, Treasurer to the Committee. This document is of such interest that sections of it are given here in the author's own words.

"AN ACCOUNT OF THE FIRE, &c.

On Monday the 30th June, 1800, about eleven o'clock in the forenoon, the shed or building [on the river bank], in which was deposited a great quantity of cordage, oakum, &c., was discovered to be on fire. The fire commenced with such amazing and irresistible fury, that the shed in which it took place, with the forge and warehouses adjoining, and a hoy with her masts and sails, that lay unlading close to the side of the wharf, formed in a few minutes one general blaze. The wharfinger, and men employed on the wharf, in endeavouring to extinguish the fire, exposed themselves to great danger, and were scarcely able to effect their escape.

Many causes conspired to extend the conflagration; the shed in which it began, was full of combustible matter, viz. cordage, hemp and oakum, the building itself, and most of those adjoining, were of wood, some of them had been recently tarred and ochered, and the whole were rendered extremely susceptible of fire from the long drought, and heat that had preceded it.

In the space of three hours, the several houses, buildings, &c. were either wholly destroyed, pulled down or damaged, and their unfortunate occupiers, being above one hundred persons with their families, bereft of their homes; and the greater part of them rendered destitute of all means speedily to obtain others. The adjoining gardens, road, fields, &c. were the only immediate places of safety to which they could fly, and these places contained the remnant of their apparel and furniture, which, in many instances, at the imminent hazard of their lives, they had snatched from the ravages of the merciless flames.

Unfortunately this dreadful scene commenced about an hour before the ebb of the tide, which prevented the removal of the hoy, and occasioned her loss, and rendered it very difficult to procure a sufficient supply of water for the engines; this with the other circumstances above stated, are the principal causes of the conflagration extending itself so widely.

The exertions which were made to extinguish the flames, can scarcely be described. The inhabitants of the town and neighbourhood, seemed to vie with each other as to who should do most to assist the unhappy and distressed sufferers in the removal of their effects, and in the prevention of their houses from being consumed, and in so doing, exposed themselves to the most severe fatigue and imminent dangers. The Commissioner of Chatham Yard (F. J. Hartwell, Esq.) immediately gave all the workmen employed there, liberty to leave their work, to assist at the fire, and had them supplied with proper implements for pulling down houses, &c. He also sent the Dock Yard engines, and (by the Dock teams) a large supply of water in butts. The Commandants of the Barracks at Chatham (Major General Hewett and Major General Innis) sent large bodies of troops to assist in the removal of goods, and the extinguishment of the flames, and also guards to protect the goods taken into the fields, &c. The Agent Victualler at Chatham (Joseph Mathews, Esq.) also sent the men employed in his department, the engines kept at the Victualling Office, and a large supply of water in butts. The gentlemen of the several breweries in the town and neighbourhood, sent very large supplies of water and small beer, and kept their teams employed in that service, during the whole continuance of the fire. The assistance of all these gentlemen, (as well of those in public, as of those in private stations.) was rendered unsolicited, and with a zeal and alacrity, that reflects the highest honor on their character, and entitles them to the gratitude of the public.

By the united endeavours of all, and the merciful interference of Providence, the flames were at length extinguished, where it least could be expected; for the buildings at the East end of the ruin on the North side of the street, and at the West end of the ruin on the South side of the street, where the fire ceased, were chiefly of timber covered with weather boarding.

Fortunately the wind was moderate at the time the fire happened;

during the conflagration, it veered from the East and South to the West.

The strength of the fire was so great, that on the falling in of the houses, large flakes of fire were thrown up a prodigious height, and carried to a considerable distance, and on reaching the ground, did considerable injury to the hay, which lay half made, and the haystacks in the fields, on the South side of the town; but the most unfortunate effect arising from this cause, was, that in the midst of the great conflagration, two or three cottages and a barn in Louch's field, at the distance of a quarter of a mile at least from the town, caught fire, and being in a great measure left unguarded, (the occupiers being either engaged at their employ, or in assisting at the extinguishment of the fire in the town) were in a very short space of time, with almost every article they contained, consumed.

To describe the calamitous scene, which this dreadful conflagration occasioned, is impossible; parents searching after their children, whole families roofless and pennyless, and such like spectacles were every where to be seen. But the most dreadful catastrophe attending it, was, the burning of William Bassett, a servant of Messrs. Best, who, in defiance of the intreaties and remonstrances of the surrounding multitude, rushed into his house, while it was burning, to endeavour to get some money he had left in it, and was immediately buried in the ruin, leaving a disconsolate widow, then far advanced in pregnancy, to lament his loss. Another catastrophe happened in the evening, after the fire had subsided, by the falling of a chimney on a Mrs. Dunk, who incautiously ventured too near it with her infant child in her arms, and they were both killed. To the divine interposition of Providence alone, can it be attributed, that no other lives were lost on this most melancholy occasion.

It is worthy of remark, as a proof of the intenseness of the fire, that many hooks, screws, nails, &c., in Mr. Seaton's house, melted, and ran into one solid mass.

Several persons suffered from accidents which befel them, in endeavouring to extinguish the fire.

General Hewett, with the same humanity that prompted him so materially to assist in saving the property of the sufferers, in the evening endeavoured to alleviate their miseries, by sending tents, and having them pitched in the field adjoining the New Road, for the reception and accomodation of those, who had not been able to provide themselves with a shelter.

A guard of the Gentlemen of the Chatham and Rochester Volunteers, was placed on that, and many succeeding nights, to watch and preserve the property, which had been deposited in the road, gardens, fields, &c. adjoining, for the benefit of the sufferers.

The loss arising from this dreadful visitation, was computed at £30,000, £25,000, of which were insured, principally in the Sun, Phoenix, and Royal Exchange Assurance Offices; the first of which sustained about three fifths of the loss.

To alleviate the miseries this dreadful calamity had created, and to soften the pangs of the distressed sufferers, several gentlemen of the town assembled a few days afterwards at the house of Joseph Mathews, Esq, the Agent Victualler, and entered into the following resolutions,

Chatham, July 3, 1800.

At a meeting of the principal inhabitants of the town of Chatham this day, to take into consideration, the most effectual means to be adopted, for the immediate relief of the unfortunate sufferers by the late dreadful fire, whereby upwards of sixty houses were totally destroyed, and a great many families reduced to the utmost distress.

It was unanimously Resolved,

That a subscription be immediately made, from house to house, throughout the town and parish, to effect the above laudable purpose.

That application be made to the respective Magistrates, Ministers, &c., of the several cities, boroughs, towns, and parishes, in the county, stating the above mentioned calamitous affair, and supplicating their aid by a similar subscription.

That one or more persons, from the neighbouring parishes, be requested to assist the Committee appointed for this parish, in examining the claims of the sufferers, and granting such relief as circumstances will allow, and the nature of their case may require.

That the Committee do meet at the Vestry-room, Chatham, on Tuesday next, the 8th inst., at ten o'clock in the forenoon, to receive statements of the losses sustained by those persons who are *desirous of receiving relief* from the Subscription, and that public notice be immediately given of such meeting.

That such statements be forthwith examined, and distribution made of the money collected, in such manner as shall be judged expedient, and will best tend to alleviate the miseries of the unfortunate.

PAWNS

A great number of persons, in very low and indigent circumstances, who had been obliged to pawn their wearing apparel, goods, &c to Mr. Thomas Frid, a pawnbroker, whose house, with the greater part of the articles it contained, was entirely consumed by the fire, applied to the Committee, stating their loss, and infinite distress on the occasion, and praying relief (Mr. Frid not being responsible for the loss). – The Committee took the same into consideration, and, after examining the accounts of the sufferers, who were burnt out, or otherwise driven from their homes, and their goods destroyed or damaged, and finding that all had been seasonably relieved, resolved, to extend the benefit of the

12

subscription to those objects who had suffered by losing the articles, their necessities had occasioned them to pledge.

The List of Subscribers are given in full, together with the District in which they resided, but are merely given here in Totals for each Locality.

	£	s.	d.		£	s.	d.
Ash	2	2	0	Maidstone	22	3	6
Ashford	23	15	6	Milton, next Sitting-			
Aylesford	23	7	0	bourne	13	13	0
Bredhurst		17	6	Minster	2	2	0
Borden		10	6	Newington	2	2	0
Boughton, near Coxheath	1	0	0	Northfleet		2	0
Burling		2	6	Pluckley	1	1	0
Canterbury and Environs	141	6	0	Queenborough		2	6
Charing	5	5	0	Rainham	20	1	6
Town of Chatham ..	477	16	5	The City of Rochester			
From a Friendly Society				and the adjoining			
held at the George,				Parish of Saint			
Globe Lane, Chatham,				Margaret	451	17	6
by Mr. Marriner ..	10	0	0	The Dean & Chapter of			
Marines	29	1	6	Rochester	20	0	0
Upper Barracks	27	17	6	Several Gentlemen			
The Officers and Work-				assembled at the Parr's			
men belonging to His				Head Tavern, in the			
Majesty's Dockyard at				City	20	0	0
Chatham	162	7	6	Sheerness	84	14	6
Chilson	20	0	0	Sittingbourne	31	12	0
Cliffe	1	1	0	Strood	56	4	3
Cobham	10	10	0	Surry	4	4	0
Cranbrook	16	2	6	Teston	1	1	0
Cuxton	1	11	6	Throwley		10	6
Deal	1	10	6	Tonbridge	22	12	8
Devon	2	2	0	Wouldham	1	5	0
Dover	10	2	6	Wye	12	11	6
Eastry	1	1	0				
Faversham	7	18	9				
Frindsbury	17	6	0				
Gillingham	131	6	6				
Gravesend & Milton ..	75	8	0				
Greenwich	14	2	6				
Halstow		10	6				
Hastingleigh	2	2	0				
Hedcorn		7	0				
Higham	3	5	6				
Hoo	1	11	6				
Lewisham	1	1	0				
London	52	6	0				

By the Ballance in the Treasurer's Hands "of the Fund of the Association of the North Division of the Lath of Aylesford and the City of Rochester, instituted 10th December, 1792, for defending Liberty and Property against Republicans and Levellers," remitted by Messrs. Twopeny £50.

Right Hon. Lord Henniker, remitted by Messrs. Twopeny £10 0s. 0d.

The following are a few of the sufferers and their claims, which in the original, are in tabulated form:–

Anderson, John – *Occupation*, Hoyman – *Families*, Wife and two children – *Loss*, One Third of Hoy, Warehouse and Wharf – *Value claimed*, £448 6s. 8d. – Paid, £200 0s. 0d. – *Observations*, Goods saved, too recent a Purchase to insure Wharf, &c.

Bassett, Rebecca – Widow – Apparel and Goods – £20 8s. – Paid £30 10s. – Burnt out, saved half – Her Husband burnt to Death in the Fire.

Bulmer, Rebecca – Washer – Widow, no children – Apparel and Goods – £37 1s. 6d. – Paid £13 – Burnt out, saved a Part.

Cameron, William – Ordinaryman – Wife and one child – Apparel and Goods – £4 14s. – Paid £4 14s. – Burnt out, saved greater part.

Capling, Robert – Ostler – Wife only – Apparel and Goods – £11 4s. 6d. – Paid £6 6d. – Wife earns her living.

Colley, Ann – Servant to Mr. Robinson – Apparel – £1 10s. – Paid £1 10s. – Saved Part.

Dawson, Darey – Slopseller – No Family – Apparel and Goods – £146 10s. 4d. – Paid £35 – Burnt out.

Easterwood, Jeremiah – Rigger and slop-seller – Wife and two children – Goods in Hoy – £6 13s. 8d. – Paid £6 – His Dealer allowed £10 per cent. on Loss.

Fullagar, Thomas – Carter – Wife and – children – Goods on board Hoy – £10 – Paid £10.

Gardner, John – Shipwright – Wife and two children – Hurt at Fire – Paid £5 – Chest of Drawers fell on him.

Gilbert, John – Wife and five children – Hurt at Fire – Paid £5 – Arm injured.

Godfrey, Thomas – Hoyman – Wife and six children – One-third of Hoy, Warehouse and Wharf – £448 6s. 8d. – Paid £120 – Goods saved, too recent a Purchase to insure.

Graham, John – Rigger – Wife and two children – Apparel and Goods – £28 15s. 6d. – Paid £28 15s. 6d. – Insured £100.

Harris, Thomas – Bricklayer's Labourer – Wife and five children – Hurt at Fire – Paid £5 – Shoulder, Leg and Arm burnt.

Jarvis, Thomas – Shopkeeper – Wife – Goods on board the Hoy – £5 8s. 6d. – Of Ability (to bear loss).

Jenner, Jane – Servant to Mr. Elliott – Apparel –£5 18s. 6d. – Paid £5 18s. 6d. – Burnt out.

Lawrence, Thomas – Shipwright – Wife only – Apparel and Goods – £31 6s. – Paid £5 5s. – Burnt out, insured £100 – Of Ability – (only three claimants appeared to have insured their goods).

Martin, Richard – Chelsea Pensioner (Lame of one Leg) – Sawyer – Wife and one child – Goods and Apparel – £8 5s. – Paid £7 12s. 6d. – Burnt out.

Masters, John – Servant at Trumpet (now Royal Exchange, next the Empire) – Apparel – £4 10s. – Paid £3 10s.

Oliff, Jonothau – Victualler – Wife and five children – Beer in Hoy – £10 – Paid £0 0s. 0d. – Of Ability.

Seaton, Benjamin – Cabinet Maker – Single – Apparel and Cash – £57 19s. – Paid £14 14s. – Burnt out – His Chest of Tools are now in the Rochester Museum.

Thomas, John – Scavalman – Wife and four children – Hurt at Fire – Paid £5 – Overrun by Engine, Leg broken.

The list of Pawns, or goods lost by the Fire in Mr. Frid's Pawnbroker's Establishment are thus set out, of which I shall only give one example:–

Sufferer's Name, Ablett, William – *Occupation,* Ropemaker – *Family,* Wife and two children – *Goods pledged for* £2 3s. 2d. – *Goods valued by Sufferers,* £4 9s. 6d. – *Paid* £1 10s. 0d.

On examining the various accounts, and consolidating them, it appeared, that the total fund subscribed was £2107 2s. 1d., and that the money already paid, with the necessary expenses incident to the collection and distribution were £2076 13s. 1d., consequently the balance of £30 9s. was still remaining in the hands of the Treasurer, which was divided amongst such sufferers of the first denomination, as to them seemed best entitled, and on the 22nd day of December, the last and final distribution of the money collected was made."

Twenty years later, the second 'Great Fire of Chatham' happened. William Jefferys, treasurer to the 1800 Committee, was once again in charge of the relief fund. His eye-witness account described the fire: "Fire broke out at 2 a.m. in a bakehouse in High Street and spread next door to a tallow-chandlers. These buildings being near the town quay, the fire was first spotted from the Medway. The boatman quickly rowed ashore and awoke all those in dangerous proximity to the threatening flames. The sentry at the Chatham barrack gate also saw the fire and soon it was attended by sappers, Artillery, the Veteran Battalion, Royal Marines, the Navy and the East India Company. However, as said, it quickly crossed the High Street and in half an hour the flames raged with so much violence as to prevent all approach to them. Though able, active and enterprising men were well supplied with water from the river, the fire bade defiance to all human exertions. Soon it communicated its devouring flames to the elegant and substantial mansion called Chatham House; in less than two hours the fire had consumed the interior of this noble edifice, leaving its walls a melancholy heap of ruins". He relates how a group of men, possibly firemen, "by their united exertions, with a plentiful supply of water from buckets and engines and through the merciful interference of a Kind Providence", made a fire-stop at the burnt-out shell of Chatham House.

The fire was now raging in the town, and the London engines arrived to help contain the conflagration. A Mr Baker took it upon himself to give orders for two houses to be demolished to make a fire-break. The fire was, in fact, got under before it reached the break, and the owner, a Mr Cohen, was unable to obtain compensation from the insurers, the Eagle, because the properties were destroyed by demolition and not by fire. He then sued Mr Baker and was granted compensation and costs.

The total loss was 73 buildings – dwellings and warehouses – and the fire continued to smoulder among the ruins for five weeks. William Jefferys, a man of undoubted social conscience and compassion, since he had for a second time agreed to take on the "arduous and invidious task" of collecting and dispursing the relief money, mentions with sadness "the villainy of those wretches undeserving the names of men, who during the awful visitation, under the pretence of yielding assistance to their fellow creatures in the hour of distress, took base and cowardly advantage of their sufferings by pillaging their houses".

In 1820, the Relief Committee was asked for help by customers of a Mr Frid's pawn shop. This business had also been destroyed in the fire of 1800 and generous compensation had been afforded those who had lost goods in pawn. Now, Mr Jefferys was beset by claims for precious jewellery, silk gowns and gold watches as well as "furniture fit for a nobleman's house" from people of obviously low means!

Part II

Insurance Brigades and Volunteers

1801–1935

Fig. 6. An early firemark of the Kent Fire Office that used to be displayed on premises insured by them.

Although the first Fire Insurance office was set up in London as early as 1690, it was not until 1750 that firemarks – metal plates fixed outside houses to show that the owners were insured – first appeared in Kent. It was not until 1802 that Kent's own first Fire Insurance company was formed. Known locally as 'The Fire Office', it maintained its separate existence for a century, merging with the Royal Insurance Company in 1901. It is indeed to the Secretary of the Royal that I am indebted for the details of the Insurance firemen in the County.

The 'Kent's' first step was to reward persons who assisted in extinguishing fires on property insured by the Office, and over many years large sums were expended in this way. At the same time, the Office was a generous donor to public-spirited persons who organised subscriptions to purchase fire-fighting equipment for their locality. Leather buckets and exes were offered to Local Authorities for use in prominent places and it was the duty of the Company's Agents, who were also supplied with buckets, to organise helpers to extinguish fires.

The first appointment of firemen by the 'Kent' was in March 1804 when 12 men were enrolled in Deptford. They were supplied with a uniform but received no pay as it was considered a sufficient reward for them to receive a Certificate which protected them from being impressed into the Royal Navy. For this purpose their names were registered with the Lords Commissioners of the Admiralty. Men clamoured for the job of firemen to get this certificate!

In the same year, the 'Kent' supplied two manual engines and enrolled men to handle them, in Maidstone. By 1821, manuals had also been supplied to Faversham, Rochester, Chatham, Gravesend, Sittingbourne, Canterbury, Malling, Tunbridge Wells and Greenwich.

Jackets, trousers, hats and badges were the standard equipment for the firemen and the uniform and the romance always associated with those who fight fire, together with the popular 'Impress Certificate', attracted plenty of volunteers. The first uniform was of Kentish Grey linen with a felt helmet. In 1816 the Directors resolved "to purchase warmer clothing at a cost of 24/- a dress, it being the opinion of the Board that the cloth will not only be warmer but better defence against fire than linen".

The uniform seems to have varied in different towns according to the demands of the men themselves! The Deptford men in particular seem to have made a nuisance of themselves as first they asked for glazed sealskin helmets. In 1809 they were awarded a uniform of dark blue with grey facings. In 1811 the Deptford Agent complained that the firemen "refused to assist owing to dissatisfaction" at a fire which cost the Office £400. The following month they were given an underjacket, breeches and boots.

Each fireman was supplied with a small oval brass plaque affixed to the door of his home so that he could be called by runners or neighbours.

19

Whilst the early firemen received no wages apart from the Engineer or Supervisor, i.e. the Captain who had 2 to 4 guineas a year, they were paid for attendance at fires. The earliest record of the fees is of 1825 when the fees were revised to:

"If the engine be had out and not used   3/- a man
If used for less than 3 hours   5/- a man
If used from 3 to 6 hours   7/- a man
If used from 6 to 12 hours   10/- a man"

Each man had to proceed to the fire with all possible speed, and a fine was imposed on any who arrived more than three minutes after the engine. Up to 2/- a man was allowed for beer or spirits, at the discretion of the Captain, when good work had been performed.

The fireman's Annual Dinner was always an occasion. On December 8th 1812, the Minutes record "The Maidstone firemen being desirous of having their annual dinner the day after Christmas Day at the Nelson's Head, the Committee request that such a dinner be limited to 3/- each man for eating and that not more than three pots of beer be allowed each man".

History relates many stories of gallantry and humour in the operation of the old Insurance Brigades and they also had their tragedies. Thus a 'Kent' Board Minute of March 27th 1822 – "Resolved that such compensation as appears proper shall be paid to the widow and family of Hayes, one of our late firemen at Rochester who was killed at the fire at Denton, and also to Hook, another who was much hurt by the Fire Engine". There was no Welfare State in those days!

The earliest manual engines were carried to the fire, rather like a stretcher, before they were put on wheels, and one of these latter, used in the early part of the last century, is displayed in the Kent Fire Brigade Museum at Brigade H.Q. at Tovil. These manuals had from two to four pumps operated by a long handle on each side to which as many men as possible attached themselves.

In January, 1810, it was decided to buy a "big new engine of the latest type" for Maidstone. The specification for this, including the equipment, is recorded in the Office, and it is noted that each fireman was to be supplied with "a large rattle to give the alarm of fire, etc". This new engine did not arrive until a year later and there appears to have been some trouble with the firemen at that time. The Minutes say – "The Committee continued the firemen who had not been refractory, restored such as appeared sorry for their conduct and filled up the list by electing others forming 21. Reception Committee formed to receive the new engine at 3 p.m. on 13th instant expected by Mr Shadgate's Waggon with the consent of the Minister and Churchwardens carefully take and place same in the church at its West End where Bucketts are also to be placed".

The firemen were newly equipped for this great occasion with "glazed hats with the Kent Fire Office painted on same with each to have a Wallet with the County Arms painted on same for convenience of removing property from Fires. Smiths, working Silversmiths of Greenwich to supply a Nickel Badge with chain to suspend same round the neck made of silver". These badges which cost 3/6 and today are valued at £15, were later worn on the left arm as became customary with Insurance Brigades.

'The Great New Engine' was kept in All Saints' Churchyard until 1820, when an engine-house was built for it by the brigade. A plan showing its position, together with the water mains of the High Street, survives. When the new Office was built in 1827, the engine was housed at the rear and became 'The Fire Station' – this is still more or less in its original state.

If a fire occurred in the Borough, the Town Hall bell rang the alarm, but if in the country, the alarm was given on the brass bell in the Office yard. The first engine was taken out when five men arrived. Later arrivals were paid 'call-money' to stand by in case the second engine was needed. A messenger on a galloping horse generally brought news of the fire before the days of the telegraph. The limit of a Maidstone call was 20 miles, a long way for the four horses kept in a nearby stable. The leading near-side horse carried a rider, and before the bell of more modern days, the way was cleared by rattles and the sounding of a brass post-horn, a proud possession of the Office.

The first and oldest volunteer fire brigade in Kent and probably in the country, was established at Hythe in 1802, the same year as the foundation of the Kent Fire Office. For a long time, controversy surrounded Hythe's claim to have the oldest brigade, with Ashford being the main contender, but records still in existence seem to prove their claim beyond any doubt. The magazine 'Fire and Water' reported in its March 1900, issue that "the Hythe Brigade celebrated its 98th anniversary with a dinner at which Honorary Captain Cobb, who recently retired from active service after 40 years work, presided". It was not until 1814 that the Ashford Fire Engine Association was formed and by then, the Hythe Brigade, now renamed the Hythe Fire Engine Association, were already amending their original brigade regulations.

In July 1814, the Ashford Fire Engine Association met and recorded in a minute that they were pleased to learn that the Institution was making rapid progress. Some confusion exists about the next few years in the history of the Ashford Brigade. It is believed that it was re-formed in 1824, and an old book on fire brigades states that the town had a population of 8,005 and a volunteer brigade of 29 men, one engine station and two engines with six inch pumps. The brigade was supported by voluntary contributions. Whatever confusion may have existed about the shape of the brigade, since 1814, was resolved when the inhabitants of the town met in the Vestry on January 16th 1826, to "form an

£300 REWARD.

FIRE AT Eastry Court.

In investigating the cause of this Fire, there appears to be no doubt that it was the diabolical act of some malicious Person or Persons. We, therefore, the Owners of the Property destroyed, do hereby offer a Reward of **TWO HUNDRED POUNDS**, to be paid upon the conviction of the Offender or Offenders.

WILLIAM BRIDGER.
RICHARD HALFORD.

January 13, 1834.

N.B. In addition, We are authorized to state that His Majesty's Government has been pleased to offer a further Reward of **ONE HUNDRED POUNDS** to any Person or Persons who may give such information as will lead to the discovery and conviction of the **Offender or Offenders**, and a **FREE PARDON**, except to the Person who actually committed the offence.

W. B.
R. H.

COLEGATE, PRINTER, PARADE, CANTERBURY.

association for protection of life, buildings and property from fire". The meeting was told that the inhabitants had belonging to them "two engines, suction pipes, three lugger pipes, two branches and 84 buckets" and it was found necessary to add to these "four hooks, two tomahawks, one hundred flambeaux, four hair strainers and lanthorns". This was a very considerable arsenal for 1826 and led, during the next 50 years, to Ashford becoming one of the leading volunteer brigades in the County.

Dartford, which already had a manual engine in 1740, and had added another in 1783, built an engine-house to accommodate them in 1786. This was in use until 1827, when the Vestry decided that a new engine-house should be built next to Holy Trinity Church. Building proceeded and finally the new engine-house was ready to receive the two parish pumps. In the meantime, however, there had been a change in the membership of the Vestry and they refused to sanction the expense, and ordered the £550 building to be demolished forthwith. The whole of the expense was thrown onto the unfortunate churchwarden, a Mr W. Shepperd. History does not record how he coped with such a crushing debt.

Further developments and improvements in fire-fighting equipment were made about this time. In 1829, the first, rather primitive steam fire engine was built in London by Braithwaite and Ericsson; a kind of breathing apparatus to enable firemen to breathe in heavy smoke was invented in France; and even the original manual engines grew larger and larger and some had to be operated by up to 40 men.

Firemen have always liked beer for its cooling and refreshing qualities, but no more so than in the days of the manual fire engines when the jets were obtained only through sheer back-breaking, exhausting pumping by muscle and sinew, beer was a must. The tough characters who manned the levers of the old-time pumps – powerful engines that took anything from 4 to 40 men to man – be they firemen, soldiers or volunteers from the crowd, needed beer in copious quantities to keep them going and to replace the sweat that literally poured off them. Beer was just as important to them as the money. "No beer, no water!" or "More beer!" were frequent cries, and if the beer didn't turn up the officer in charge probably found that he had a strike on his hands.

The importance with which beer was regarded is indicated by the fact that the rules and regulations of the old fire brigades of the 1880's usually made specific reference to it.

The Kent Fire Office Regulations for the Payment of Firemen, made in 1830, laid down: "No beer, spirits or other refreshments to be paid for, except such as may be thought necessary and ordered by the Agents, Foreman or Engineer, for the Firemen and the twenty extra men authorised to be employed – but such allowance in no case to exceed Two Shillings for each person". You could buy a lot of beer in 1830 for 2/-!

The Regulations for the firemen belonging to the Phoenix Fire Office, Canterbury, in 1849, had the clause: "No beer, spirits or other refreshments shall be paid for unless ordered by the Engineer, or his Deputy, and only to be used for the Firemen and extra hands employed by him. And as intoxication on such occasions is not merely disreputable to the establishment, but in the highest degree dangerous, any Man who may be discovered in that state shall not only forfeit his whole allowance for the turn-out and duty performed, but will be forthwith dismissed from the Establishment".

Hythe Fire Engine Association, formed in 1802 and having successfully established their claim to be the oldest Brigade in Kent, continued their work for nearly 30 years. But then, early in 1832, the town and its brigade were split into opposing factions. The cause of the row is unfortunately not known, but by October 1833, there were two brigades in the town, one quaintly called the "Scot and Lot" brigade and the other the "Corporation" brigade. This division appears to have continued until 1867 when the two brigades reunited as the Hythe Volunteer Fire Brigade. The Rules and Regulations of the Scot and Lot fire brigade, dated October 15th, 1833 are still in existence, extracts from which I quote:

"Rules and Regulations of the Hythe Scot and Lot Fire Engine Association. These set out the names of the Pipe Conductors, Inspectors of Premises on Fire, Superintendent for Procuring Water, Inspector of Pipes. Duty of the Pipe Conductors (Branchmen) will be principally to attend to the proper disposal of the pipe and the instructions of the Inspector of Premises on Fire as to what part the water is to be directed to. Inspectors of Premies on Fire will immediately on alarm being given repair to the spot and examine the premises on fire or in danger and give instructions to the Pipe Conductors and also for the use of fire hooks when necessary.

The Superintendents for Procuring Water will immediately direct their attention to that need; and with all despatch form lines if necessary for the conveyance of water, and when a proper supply is established they will place themselves at suitable distances to protect and take care of the pipes. Officers not on duty will relieve each other at appropriate intervals and as a matter of course render assistance in all cases. 8th Rule of the Association: That a badge as a mark of distinction be worn by members when ever they meet in the Association and in case of fire. The Brigade shall consist of 18 members. The composition of the Brigade shall consist of one captain, one lieutenant, one engineer, two branchmen and 12 firemen. The election of officers shall be by ballot annually in January. Any member neglecting or refusing to attend a fire without giving the Committee a satisfactory reason shall be liable to a fine not exceeding 10/- or to be dismissed from the Brigade.

That members do meet at the engine house as heretofore for the

TOWN AND PORT OF
NEW ROMNEY.

Rules and Regulations
RESPECTING THE
FIRE ENGINE.

THE Engine is under the care and direction of JOHN WILES, and the Keys of the Engine House are kept at the Gaol, by the Police Officer, and JOHN WILES, where, and to whom, in case of a Fire, application is to be made.

NAMES OF THE FIREMEN.

JOHN WILES, Foreman,

1 JEREMIAH WRAIGHT, Carpenter,	7 ALFRED HUTCHINSON, Labourer,
2 RICHARD PEARSON, Carpenter,	8 WILLIAM BOURN, Wheelwright,
3 WILLIAM MASEY, Bricklayer,	9 STEPHEN TURNER, Labourer,
4 WILLIAM JONES, Brazier,	10 JOHN DROWLEY, Carpenter,
5 HENRY PAGE, Coal Merchant,	11 WILLIAM MASEY, Labourer,
6 WILLIAM HUTCHINSON, Labourer,	12 EDWARD CATT, Labourer.

The Firemen on being called out, and attending and discharging their duty in strict conformity with the Rules laid down by the Foreman (and approved by the Mayor and Deputy-Mayor for the time being), are to be severally paid as follows:---

For the first Hour, 2s. 6d.; and for each Hour afterwards, 6d.

Whenever the Engine is required out of the Town, be the distance and the length of time what it may, Mr. THOMAS BUSS of the New Inn is to be paid for providing 4 Horses with drivers for the same, pursuant to his engagement, £1. 5s.

In the event of the Engine and the Services of the Firemen being required out of the Town, the above Charges are to be paid by the person or persons requiring the same.

The Foreman is to be allowed to employ, if necessary, in addition to the Firemen, any number of Labourers not exceeding 12, who are to be subject to the same Rules and Regulations, and be paid in like manner as the Firemen for their Services. No Beer, Spirits, or other Refreshments are to be paid for, except such as may be thought necessary, and ordered by the Foreman (and approved by the Mayor and Deputy-Mayor for the time being) for the Firemen, and extra Men employed; such allowance in no case to exceed 2s. for each Man.

The Engine is not to be detained at Fires after the Foreman is satisfied it is no longer requisite.

By Order,

WILLIAM STRINGER,
TOWN CLERK.

22nd April, 1845.

TAYLOR, PRINTER, &c., LIBRARY, HIGH STREET, RYE.

express purpose of duly examining by playing the fire engines belonging to the Parish on the Monday after each Quarter Day Old style: on the Lady, Michaelmas and Christmas Quarters at 4 o'clock and on the mid-Summer Quarter at 7 o'clock: or at other such time as may prove most convenient and be stated in the circular notice issued by the Secretary previous to such quarterly meetings. That every member absent at the hour appointed do forfeit 1/-: if the weather will permit, the engines to be then taken out and played for one hour: and every member who does not attend before the commencement of the second half hour to be fined 1/6d · additional, making in the whole 2/6d. Members absenting themselves before the engines are housed to be fined 1/-. Sickness only to be considered an exemption".

It is a matter for speculation why, during the 17th and 18th centuries, when many towns in Kent were devastated by huge conflagrations, Maidstone should have escaped such a fate. I have already recorded that as early as 1591 reference was made in the Borough's Burgmote book to the citizens having to buy buckets, chains and hooks for the defence against fire. For the next 200 years, practically nothing is known how the town defended itself against fire and how it managed to escape destruction in an age of flimsy buildings, open fires, candles and oil lamps. One must assume that Maidstone, like other and often less important places in the County, had some kind of equipment apart from the old hooks and buckets, such as one or two manual pumps. More organised fire protection started in the town with the establishment of the Kent Fire Office in 1802. The 'Kent' provided two manual engines in Maidstone in 1804 and engaged men to operate them. By the 1830's other insurance companies, such as the Sun and the Norwich, had clients and equipment in Maidstone, and an interesting policy by the Sun Fire Office, issued to the Earl Cornwallis of Linton Place, is preserved in the Kent Fire Brigade Museum.

About the same time, the Kent Fire Office issued a "Caution" to servants "against negligence with fire". This proclamation threatened them with fines of £100 or prison with hard labour for 18 months if, "through their carelessness dwelling houses, outhouses or other buildings be fired".

By 1850, Maidstone was protected by engines belonging to the 'Kent' and the Norwich Union; during major fires, these were assisted by an engine from the Cavalry Depot. Water was in short supply and in 1855 a public house in Earl Street, the King's Arms, was burnt down because of lack of water. This shortage caused several more buildings to be destroyed during the next few years and it was not until 1859 that the Maidstone Spring Water Company was set up which, after sinking new wells, finally supplied the town with an adequate water supply both for domestic and fire-fighting purposes.

KENT
Fire Insurance Office,
MAIDSTONE.

A CAUTION

TO

SERVANTS

Against Negligence with Fire.

Whereas it is enacted by Statute of the 8th Geo. 3rd, Chap. 78,

"**THAT** if any menial or other SERVANT or SERVANTS, through negligence or carelessness, shall FIRE or cause to be fired. anv Dwelling House, or Out-house, or Houses, or other Buildings, such **SERVANT or SERVANTS**, being therefore lawfully convicted by the Oath of one or more credible Witness or Witnesses, made before two or more of His Majesty's Justices of the Peace, shall forfeit and pay the sum of **ONE HUNDRED POUNDS** unto the Churchwardens or Overseers of such Parish where such Fire shall happen: to be distributed amongst the Sufferers by fire, in such proportions as to the said Churchwardens shall seem just; and in case of default or refusal to pay the same immediately after such conviction, the same being lawfully demanded by the said Churchwardens; that then in such case such Servant or Servants shall, by Warrant under the Hands and Seals of two or more of His Majesty's Justices of the Peace, be committed to the common GAOL or HOUSE of CORRECTION, as the said Justices shall think fit, for the space of EIGHTEEN MONTHS, there to be kept to hard Labour."

The **DIRECTORS** of this Office having ascertained that several Fires which have lately happened in this County were owing to such negligence, they hereby order this **PUBLIC NOTICE** as a Caution to Servants that they may not subject themselves to such Penalty.

By Order of the Directors,
CHAS. HUGHES,

Secretary.

27

With the new awareness of fire through the insurance brigades, the authorities and citizens in more and more Kent towns and villages decided to set up their own volunteer brigades. During the period 1840–1870 at least 14 of such brigades were formed. First evidence of the Hawkhurst Volunteer Brigade goes back to 1843, when the town had an engine "worked by hand by four persons using a see-saw arrangement" and drawn by horses. This crude apparatus saw service for 40 years, and was then replaced by a more modern engine of the manual type under the captaincy of Walter Mascall. The Mascall family kept a tight control on the Hawkhurst Brigade; Walter Mascall and his nephews, Thomas, Ken, George and Charles Barnes, were, in succession, chiefs of the Brigade until Charles Barnes retired in 1921.

Little is known about the beginnings of fire-fighting in the Parish of Cranbrook, although it is certain that, as in other places, the duties for providing buckets and hooks were in the hands of the parish overseers (created as long ago as 1601). There are no records of manual pumps or organised volunteers in the town. However, by 1844, it was reported that Cranbrook Fire Brigade took an important part in the "Great Fire" which destroyed the entire north side of the High Street. Gravesend, which already had been nearly destroyed by a disastrous fire in 1727, was again devastated by huge conflagrations in 1844, 1846 and 1850.

The fire of 1844, which led to general conflagration over an extensive area, started in West Street. This was a narrow thoroughfare running parallel with the river and intersecting a number of small streets. No. 51 West Street was occupied by Mrs Susan Sandford who was in the fish trade. Here, shrimps were boiled over a sizeable furnace under conditions that were probably not very safe. It was subsequently considered that Susan's stoker had been the unwitting cause of the conflagration. It was his job to rake out the furnace after use, and to see all was safe. He must have left some cinders unextinguished.

At about a quarter to eleven in the evening of Sunday June 2nd, 1844, Henry Wickham of the Gravesend police force noticed flames issuing from the shrimp boiling-house and he raised the alarm immediately. The rest of his colleagues were quickly on the spot as were soldiers stationed in the town. The news was carried across the river to Tilbury Fort, and soldiers were also sent from there.

Gravesend Corporation possessed three engines, the Kent Fire Insurance Company had engines at Dartford and Rochester and the Royal Exchange Assurance had an engine at Crayford. All machines arrived in speedy succession at West Street in Gravesend where the scene was indescribable.

West Street consisted mainly of wooden houses and buildings used as warehouses where some dangerously flammable materials were stored. When Policeman Wickham discovered the fire, the wind was blowing 'rather fresh' from the north or north-east, and this assisted the rapid

28

spread of flames amongst the congested and easily-ignited buildings.

People living in High, Kempthorne, Bath and Wakefield streets soon joined those of West Street in moving their belongings to places of safety. The majority of the inhabitants of the area were very poor people and there were scenes of distress and, indeed, of tragedy. As the flames began to threaten the house in which lay the dead body of his daughter, a shoe-maker named Hooker re-entered his house, took up the body, and carried it out to safety. When the house of a plumber and glazier named Brightwell had to be demolished to check the spread of the fire, his son and daughter, both in the last stages of consumption, had to be moved hurriedly from their beds. This had an immediately fatal effect on the boy; the girl also died shortly afterwards.

Firemen, police and soldiers were confronted with a formidable task. The flames extended from Susan Sandford's place westwards to Union Wharf which was owned by a brewer named Beckett. The Wharf was tenanted at the time by the Star Steam Packet Company and used as a store for pitch, tar, timber and other articles needed for boat building. Naturally, the place burned furiously and was rapidly destroyed. Flames then spread to a storage for salt where there were also stored five or six barrels of gunpowder and a large quantity of sulphur. Two of the barrels of gunpowder were rolled into the Thames before the warehouse caught fire, but the remainder exploded with great force and blew the roofs and walls of adjoining houses to a considerable distance.

Firemen and soldiers worked ceaselessly at the pumps but they made little headway against the flames. Seven houses on Horncastle Quay were now alight and soon destroyed, Elsewhere, as the flames spread, three public houses – the India Arms, the Cook and the Fisherman Arms – were destroyed.

Extensive premises belonging to a man named Matthews, a maker of masts and blocks, were also seriously damaged, most of the stock of timber, spars and blocks being destroyed. It is interesting to record, though, that when he later searched the ruins he discovered that his books and papers had survived through being in an iron chest. Other sufferers included the owners of a marine stores, a bakery, a grocery, a clothiery and a plumbing and glazing works.

Soon after three o'clock in the morning of Monday June 3rd, the wind lulled and for the first time during the anxious night the fire-fighters began to achieve some mastery over the flames. Within two hours the conflagration was nearly subdued, although the fire engines continued to play water on the ruins for the rest of the day. In all, three warehouses, four licensed victuallers' establishments and 19 private houses and shops, with most of their contents, were destroyed.

In view of the extreme poverty of many of the people involved in the conflagration, the authorities knew that they had to act quickly. The Board of Guardians possessed some cottages which were empty and into these were hurried those people who could not find a roof with friends or relatives. At 11 o'clock on Monday morning, the magistrates met at the Town Hall and they decided to start a fund for the unfortunates who had lost nearly all they possessed.

Two years later, Gravesend was again devastated by a fire which, as on previous occasions, having started in West Street, rapidly spread and engulfed much of the town. An eye-witness account, published in November 1846 in the "London Illustrated News", gave a graphic description of the conflagration.

"Singular to say, the locality of the fire was the same as the former fires, West Street, extending along the water side from the Town Pier towards the Rosherville Gardens. The fire was first observed from a body of smoke hovering over the premises occupied by Mr Garratt, grocer, adjacent to the Pier Hotel, at the corner of West Street. The inmates having been got out in safety, steps were taken to bring the Corporation engines, which were soon on the spot, into operation; but the defective state of the water mains enabled the flames to extend themselves to the buildings on each side. The military at Tilbury Fort were mustered by the commanding officer of that fortress who with every promptitude forwarded them to the assistance of the townspeople. Their efforts, however, were of little avail in stopping the conflagration; for at least four hours the wind, which was blowing a violent gale, completely baffled their operations, and increased the magnitude of the fire to a frightful degree.

The scene by 4 o'clock was most awful; the flames had crossed the street and seven or eight houses were in flames, besides the whole of the premises from the Town Pier to considerably below the Talbot Inn, which was also amongst the number. From the south side of West street the fire raged upwards, in the direction of the centre of the town, destroying in its course a great number of low dwelling houses in the various courts. These were principally tenanted by poor fishermen, hawkers, labourers, etc, etc. In one court there was no thoroughfare, except from the approach of West Street, and that being stopped by the dense body of fire, the greatest anxiety was entertained for the safety of the poor creatures who tenanted it.

The police and soldiers, however, bravely exposed themselves in rescuing them, in which they succeeded, by dragging them in at the back windows of adjacent houses. It was reported, notwithstanding, that one or two persons were missing. Happily this is not the fact. No check to the fire was effected until near 7 o'clock in the morning. At 10 o'clock, however, an immense body of fire existed in every part of the ruins.

The principal portion of the houses that were erected on the site of the fire in West Street was consumed, together with both sides of the street from High Street to King Street. Amongst the buildings destroyed or materially injured we may mention the Pier Hotel, Talbot Inn, Punch

BOROUGH OF GRAVESEND.

THE LATE
CALAMITOUS FIRE
In High Street and East Street.

It having been deemed advisable that an official enquiry should be made with reference to the Origin of the above Fire, I hereby give Notice that I intend holding an

INQUISITION

for that purpose at the

TOWN HALL,

On Friday Morning next, 30th Instant,

at Ten o'Clock, at which time and place I earnestly request all persons who can give any information upon the subject to attend.

E. A. HILDER,

Coroner for the Borough of Gravesend.

JANUARY 28th, 1857.

CADDEL AND SON, PRINTERS AND STATIONERS, KING STREET, GRAVESEND.

Bowl Tavern, and all the intermediate wharfs and buildings.

When the ruins were sufficiently cooled to permit any person to pass over them, not the slightest vestige of a street remained – not one wall stood; the bricks, mortar and stone of not less than 20 houses in the eastern part of West Street, being all turned into the carriage-way, which was completely choked up by them. Nothing remained standing except clumps of chimneys, most dangerous to pass, and tottering in the wind. It is almost unnecessary to state that the whole of the stock in the several houses is completely destroyed, and that the poor creatures in the alleys leading from West Street, several of whom are burnt out, are deprived of house and home, and left consequently dependent upon the humanity of their fellow townsmen.

The greatest dissatisfaction prevails in the town, from the fact of the fire having, as in the previous case, made such fearful havoc before it was got under. In general measure that may be accounted for by the large quantity of timber in the premises. In West Street there were not fewer than 25 houses burnt, the major portion of which consisted of wood; whilst there were but two or three brick buildings in the same street that were totally destroyed. The Pier Hotel and Nos. 83 and 84 High Street, were also brick built, and the fire was at first confined to the top part of these premises. On Friday night (last week), however, owing to the great body of heat in the place, a fresh outbreak occurred in the Pier Hotel, and Loder, the engineer, who was left in charge of the place, was obliged to break open the front door, and set the engines again to work, and it was owing only to the extraordinary exertions of the police and firemen that the work of destruction has not again proved most disastrous. To add to the misfortune, whilst the engines were working on Friday night, the main water-pipe in the district burst, so that for the last three hours no water could be obtained from that source".

Four years later, in August 1850, the "London Illustrated News" once again had to report a "most extensive and destructive fire" at Gravesend. So intense was the fire that two engines from the London Fire Engine Establishment were sent all the way to Gravesend to assist.

"The fire was first observed at 2 a.m. in the house of Mr J. Adlington, a grocer and tea-dealer, in the High Street, nearly facing the Town Hall, and it was at that time very inconsiderable; but in the absence of a supply of water it made rapid progress, and before the residents became aware of its existence the back of their dwellings in Church Ally, High Street and Princes Street were cracking with the intense heat.

The High Street is, considering it is the principal place of business in the town, an exceedingly narrow thoroughfare, not sufficiently wide in any part for two vehicles to pass without inconvenience. At the back of this street was Princes Street, whilst West Street bounded the northern end, and Church Ally ran at the southern extremity of the White Hart Inn. The whole clump of buildings standing within these boundaries was

32

about 50 or 60, and covered probably a couple of acres of ground.

Many of these, notwithstanding that they were three or four storeys high, and contained goods of some thousand pounds in value, were constructed principally of timber, so that the officers of police became aware that, unless strenuous exertions were made, some of the inhabitants must lose their lives. They therefore aroused the whole of the occupants of these premises. In a very short space of time the town engines, together with those of the Custom House and of Mr Plane's (the Mayor) Brewery, were on the spot; and a supply of water from the mains of the water-works having been promptly got, every effort was made to subdue the fire, which by this time had extended itself to the house adjoining Mr Adlington's. The wind blew rather fresh from the south-west, sweeping the flames over the houses down the High Street towards the Town Pier.

The engines, though well worked and abundantly supplied with water, gained no influence over the fire, which had at about 3 o'clock extended to seven houses on the (the western) side of the street. The engine from Tilbury Fort, accompanied by a body of troops, having now arrived, more vigorous, but equally unavailing efforts were made to stay the further progress of the fire, which had, at soon after 3 o'clock, crossed the street, seizing first upon the extensive premises of Mr Young, butcher. From there the flames spread to the houses all down the eastern side of the street, including the County Bank, the Savings Bank, the Kent Tavern, Brinchley's Distillery, etc.

The High Street, on both sides from the Town Hall downwards, to within a short distance of the Town Pier, was at 4 o'clock completely in flames, which, when they involved the premises of Mr Troughton, tallow-chandler, and an oil-shop and chemist's shop contiguous to it, formed an awful conflagration. At this time, all hope of preserving a single house between the Town Hall and the pier was abandoned by all parties, notwithstanding that the Dartford and Rochester engines had arrived, and a prodigious volume of water was discharged on the whole line of burning houses on both sides of the street. There was, fortunately sufficient time to save the cash-boxes and the securities and other documents of the County and Savings Banks, which were taken to the Custom House, all the officers of which were actively engaged, with the military, police and townspeople, in working the engines. Comparatively little property was saved from the fire, which, between 5 and 6 o'clock, had completely destroyed 24 houses on both sides of the High Street, independently of several houses in Princes Street and the courts leading out of the High Street, between the Town Hall and the Pier.

A telegraphic communication from the railway station, at the instance of the Mayor (Mr Plane), having been made to the London Bridge station, a body of the Fire Brigade and two engines were as soon as possible despatched from London, and arrived in Gravesend at about 27 minutes to 7 o'clock. The work of destruction was then done, the fire having been providentially stayed in its progress down the High Street, and extending backwards to Princes Street, by a change of wind to the north and westward at 6 o'clock. The assistance of the Brigade, with their powerful engines and practised skill, was, however, effectual in suppressing the fire still bursting forth from the mighty mass of ruins – all that remained of the property destroyed.

The general body of tradespeople and inhabitants of the town are loud in their complaints against the corporation in not having an efficient corps of firemen and engines established, after the warning they received by the two previous fires, which it will be recollected consumed the greater part of the lower portion of Gravesend".

By the mid 19th century the Phoenix Fire Office seem to have been well established in Kent as is shown in their regulations for firemen at their Canterbury office, dated July 1849:

"On an alarm of Fire being given the whole of the Firemen shall assemble at the Engine House and act with spirit under the order of the Engineer in getting everything ready for service. Each man will get a Badge with the Phoenix on it, and on all occasions when on duty will wear it.

No beer, spirits or other refreshments will be paid for unless ordered by the Engineer, or his Deputy, and only to be used for the Firemen and extra hands employed by him. And as intoxication on such occasions is not merely disreputable to the establishment, but in the highest degree dangerous, any man who may be discovered in that state shall not only forfeit his whole allowance for the turn out and duty performed, but will forthwith be dismissed from the Establishment.

As nothing is so hurtful to the efficiency of an Establishment for extinguishing Fire as unnecessary noise, irregularity, and insubordination, it is enjoined on all to observe and execute whatever orders they may receive from the Engineer, or his second, with quietness and regularity, and to do nothing without orders".

As already mentioned, about this time a number of new volunteer brigades were formed throughout Kent, but often the exact date of formation cannot now be established. In records, one frequently comes across mention of a meeting to discuss the acquisition of a fire engine when no previous mention of a brigade had been found. For example, a meeting of dignitaries at West Malling in 1850 was shown a new fire extinguisher, graphically called the "Fire Annihilator", which suggests that some sort of fire organisation existed in the town before that date. A Vestry meeting was called in 1852 to discuss the raising of money to buy an efficient fire engine and there is a suggestion that a pump was acquired by 1854.

Again, no records exist about the beginning of the Edenbridge Brigade, but already in 1850, the town had a Tilley engine which had to

REGULATIONS FOR THE FIREMEN
BELONGING TO THE
PHŒNIX FIRE OFFICE,
41, St. George's Place, Canterbury.

1st.—On an alarm of Fire being given the whole of the Firemen shall assemble at the Engine House and act with spirit under the order of the Engineer in getting everything ready for service. Each man will get a Badge with the Phœnix on it, and on all occasions when on duty will wear it.

2nd.—Each man, on giving his attendance at the Engine House, in the day time, before such alarm is discovered to be unfounded, to have Two Shillings.

Ditto	ditto	at night	....	....	....	3 Shillings.
Ditto, attending Fire (but not working engine), any time under One Hour						3 „
Ditto, One and under Three Hours			....	....	....	4 „
Ditto, working Engine, any time under Five Hours			....	....	....	5 „
Ditto, Five Hours and under Seven			....	....	....	7 „
Ditto, Seven „ Ten			....	....	....	10 „
Ditto, Ten „ Twelve			....	....	....	12 „

and 1s. for every additional Hour after Twelve Hours.

3rd.—Each man to repair with the Engine to the Fire with all possible speed; and if not there within half-an-hour after the arrival of the Engine a deduction on the regulated allowance to be made at the discretion of the Engineer.

4th.—The Engine not to remain at Fires after the Engineer is satisfied it is no longer necessary, it being considered of the utmost importance that it should not be off its station longer than is absolutely requisite. And on an alarm, the Engine not to be taken out without the knowledge of the Engineer, and until the situation of the fire is correctly ascertained.

5th.—No beer, spirits, or other refreshments will be paid for unless ordered by the Engineer, or his Deputy, and only to be used for the Firemen and extra hands employed by him. And as intoxication on such occasions is not merely disreputable to the establishment, but in the highest degree dangerous, any Man who may be discovered in that state shall not only forfeit his whole allowance for the turn out and duty performed, but will be forthwith dismissed from the Establishment.

6th.—As nothing is so hurtful to the efficiency of an Establishment for extinguishing Fires as unnecessary noise, irregularity, and insubordination, it is enjoined on all to observe and execute whatever orders they may receive from the Engineer, or his second, with quietness and regularity, and to do nothing without orders.

7th.—The men not to allow their attention to be distracted from their duty by listening to directions from any persons except the Engineer, or his second; and will refer every one who applies to them for aid to the Engineer.

8th.—The Firemen to be careful to let the Police know where they live, and to notify any change of residence to them.

9th.—Careless conduct, irregular attendance at exercise, or disobedience of the Engineer's orders, will be punished by dismissal.

10th.—No person will receive any remuneration for alleged assistance given at a Fire whose names are not taken by the Engineer.

11th.—Messrs. T. and H. Cooper, Agents, reserve to themselves the control over the whole Establishment.

Phœnix Fire Office, Canterbury, July 6th, 1849.

be dragged to the fire by hand. A splendid bugle, inscribed "Edenbridge Fire Brigade" is preserved in the Kent Fire Museum at Maidstone, but it is not certain when it was used to clear the way for the Brigade to the fire. By 1852, three different insurance brigades were working in the Dartford area, but when a big fire broke out in that year in a paper and oil mill at Dartford Creek, engines had to be sent from London by train to fight the blaze. About the same time, canvas hose began to supersede the heavy and cumbersome leather hose which was difficult to roll and liable to crack.

Some confusion exists about when the Margate Fire Brigade was formed. Dates vary between 1852 and 1862, but during that time, Margate had two colourful, nationally-known chief officers, two rival brigades and some of the finest fire-fighting equipment and machines in the County. The most probable founder and first captain of the Margate Brigade was Frederick Hodges, a German, who later became famous as the chief officer of the Lambeth Distillery Brigade in London and, with his men and powerful pumps, quickly outshone the work of the London Fire Engine Establishment. What seems certain is, that by 1864, Margate had a brigade consisting of 24 members with an engine-house in New Inn Yard, two engines, (one for 30 men and the other for 20), a fire-escape and 500 feet of leather hose. The total value of the equipment which was the property of the Town Council was assessed at £350. The Council also provided the uniforms and equipment for each volunteer. Fire alarms were given by maroons and a contemporary record stated that the noise of these maroons "could be heard even in a half gale of wind at a distance of one mile to windward of the Station". On hearing the alarm, the police on their various beats were required to call immediately on all the firemen who lived in their district, and it was claimed that an engine could be got to the scene of a fire a quarter of a mile distant from the engine-house in about $7\frac{1}{2}$ minutes.

Captain Hodges, and it is not clear how he divided his duties between London and Margate, was certainly an innovator. His volunteers had to participate in complicated training drills, and wet drills were carried out in the grounds of Holy Trinity Church with water jets directed against the Church tower. His name is still remembered by "Hodges Gap" and "Hodges Flagstaff" on the seafront at Cliftonville. A friend of the Prince of Wales (later King Edward VIIth) appears to have retired from London in the mid-1870's and lent a magnificent presentation manual pump (given to him earlier by the people of London), to the Brighton Fire Brigade. Again it is not clear when Hodges relinquished the control of the Margate Brigade, but for a period a Mr Fasham is on record as captain. Next on the scene was another enthusiastic fire 'buff'. He was a Mr Davies, a wealthy young man who, after a spell attached to a Canadian Fire Department, returned to London and founded the Westbourne Park Fire Brigade. On a date not recorded he moved to

Margate, taking his engine with him and set up in opposition to Mr Fasham's town brigade with his own private fire station, equipment and men. Troubles quickly started when it was shown that the Davies Brigade was quicker and better equipped than Fasham's.

They usually arrived first at a fire and were more efficient in putting it out. The town became divided and so great was the ill-feeling that his hose was cut at fires and the windows of his private fire station smashed. Davies moved his brigade to Westgate-on-Sea, but to the fury of the town brigade, continued to attend fires in Margate. The situation became untenable, and after a series of stormy meetings of the Town Council, he was made chief of the town brigade. One of the first actions of Captain Davies was to amalgamate the town brigade with his own and to force the resignation of the unfortunate Chief Fasham. Described at the time as a "good, kind-hearted man but possessing no aptitude for command and little experience", he was sent away with nothing more than a vote of thanks for his services. Davies in the meantime had persuaded the Council to buy a new engine which in due time was brought from London. According to the custom of the time, the new engine, decorated with garlands and flowers, was paraded through the streets of Margate for a christening ceremony. In the procession were the Mayor, Captain Davies and members of the Town Council; and the streets were lined by large numbers of the population. But ex-Captain Fasham, who still had many friends in the town who thought that he had been treated badly by the Council, was not yet quite ready to give up. Together with his volunteers he dragged his old engine to meet the parade of the new, head-on. Scuffles started, which quickly developed into a full-blown riot. The police, many of whom were also fire volunteers, were mobilised in large numbers and had considerable troubles in breaking up the fighting factions. Davies proved not only a good fire chief, but also a man keen on international co-operation between fire brigades. Soon after the Margate Fire Brigade riots, he took his whole brigade to France by ferry steamer to visit the brigades of Boulogne and Dunkirk and later entertained 60 French pompiers at a great competition in Margate.

By the mid-19th century, great progress had also been made in the Ashford Fire Engine Association. Already an important brigade soon after its foundation in 1826, by 1840 the Brigade had 40 members and at least two engines. There were four inspectors, four branchmen, four foremen, four engineers, a secretary, and 27 ordinary members. The Ashford Association prided itself that, unlike most other members of brigades, their members never received the smallest remuneration for their services. Their account books, still in existence, show that persons whose property was on fire were charged for the use of the engines only – five guineas for the large and three guineas for the small engine. The rest of the funds were obtained through private subscriptions and

contributions from the fire offices of the Kent, Phoenix and Norwich Union insurance companies. Although the accounts show that the members received nothing for their attendance at fires, not even a sixpence for refreshments, they were fined for non-attendance. However, from the Brigade's Minute books, it is obvious that these fines had been devoted to 'conviviality at the Saracen's Head', a hostelry apparently much frequented by the thirsty fire-fighters.

By the 1860's the Ashford Brigade had become famous not only in Kent but throughout the south of the country. Captain Shaw, the Chief of London (and of Gilbert and Sullivan fame), was taking a great interest in what was happening in Ashford, and on several occasions visited and drilled the Ashford men, complimenting them on their efficiency and giving them valuable advice and information. A letter from him, addressed to the Ashford Superintendent James Benton and dated June 29th 1869, following one of Captain Shaw's visits, states:

"I had great pleasure in looking over your arrangements for the suppression of fires in Ashford and the neighbourhood, and am of opinion that you and the other gentlemen voluntarily associated with you in this work are entitled to very great credit, not only for what you have already done, but also for what you propose to do in the way of increasing and improving your stock of appliances. You have certainly made the best of everything, and I have no doubt that, with a moderate expenditure, you will be enabled to put your brigade in such a position as to be of very considerable credit both to yourself and to your town. Assuring you that it will always give me great pleasure to assist you in any way in my power and wishing you and your brigade every success in your most praiseworthy exertions, I am, etc, etc. Captain Shaw''.

Earlier, however, two fires occurred in 1857 and 1858, one of which resulted in a public inquiry because of "certain shortcomings in the efficiency of the Brigade''. The first, on July 6th 1857, broke out at the station of the South-Eastern Railway and was reported in the "Ashford and Alfred News'', which recorded:

"The fire occurred in a building close to the station, used as a carpenters shop and paint shop and spread with great rapidity and fears were at one time entertained for the safety of the station. Two fire engines belonging to the South Eastern Company were promptly engaged in extinguishing the fire, it was got under about 1 o'clock, but not before the building was completely destroyed with its contents and a quantity of timber adjoining much damaged.

Further destruction was only prevented by the efficient working of the engines. It was materially checked in the first stage while the engines were being got ready, by a tank of water, which was in close proximity being poured upon it. The Ashford engine was speedily in attendance; but its services were not required, there being a deficiency of water to supply it, although great assistance was tendered by several residents of the town''.

The second blaze, much bigger, and which led to the enquiry, happened on January 26th 1858, and was again reported in the Ashford and Alfred News: "On Tuesday night, shortly before 11 o'clock, a fire broke out in a carpenters shop belonging to Mr Boulden, situated behind his house at Mill Bridge. It was first seen in the upper room of the building and in consequence of the inflammable nature of the contents soon reached the outside. The workshop was surrounded with other wooden buildings which had also tarred roofs and some being thatched and a strong wind raising the fire with fearful violences, these speedily caught the blaze. In half-an-hour from their discovery a terrible spectacle was presented by the height and extent of the flames, which had spread to the stables of the Queen's Head public house adjoining Mr Kingsford's garden on one side to a lodge of Mr Watson's wool store close to the bridge on the other, a space of more than 300 feet in length by about 100 in breadth and which included, besides the carpenters shop, a small shoemakers workshop, numerous outbuildings, stables and lodges, one more than 60 feet in length belonging to the wool stores.

The Ashford engine No. 2 arrived about 20 minutes after 11 and the efforts of those who worked it prevented the conflagration spreading along the range of stables belonging to the Queen's Head and saved the dwelling houses that face the mill and the backs of which were round the carpenters shop, from destruction. The greatest endeavours were made

39

to get the wool out of the building but such was the rapidity with which the fire raged that comparatively only a small portion was saved. It was speedily enveloped in flames which reached a great height and could be seen for many miles around.

The South Eastern engine from Alfred however was promptly brought to the spot. By this time the fire had caught Mr Watson's house which adjoined and from which the furniture was being removed. Such a stream of water was poured upon it however by the South Eastern engine that the house was saved. Meantime the other Ashford engine had arrived, which, although it was sometime before the hose was adjusted, aided greatly in extinguishing the rest. The property destroyed may be estimated at from £1,200 to £1,500.

We understand that a public enquiry is likely to be made upon this occasion and it would be desirable to have it as early as possible. The Ashford engine which arrived first was not efficiently directed and the South Eastern engine by the promptitude by which it was got to work and the able manner in which it was directed was certainly the means of saving Mr E. Watson's dwelling house and possibly the whole block. The other town engine also did good service after it commenced playing, although through some confusion at first in fixing the suction pipe it was considerably delayed".

A few days later on February 1st, the enquiry was held, and I have taken extracts from a contemporary record.

"A public meeting was held at the Saracens Head Hotel for the purpose of investigating the cause of the fire and also to enquire into the efficiency of the present means in this town of suppressing such calamities. The members of the Ashford Engine Association and all who could aid the enquiry were requested to attend. H. Whitfeld Esq. occupied the chair and most of the leading inhabitants and tradesmen were present, making a very large meeting. The chairman stated the object for which they were met together, and called upon any gentleman who could give any information which would explain away any suspicions which might be afloat, or aid in the more prompt extinction of such unfortunate occurrences, to stand forward.

It was resolved to endeavour first to ascertain the cause of the fire and to obtain such testimony as anyone might be willing to come forward voluntarily and give; in order, as several gentlemen said, that the character of a fellow townsman might be relieved from such ill-natured and unsupported imputations which had been cast upon it; among them, one to the effect that he had left the Marlborough Inn – where he was spending the evening at a meeting of the Foresters Club – for half an hour between 10 and 11 o'clock on the evening of the fire.

As Mr Boulden, carpenter, was not present, his attendance was requested and he shortly afterwards entered the room. In the meantime it was stated by Mr F. Paine and some other gentlemen that Mr Boulden had passed the evening at the Marlborough and Mr Paine said further, that about a quarter to 11 o'clock he met Mr Boulden returning to the room in the Duke of Marlborough; but he had not seen him quit the room. Mr Boulden was then asked by the Chairman if he would favour the meeting with any information and in reply to questions he said he had left his house at a quarter past eight on Tuesday evening and went to the Duke of Marlborough to a meeting of the Foresters Club and with the exception of an absence of about two minutes, did not quit the house until called by his daughter about 11 o'clock. He sat all the evening between a person called John Watson and Mr Gibbs, the butcher. Mr Gibbs, said he was with Mr Boulden at the club all evening.

An anonymous letter was here handed the chairman, stating that a Mr Prebble, employed at Mr Elliot's brewery, could prove that Mr Boulden was absent for half an hour from the room between 10 and 11 o'clock. Mr Prebble was sent for and said he saw Mr Boulden leave the room about 10 o'clock he was absent some little time, perhaps ten minutes but certainly more than five. He denied having said he was absent for half an hour. Mr Boulden mentioned some songs that were sung and other circumstances that passed during that period, showing that he must have been at the Marlborough at the time. Several gentlemen expressed their opinion that all suspicions and doubts had been cleared away by the evidence that had been heard. Mr Furley proposed and Mr Ramsay seconded two resolutions; one declaring the option of the meeting that the fire commenced on Mr Boulden's premises, the other that Mr Boulden did not quit the Marlborough premises from 8 o'clock until 11 on the evening of the fire. The Chairman then asked whether anybody wished to put any more questions and he put the proposed resolutions to the meeting and they were unanimously carried.

The meeting then proceeded to enquire into the efficiency of the present means for extinguishing fire. Mr Bird, secretary to the Fire Engine Association, said that the engine arrived at the fire in ten minutes from the alarm being given. The whole of the Association were not there; some did not know of the fire until the next morning; the police had neglected to call them. He had supplied Superintendent Dewar with ten or 12 printed cards containing the names and addresses of the Fire Brigade. He and Mr Fowler ran together to get the engine out, but they had some little difficulty in doing so from the locks of the engine house. The engine No. 2 was a very good one; although the South Eastern was more powerful. The cause of the delay in getting the engine No. 1 to work was that some person had taken an old hose which was kept at the top of the engine house, although the right one was strapped to the engine. The fire-cocks would not supply more than one engine.

Mr Richardson went and told Mr King to turn the water on. Mr Wilks had told him upon one occasion that they would not be allowed to have water from the Company; but he had told him that he (Mr Bird) would pay for it. He thought that the town would have no reason to find fault with the Association, if the police had a regular plan of calling them and a more convenient place were provided for the engine house. The engines were in very good order. Mr Thurston said the water belonged to a private Company and it was formerly left on at all times, but through the dishonesty of many individuals they had been obliged to turn it off at night. Mr Furley suggested that a space in Bank Street would be a desirable spot for the erection of an engine house but the materials and ground of the old one might be sold to build on. He thought a deputation should wait upon the Commissioners of the town and ask for a yearly grant of money in aid of the Engine Association, as he was in favour of paid services, for then a right to grumble were given if they were not efficiently performed".

About this time too, steamers made their re-appearance, with one being built by Shand Mason in London in 1858, and another in 1861 by Merryweathers. I say re-appeared intentionally, because, already in 1829, John Braithwaite, a London engineer, had invented the first steam fire engine. With a ten horse-power engine and weighing 45 hundredweight, it could raise steam in 13 minutes and could throw 170 gallons a minute to a height of 90 feet. Although the new steamer proved itself at a big fire in London the following year, fire chiefs throughout the country showed little interest in the invention. Too heavy, too expensive, too slow to raise steam, were some of the objections and it took another 30 years before steamers were accepted and gradually brought into use. Few records remain to show where the first steamers were in use in Kent. Ashford Brigade was probably the first in the County when they acquired a Merryweather direct-acting steam fire engine holding 320 gallons, at a cost of £450. The whole of this money was raised by voluntary subscription. The only other early reference to a steamer in Kent was found in an old vellum-bound book of the Phoenix Insurance Company at Maidstone which shows that, in 1897, five guineas were contributed to Sittingbourne for a new steam fire engine. Folkestone, always an important harbour, seems to have had a rudimentary fire brigade in 1864. The population then was 9,400 and the brigade consisted of 13 men, one three-inch manual for 12 men, 130 feet of leather hose and they had to take water from plugs in wooden mains. Just as well that they only averaged one fire per annum!

From the beginning of the 19th century, fire-fighting methods and appliances gradually improved, and with the introduction of the steam fire engine, with its considerable output of water, conflagrations could more easily be contained. However, with the exception of London and the bigger cities of the country, the rescue of persons trapped in fire was still rudimentary, and relied mainly on builder's ladders, ropes, and the courage of the rescuers.

In 1836, the Royal Society for the Protection of Life from Fire was

Fig. 7. Gillingham Fire Brigade's Merryweather Steam Fire Engine.

formed in London and provided a number of wheeled escapes, very similar to the escapes carried on appliances in brigades until recently. The Society obtained its funds through subscription, and in 1837, Coronation Year, Queen Victoria became its patron. In London, escape stations were provided during the night with a conductor who, to assist with the heavy escape, could order passers-by or policemen to help push the escape to the fire. Thus, in London, the Society was responsible for providing protection to people in case of fire, while the Metropolitan Board of Works protected property. In 1865, "an act for the establishment of a fire brigade in the Metropolis" became law, and with new rate for fire protection being imposed, the contributions to the Society dwindled. In the same year the Society, still owning many escapes, offered these to the provinces under certain conditions of maintenance and inspection; and Canterbury was one of the very first towns to take advantage of this offer.

It will be recalled that fires in Canterbury were among the very first to be mentioned in this book, with records going as far back as the 7th and 12th centuries. And while it is certain that the City had the usual basic fire protection provided by the Vestry and Commissioners (probably adding wooden manuals to the array of buckets, hooks and chains) it is interesting to note that very little is known when the first properly organised volunteer establishments were formed. In a book "Fire

43

Engines and Brigades", published in 1865, reference is made to Canterbury having a volunteer brigade in 1815, but does not give any details of its organisation or equipment. The same book states however, that about the time of publication, Canterbury had a population of 22,000, two paid fire brigades, two engine stations and two engines. One brigade, consisting of a foreman and eight men, is kept up by the Kent Insurance Company, and the other, consisting of a foreman and nine men, by the Phoenix. Each establishment, including rent of engine-house and salaries, cost about £30 per annum; and the expenses of attending fires were paid by the offices interested.

Each engine is for 26 men, and is provided with 180 feet of leather hose. The value of the plant and appliances of each brigade is about £120. In addition to the above engines, there is one at the station of the London, Chatham and Dover Railway, one at the barracks, one at the cathedral and one in the parish of St Margaret. The supply of water in case of fire is very uncertain, and is derived from the river where accessible, and also from the waterworks.

Although Chatham had two disastrous fires in 1800 and 1820, both of which nearly destroyed the town, it was not until 1866, following another big blaze at a wharf (which it was said burnt for seven days), that a meeting of the town's people was called at the house of Mr Ralph in the High Street. Present among others was the High Constable of Chatham, and a resolution was passed that "a volunteer fire brigade should be formed with Mr D. Barnard as Captain". The Kent Fire Office made a donation of £25 to the new brigade and the men attended their first serious fire only three weeks after the brigade's formation when several shops in the High Street, including one owned by Captain Barnards (who also owned the famous Barnard's Music Hall), were badly damaged. In 1870, the Society for Protection of Life from Fire presented a fire escape to the town and members of the brigade were instructed in its use. One year later in April 1871, all the fire-fighting resources of the area had to be mobilised to assist the Chatham Volunteers when fire broke out at Neylor's oil and colour store in Hammond Place. Despite the combined efforts of the Chatham Brigade, the Dockyard Police Brigade, the Royal Marines with a floating engine, the Kent Fire Office Brigade and the Railway Company's engine, further assisted by the Gun Wharf and Rochester Police hose-reels, and a detachment of troops from the local barracks, the fire destroyed a dozen houses.

As happened so often in those days, it needed a destructive fire before people decided to find better ways of fire protection other than by buckets of water and primitive engines. This was the case in Whitstable when, in October 1866, a serious fire destroyed two public houses, the "Duke of Cumberland" and the "Red Lion", together with dwelling houses and various stores. A public meeting was called "to consider the desirability of the town possessing a fire engine". It appears that no conclusion was reached at that meeting but at a second meeting, it was reported that the Norwich Union had offered to provide an engine if a suitable building to house it and the hose could be found.

Once again the meeting adjourned, the good citizens of Whitstable having decided to approach other insurance companies for help and no doubt hoping for a better deal. It was not until July 1867, that an engine was finally installed and a volunteer brigade of 26 men formed. Whitstable was fortunate not to have delayed the formation of their own brigade any longer, for two years later, on November 16th 1869, a "great fire" devastated the town. A contemporary account gives a graphic and colourful description of the fire:

"About a quarter to 11 o'clock at night, a coastguardsman named Edwin George Lane, while on duty near the locality, first observed flames issuing from the roof of Mr Hoult's shop. He at once raised the alarm, and in a short time a considerable and excited crowd of people had hurried to the spot, though amid the general confusion little could be done effectually to arrest the progress of the fire, which, as soon as it had burst through the shop roof, rapidly spread to other parts of the building under the aggravating influence of a brisk north-east wind that was then blowing. In the meantime, however, not only had telegrams and mounted messengers been sent to Canterbury and Faversham for the fire engines, but the Whitstable engine had made its appearance on the scene. Some time was unavoidably lost in obtaining water and getting the hose into play, and even when this had been accomplished, the work of repressing the momentarily increasing conflagration was, after a short time, brought to a premature standstill by the fouling and choking of the engine by the sand and weed drawn up with the seawater from the beach.

The flames now had it all their own way, and they devoured the inflammable, dry timbered and tarred buildings with a terrible avidity which it was next to impossible to withstand. The excitement and the crowds every moment increased, the confusion and distress being heightened by the terrors of the unfortunate people whose dwellings and property were either being consumed, or were in imminent danger of sharing what then threatened to the common fate. At this crisis of the sad disaster, Mr Superintendent Walker (of the Home Division), with a number of the constabulary under his direction, arrived on the spot, and he, with characteristic coolness and energy, at once began to take the requisite steps not only for assisting the unfortunate persons who were fleeing from their endangered dwellings in alarm, and of protecting their scattered property from the hands of adventurous marauders, but also of discovering sources of water supply preparatory to the arrival of the fire engines from Canterbury and Faversham, which were now anxiously and eagerly looked for.

In this task, as may be supposed, Mr Walker encountered great difficulty, but his efforts were not without success – success to which it would be unfair of us did we not add that the coastguardsmen largely contributed, by the hearty readiness with which they placed themselves under his orders. At length the engines of the 'Kent' and 'Phoenix' offices from Canterbury, and the 'Kent' and 'Norwich' from Faversham arrived, and were as soon as possible posted in available positions for contending with the fire that was now raging furiously around. The spectacle presented by the great mass of blazing buildings was magnificently terrible, and, if the spectator could only divest his mind of the thought that it entailed so much destruction and distress, he could hardly look upon it as it lit up luridly the surrounding country, and reflected itself in the waters of the Bay, that lay beneath the gloomy reddening clouds like a sea of molten gold, without a feeling of mingled admiration and awe.

It was indeed a sight fearfully impressive, and once seen could never be forgotten. The flames despite all that the united efforts of the four engines could effect, continued their devastating march without any material check, from the harbour gates on the right, as far as the premises of Mr Josiah Reeves, mast and block-maker, on the extreme left, where, owing to the interposition of a wider break than usual between the line of buildings, its further progress in that direction was providentially arrested. It had, however by the veering of the wind to the north, and subsequently to the north-east, been carried across Marine Street into Harbour Street beyond, and had in both localities done great damage, especially in the intervening space, where almost the whole of the buildings were destroyed, and many were more or less seriously injured by the furnace-like heat to which they were subjected.

The fire extended along Harbour Street to a point nearly opposite the residence of Mr Hayward, surgeon, which was greatly damaged by the extreme heat of burning buildings opposite, and the adjoining house and shop of Mr Goodwin, greengrocer, suffered in the roof and upper rooms, it only being by the incessant exertions of the occupier that it was saved from destruction.

The total number of buildings consumed is stated to be no fewer than 71, of which 25 were inhabited houses of various dimensions, the remainder being stores, workshops, etc. Along the "Sea Wall" and in Marine Street there were destroyed 36 stores, 16 cottages, three sail-lofts, two inns (The Victoria and The Spread Eagle), one blacksmith's forge, one ship chandlers shop and timber yard, one auction mart, one shipping office, and three shoemakers shops; and in Harbour Street there were consumed four dwelling houses and shops, and three private dwelling houses".

Cranbrook Fire Brigade, already established during the great fire of 1844, seems to have developed considerably during the next two decades.

The regulations for the Cranbrook Fire Engine Establishment, dated October 1867, are still in existence and make interesting reading.

The colourful career of Hythe Fire Brigade (the oldest in the County having been formed in 1802), took another interesting turn in 1867. Having split in 1832 – for reasons unknown – into two brigades, the oddly-named 'Scot and Lot' brigade and the 'Corporation' brigade, they decided again without any reasons being recorded, to re-unite as the Hythe Volunteer Fire Brigade. A book published at that time describes the fire protection at Hythe, one of the Cinque Ports, as having an engine station with two engines for a population of 3,000. "The Association consists of 40 volunteer members who give their time and subject themselves to fines for non-compliance to the rules, and honorary members who pay a subscription of 4s. per year. The Kent office subscribes £5 per annum and the Norwich Union gives donations from time to time. The engines are two very old ones, for 20 men each and are constantly requiring repairs to keep them in working order and there are 90 foot of leather hose for each engine. There is no fire escape in the town, but a long worn out ladder does duty as such. The supply of water in case of fire is derived partly from a canal running along the town, and from pumps, ditches and waterworks. The fires average about two a year".

The citizens of Bexley Heath, who seem to have made do with a manual engine first supplied to them in 1776, apparently became restive 90 years later, and in 1867, 16 ratepayers got together to ask the parish to buy a fire engine out of the 'poor rate'. The following year, the Christ Church wardens met to discuss the problem, and a public subscription was started. Amongst the chief supporters were the then editor of the "Bexley Heath Observer" and, curiously, the Gas Inspectors. Soon after, the town was able to buy a new curricle (horse-drawn pump) costing £62, and for another £53 the Brigade acquired belts, axes and hose. 1868 and 1869 were vintage years for the formation of new volunteer fire brigades. Bromley, until that time poorly equipped with two small manuals and some ladders, was developing rapidly; and following several big fires, decided that their fire protection was totally inadequate. A public meeting was convened in the Town Hall in 1868 to approve and organise a volunteer fire brigade. A voluntary subscription fund was set up; a brigade with 17 officers and men, and captained by Mr C. Satterthwaite, was formed in November; a new up-to-date manual engine arrived and was escorted through the town with much pomp and ceremony. In 1873, Mr Conrad Nickalls became captain, and under his command the Bromley Brigade achieved great efficiency. In 1874, during the open competitions held at the Crystal Palace, Bromley won the four-man Drill Championship against competition from brigades all over England.

Little is known about fire-fighting in Bexleyheath until 1869 when some kind of volunteer brigade was formed in the town. In the same year a town meeting at Sandwich decided to purchase a new fire engine by subscription. The money was raised, the engine was bought, and members of the second Cinque Port Artillery Volunteers became voluntary firemen.

In 1870, Edenbridge, which had had a Tilley manual for the previous 20 years, decided to form a proper fire brigade and elected as its first captain a Mr Arthur Hoare, a headmaster of a local school, famous cricketer, and suspected spy. According to a book published in 1912, Captain Hoare played cricket for Kent and Sussex and in 1873 scored 468 in three consecutive innings for Ford Park v M.C.C. Despite his duties as captain of the fire brigade and headmaster of his school, he apparently was a great traveller, and narrowly escaped being shot as a Prussian spy in the Siege of Paris – he was saved from that fate by the prison doctor who knew some members of Hoare's family and declared his innocence; but before being released, Hoare had to witness the shooting of six men who had been convicted with him.

In the 1870's, Maidstone, although the seat of three Fire Insurance Offices, still had no regular volunteer fire brigade. Suggestions for the formation of such a brigade were first made in 1855 and that it should include in its members "the more respectable classes in the town". Nothing came of this, and an attempt in 1862 by the local Army Volunteer Reserve to form a brigade, also failed. In July 1870, the Royal Society for the Protection of Life from Fire granted an escape to Maidstone "under the usual conditions, to stand against the Town Hall, railed in, and the management of the escape at fires to be made under the Constabulary". In July 1873, a meeting at the Town Hall to "discuss matters relating to the proposed formation of a thoroughly efficient brigade for the town" was attended by 30 people. A committee was set up and it was decided to ask Ashford, Canterbury and Rochester for advice on how their brigades were managed. In November 1873, all was ready and the Maidstone Volunteer Fire Brigade started life. The Mayor of Maidstone, Charles Ellis, was its first captain and the uniform of the officers and men was modelled on that in use in the Canterbury brigade.

One of the largest fires Ashford had experienced for many years happened on the Saturday night of April 9th 1870, in the premises of a Mr Burnett, carriage builder and harness manufacturer in the High Street. It took more than ten hours to put out and there was some criticism of the brigade afterwards. Usually the best descriptions of old incidents are to be found in contemporary documents and the following is taken from the actual log book of the Ashford Brigade for the year 1870:

"Mr Burnett's workshops extend about 230 feet in depth from the High Street. They were substantially constructed of brick with slate roofs. The fire was first noticed in the paint shop on the top floor about

8 o'clock and soon got a considerable hold and spread with great rapidity. The new engine of the Fire Brigade was brought into North Street and played on the fire from the yard of Messrs Hart & Tatnell, corn dealers. The second engine was taken into the High Street and was drawn through Mr Burnett's front shop and brought to bear upon the flames from the inside of the building.

In the meantime the South Eastern engine had arrived in High Street and the hose from this was laid along the passage between Mr Burnett's and Mr Field's premises. By this time the whole of the factory was in a blaze from top to bottom and the glare could be seen for many miles around.

The Godinton Park engine belonging to the Earl of Mount Charles arrived about half past nine. His Lordship accompanied the engine and although it was not set to work owing to all the fire plugs in the neighbourhood being occupied, yet his lordship actively exerted himself with the other members of his Brigade to bring the fire to a conclusion. The damage done was immense and we understand it does not fall short of £6,000.

The Ashford Fire Brigade did not receive the alarm until a quarter past eight although it was given in the town almost as the clock struck eight. The time of arrival of the first engine is put down in the report as half past eight and the second engine is put down as arriving at 8.40. Mr Benton was in charge of the first engine and Mr T. L. Elliott of the second and 15 members of the brigade were present. The course adopted by the engine on the west side was much criticised. With regard to the South Eastern Railway Co's engine we may state it was sent for at 8.30 and was in the town with a full complement of the Brigade at 8.50 but owing to the defective standpipes of the old town eight or nine minutes were entirely lost. The pipes were quite useless and a connection could not be formed until the New Town Brigade attached their own canvas tank. The circumstance is much to be regretted as there was an abundant supply of water.

The Brigade was under the direction of Mr Cudworth who was present the whole time and Mr Mansell was also present and took a very active part in the operations. We cannot conclude our report without noticing the complete success of the arrangements of the new Water Co for providing water for extinguishing fires. So good a supply of water was never known in Ashford on any similar occasion".

The log reports another big fire on October 7th 1870, when an arsonist set fire to the farm of a Mr Thomas Kennett at Westwell, some miles outside Ashford. Once again the private fire brigade of the Earl of Mount Charles, who seems to have been a keen fire enthusiast, arrived with the Godinton Park engine and the Earl in charge. "The fire was discovered soon after 8 o'clock in a straw stack forming one of two rows containing nine in all, standing in a stackyard behind a large barn. A mounted messenger was despatched to Ashford for the Fire Engine and the No. 1 Engine with Superintendent Benton and 16 firemen was despatched and arrived at the spot at about ten minutes to nine. By this time the fire had spread to the adjoining stacks and assumed the dimensions of a large conflagration. The flames could be distinctly seen at Tenterden. Many hundreds of people from Ashford and the surrounding country hastened to the scene, which soon became a grand description.

The exertions of the firemen were directed in the first instance to saving the barn and adjoining buildings, as it was probable the whole homestead would be destroyed if the buildings caught alight. In this they were successful with the aid of the Earl of Mount Charles, who came at half-past ten with the Godinton Park Engine and eight firemen. The Godinton Park Engine worked till about half-past one when it completely exhausted the pond from which it was supplied.

The Ashford Brigade had connected the entire length of their hose so as to get water from another pond at a considerable distance from the premises, and they continued pumping until the fire was completely subdued, which was not until 6 o'clock on Saturday morning. The whole contents of the stack yard are reported as destroyed, the damage amounting to £800 or £900. Mr Kennett was insured in the Norwich Union Office. It will be seen from our Ashford Petty Sessions that a man was charged with setting fire to the stacks, and discharged".

Canterbury Cathedral, the Mother Church of Christianity in England, was once again nearly destroyed by fire in 1872, had it not been for valiant efforts by local firemen under Captain W. G. Pidduck, a colourful character and chief of one of the County Volunteer Brigades. The blaze broke out on September 3rd, 1872 – when plumbers were at work in the Cathedral roof – and quickly got a hold in the accumulated rubbish. The local volunteers were quickly mobilised and telegrams of help were received from the Secretary of the Admiralty, the Naval Commander, Sheerness, the Officer Commanding Chatham; and the Superintendent Chatham Dockyards whose message read: "Hear Cathedral is on fire. I am sending a steam fire-engine by rail at once. What other assistance is needed?" In the Kent Brigade Museum, there is still a photograph, too faded for reproduction, which was taken immediately after the fire was brought under control. It shows the fire-fighters standing in stiff, heroic poses under the charred roof-timbers and melted lead. The photo has the printed caption "The Roof of Canterbury Cathedral (one o'clock p.m. Tuesday September 3rd 1872). Photo taken as soon as fire was stopped. This copy was presented to the Very Rev. Dean Farrar, by Capt W. G. Pidduck, C.V.F.B., Dec 1896", and underneath are the names of the fire-fighters, who included members of the Cathedral staff, the Canterbury Fire Brigade, the Kent Brigade and the Phoenix Brigade. The frame, according to an endorsement on the back signed by Captain Pidduck, is made from oak rescued from the seat of the fire, and the photograph was respectfully presented to the Very Reverend the Dean of Canterbury, December 1896.

The account of the fire and how the photograph was taken appears in Captain Pidduck's own handwriting and shows the difficulties he had in obtaining his expenses from the Sun Office.

Fire at Canterbury Cathedral
Tuesday, 3rd September 1872

This photo was taken at one o'clock by someone who asked me to allow him to pass into the roof, the means of access being closed excepting to Firemen (a few onlookers had previously got into the roof). The photographer was a stranger to me but I allowed him to be passed on condition that he did not attempt to hinder the men until the fire was beaten down.

The fire broke out at 10.30 a.m. and extinguished at 1.30 p.m. Plumbers were at work in the roof, and no doubt a spark had found its way into one of the large accumulations of sticks and twigs which had been carried there by rooks, jackdaws and pigeons and which must have been allowed to accumulate for years, as I saw enough to fill two or three cart loads, there being several heaps from 18 inches to 2 feet in height. My bill of expenses paid out of pocket was £4.8.8d. The roof was insured in the "Sun" for £20,000, the loss was under £3,000. Salvage from melted lead about £500. After several weeks the 'Sun' Directors sent me a cheque for £4.8.6d. It must thus be said that I was fined 2d for saving the Office from a great loss, to say nothing of preserving a National Monument. Well! my men only did their duty – but we give a sentiment at our annual dinner, over empty glasses, as follows –
May the sun never shine on that Office intense
Which too utterly too too still owes us two pence.

W. G. Pidduck, Capt C.V.F.B.

The letter of appreciation from the Vice-Dean too, is a most interesting document. The facsimile has engraved around the edges illustrations of the County Fire Office, London; the actual fire at the Cathedral, with firemen at work in the roof and ladders pitched; the County Fire Office, Canterbury; Captain Pidduck himself; the Volunteer Fire Brigade on its horsed engine, apparently dashing past the Cathedral gateway; and 2nd Lieutenant G. De Lasaux. It reads:

"Canterbury, September 6, 1872
Sir,
I am desired by the Chapter to return their grateful thanks to you and the Fire Brigade under your direction, for your most praiseworthy efforts on Tuesday last which were so eminently successful in

51

Fig. 8. The Canterbury Fire Brigade, passing the Westgate Tower, 1872. (This engraving probably made following the fire at the Cathedral on 3rd September 1872.)

extinguishing the fire that broke out in the roof of our Cathedral.

Our thanks are due to others, who zealously co-operated with your endeavours, but more especially to yourselves, on whom the chief duties of the day devolved, and to whom, above all, we are indebted for the preservation of the Cathedral. Considering the great difficulties with which you had to contend, the skill and ability with which they were overcome, and the zeal, energy and activity with which you performed your duties, we owe you our warmest gratitude, which I have now pleasure in expressing.

I am, Sirs,

Yours faithful Servant,

J. Thomas, Vice-Dean

Captain W. G. Pidduck,
Volunteer Fire Brigade."

Below is printed:
"The above letter was ordered to be engraved by the Directors of the County Fire Office and a copy presented to each member of the Brigade as a souvenir of the Fire, and in recognition of the services rendered by the Corps whereby much greater damage to a National Monument was providentially averted.

Members of the Brigade, 1872

Mr William Gilbert Pidduck, Captain
Mr Thomas Willm. de Lasaux, 1st Lieut
Mr George Henry de Lasaux, 2nd Lieut
Mr Edward Beer, 3rd Lieut
Earl Mount Charles, 4th Lieut
Mr Robert Pidduck, No. 5
Mr Henry George Trimnell, No. 6
Mr William Banister, Foreman
Mr Edward Eves, Engineer."

It is understood that the Phoenix Insurance Company also holds a photograph of a similar letter of appreciation sent by the Vice-Dean to that office.

The birth of the Deal Volunteer Fire Brigade was not without problems and complications. In May, 1874, active steps were being taken to organise such a brigade in the town and it was hoped that some of the Artillery Volunteers would join as members. At the time, Deal seemed to have had very little in the way of fire protection, and had to rely on the Garrison engine for fire-fighting. In July, a public meeting was held at the Deal Castle Inn to discuss the matter and "several gentlemen were enrolled". (It is interesting to note that throughout the 17th and 18th centuries it was only 'Gentlemen' who were considered to be fit to form a volunteer fire brigade in the County, while ordinary folk were only good enough to be general handymen and fetchers and drawers of water.) Dr

T. F. Mason was elected superintendent, and among the officers was a Mr Dunn who had been for some time in the London Metropolitan Fire Brigade. It appears that the main reason for starting the Deal Brigade was the offer of an escape from the Royal Society for the Protection from Fire, which duly arrived by train from London at the beginning of August.

The escape was accompanied by an officer of the Society to show the newly-organised brigade how to work it. The first training session with the new escape was graphically described in the "Deal Telegram" as witnessed by one of their reporters: "We were fortunate to witness the evolutions of the Brigade at the Town Hall, where we were highly gratified by the agility displayed by Messrs Selth, Dunn and Harvey. It was proposed that the Superintendent of the Police and P.C. Cox should ascend the ladder and run down the canvas, but the latter gentleman declined, on the plea that he might stick fast in the descent and raise the risible faculties of the spectators – discretion in this case obviously being the better part of valour.

"The Brigade has been in active practice during the present week and may now be considered to be tolerably proficient in the management of the escape." So now the town had a volunteer brigade and an escape but no engine. Having had seven days practice on the escape, they met again at the Town Hall on August 6th for the grand display and drill where they "performed admirably well". This consisted of extending the ladder to houses, a store, and the Clarendon Hotel, where some of the volunteers "threw themselves from windows into the canvas trough".

But soon their enthusiasm was to become dampened. Although the escape did not cost the town anything, certain conditions were attached to it, such as uniforms for the operators and a standing-place for the machine. Two months later, the "Deal Telegram" already described the escape as "a rather costly toy" and "the expenses already estimated as a very serious item". The paper continues: "it is questionable whether the money might not be better devoted to the purchase of a fire-engine rather than on uniforms for a Fire Escape Brigade at so early a date. As things stand at present we are dependent upon the Garrison engines in case of fire, and it is not at all likely that the military would allow a volunteer corps to take charge of their engines, therefore there is an impression abroad that the money voted for an escape might have been advanced for other purposes of a more pressing character".

However, a year later, in November 1875, a powerful engine, well-equipped in every respect, was at last delivered to the town and paid for by voluntary contributions. The first real test of the Deal Brigade and their new engine came at the beginning of December 1875, when a fire badly damaged a range of buildings storing large quantities of farm implements, wagons, carts and seed potatoes, at the north end of the town. The Deal firemen had already been called out to another fire at

54

nearby Sholden, and the engine from Mr Hill's brewery was therefore first on the scene under the direction of the Superintendent of Police. By the time the Deal Brigade had been re-routed, the fire had spread to other buildings and "seeing that the store was hopelessly doomed, they directed their efforts to the dwelling house and adjacent buildings to prevent the fire extending to them". Finally, the Barrack engine was also sent for and arrived with a detachment of marines who gave excellent service.

Goudhurst has always been an important and attractive village in a county that is world-famous for its historic and beautiful places, but as far as the fire-fighting business is concerned, Goudhurst was always a bit of a mystery. No records whatsoever exist about the early days and, although by the middle of the 19th century some sort of volunteer fire brigade existed with the imposing name of "Weald of Kent Brigade", the date of its formation or beginnings are unknown.

Reference is made in the Goudhurst Coronation Book to one Benjamin Wilmot who, for some years prior to 1874, was Captain of the Goudhurst Brigade. He was a generous supporter of the Brigade and apparently was also the officer-in-charge of the local Yeomanry which he commanded when they provided a guard of honour and bodyguard for the Duchess of Teck (the mother of Queen Mary) when she visited Hawkhurst to open Dr Barnardo's "Babies Castle". When Captain Wilmot resigned in 1874 because he was leaving Goudhurst, he was succeeded as Captain by a Mr Albert Smith. At that time, the President was Mr A. J. B. Beresford Hope, and the Superintendent, Mr John Thurgood who kept "The Vine" inn. Before 1874, the Brigade seemed to have had a manual engine which required 20 men to operate and the Captain had to hire pumpers (which was costly) who had to be paid one shilling an hour for their work.

It was in July 1874, that a meeting of the Weald of Kent Fire Brigade was held in Goudhurst where, "the principal subject for consideration was the expected arrival of a steam fire engine. It was decided to adopt new rules better suited to the improved powers of the Brigade, which is now replacing the old manual power engine by one to be worked by steam, and the most efficient of its kind. The steam engine will do its work in a more effectual way at a fire and do away with one of the greatest nuisances for any brigade – the hiring of pumpers". Another Captain of Goudhurst Fire Brigade, whose descendants are still prominent residents of the village, was Mr Benjamin Wickham of Gore Court, who commanded his men shortly before the turn of the century.

Coombe Bank Fire Brigade was founded in 1875, when estate workmen and traders from Sundridge got together to form the rudiments of organised fire-fighting. In 1880, the Brigade was re-formed and the men were supplied with proper uniforms to take the place of the original caps and badges. The equipment at that time consisted of a

Mansion engine with scaling ladders, but this was found not powerful enough when a serious fire broke out at Sundridge Church on March 9th, 1882. The jet of water failed to reach the church roof and a "fire extincteur" had to be carried up by Captain Blyth. For their services on that occasion, the Vicar, the Rev E. D. Hammond, presented all members of the Brigade with a handsome medal. Soon after, a new six-inch manual was bought for the Brigade by a Mr William Spottiswoode who bore the whole of the expenses until his death in 1886.

In 1875, the inhabitants of Wingham decided to protect themselves from uncontrolled fire, and formed a brigade which quickly became known as the "Hunting Brigade". It consisted of a chief officer, three lieutenants, four district officers, ten men and a caller. The caller received 2s 6d from the district officer in whose district the call originated, for passing on the news to him. This fee the district officer had to find from his own pocket. But a fire, always a spectacular sight, must have had a special splendour in Wingham and district. On receipt of a fire call, maroons were sent up and people streamed into the streets to see the appropriate district officer, splendidly arrayed in hunting kit and mounted on a horse, galloping at full speed over meadows and fields to the fire ground. He was followed by the manual pump, drawn by horses and manned by a lieutenant and firemen, shouting the usual warning of "Hi! Hi! Hi!". Bringing up the rear, also in full hunting gear, came the chief officer. Wingham people loved their fire brigade which, from time to time, provided them with a most spectacular "point-to-point".

Fire-fighters, still today, belong to a service universally well liked and respected for the brave and humanitarian work they carry out without thought for their own safety or comfort. And in the old days, too, they often were the darlings of the populace, providing not only a defence against the ravages of fire, but also a colourful part of life which, especially in some rural areas, could be dull. We often read about brigade festivals, bands, and parades; and in music halls, ballads about firemen were frequent and popular. One such ballard is here reproduced from Victorian days, but although not necessarily from Kent, it may have been performed in Barnards Music Hall in Chatham which itself was badly damaged in a fire in 1866.

The scene was a station, the time was midnight,
The fatal word fire on the lamps glittered bright;
The firemen are dozing, while, safely at hand,
The horses were waiting the words of command.
Click goes the message of danger and death,
Down dash the firemen not pausing for breath,
In go the horses. Hi! Hi! Hi! clear the way,
While borne on the zephyrs a voice seemed to say:

Heaven speed the members of the Fire Brigade,
Heroes true as steel, hearts that never fear,
Ready, steady, and undismayed,
Are the noble-hearted members of the Fire Brigade.

On like the wind, how the horses perspire,
See they arrive at the scene of the fire;
Crash go the beams of the roof to the ground,
Scorching the people standing around.
Hark! how that cry of dismay rends the air,
Look at yon window, a woman's up there;
Up goes a fireman, with resolute will,
Hushed are the people, the boldest are still.

Heaven speed the members of the Fire Brigade,
Heroes true as steel, hearts that never fear,
Ready, steady, and undismayed,
Are the noble-hearted members of the Fire Brigade.

Steadily upward, still higher and higher,
Choking and scorched by the smoke and the fire,
Onward he goes till the woman he nears,
Stop – see – she falters, and then disappears.
Down go the sashes, he's in through the frame,
Out with the woman he comes once again;
Faint and half blinded he reaches the ground,
While to the skies goes the echoing sound:

Heaven speed the members of the Fire Brigade,
Heroes true as steel, hearts that never fear,
Ready, steady, and undismayed,
Are the noble-hearted members of the Fire Brigade.

Pause and reflect ere you venture to doubt
The truth of the scene I'm singing about;
I know the fireman who ventured his life,
The woman he rescued to-day is his wife.
My only object is simply to say,
England has heroes who're living today,
Men who belong to that life-saving band,
Facing King Death with their lives in their hand.

Heaven speed the members of the Fire Brigade,
Heroes true as steel, hearts that never fear,
Ready, steady, and undismayed,
Are the noble-hearted members of the Fire Brigade.

In 1876, Ashford Fire Brigade arranged a grand concert in aid of their funds in the New Corn Exchange, under the Royal Patronage of the Duke and Duchess of Edinburgh, and other high dignitaries. Performers included the English Glee Union, a military band, and an artiste member of the Hastings Fire Brigade who had come to assist. A typical Victorian performance, it included sentimental songs full of "tearful sighs, sorrowful times, rejoicing hearts, shepherds swains, rustic beauties and parting hours". Surprisingly, none of the fire brigade ballads were included, but I think it worthwhile to reproduce here the front page of the Book of Words which included all the lyrics of that memorable occasion.

In the 1870's, Gillingham was still a small village, and records reveal that even so, it was left far behind in fire brigade activities which by then were flourishing in many parts of Kent. Following a destructive fire there in 1876 which wrecked a carriage and paint workshop, 24 shopkeepers and tradesmen clubbed together and bought some leather hose and a hose-cart which were kept in a shed at Gillingham Green. No brigade was formed; and although the local council took some interest, it was not until their surveyor, a Mr Hammond, urged the council to more positive action, that a small single-storey building was erected in the council yard. No date can be found for the formation of the Gillingham Brigade, but Mr Hammond became its first chief officer. Gradually, more hose-carts (and presumably hose) were acquired; and finally a Merryweather horse-drawn manual pump was purchased.

The people of Sittingbourne, who lost their parish church through fire in 1762 and had to petition the King and his subject for help to raise money for its replacement, seemed for a long time to have learnt little about the dangers of fire. Although there seems to have been a manual (provided by the Kent Office) in the town since 1821, a reader's letter in the "East Kent Gazette" in 1872, complained about the lack of fire protection provisions, and gave a description of what would happen in the town in the event of fire: "The three engines – or rather the two water squirts and the one engine being taken by a crowd of shouting men and boys to the scene of the conflagration, a vain search for the water plug would be made while the fire was gaining ascendency. There would be an insufficiency of hose, a confusion of direction, a vast disruption of property and perhaps life and a general scramble by street roughs for salvage." The 'Gazette' advocated the formation of a volunteer fire brigade for the town and asked the various fire officers in Kent to "bestir themselves". Sittingbourne finally got a brigade in 1878 under the captaincy of a Mr George Payne.

Little is known about fire-fighting in Broadstairs, but it appears that the first volunteer brigade was formed in 1877. In 1882, the deputy clerk to the council reported that "a volunteer brigade has been established for the last five years, under the superintendance of Captain Large, and

Fig. 9. The Broadstairs Fire Brigade, taken outside the Tartar Frigade Inn. 1880s.

its services have been required about 20 times during that period". During the next ten years, there seems to have been several attempts to bring the brigade under the control of the Broadstairs Local Board, for when the Captain asked the Works Committee in 1892 for the Brigade to be supplied with proper firemen's boots, the Board resolved that "the application stand over until some understanding has been arrived at as to the Brigade coming more under the control of the Board than it is at present". It appears that the Board won the battle, because in 1895, a special meeting of the Works Committee recommended that "the full control of the Brigade be vested in a Committee of the Council to be called the Fire Brigade Committee (probably the first special committee given that name in the County) and that a set of rules and regulations for the management of the Brigade, together with a scale of charges be formulated and that the Brigade should consist of 12 men, including a Superintendent, Foreman and Engineer and that they be paid, Superintendent three guineas per annum, Foreman and Engineer two guineas and nine firemen one guinea per annum."

Deal Fire Brigade, formed in 1874, quickly developed in strength and equipment. During 1877 and 1880, they attended several fires and drew into their area the neighbouring Walmer. They earned the praise of the community in February 1877 when a stackyard at Walmer Court was on fire; and the Deal Brigade managed to reach the blaze with their engine and gear, "drawn by a pair of Mr Samual Old's galloping horses", in under ten minutes. The Deal Brigade experienced greater difficulties when, in September 1880, they were called by telegram to a coach builder's workshop again in Walmer.

When they arrived on the scene, they had difficulties in "getting the engines to the water" and similar troubles were experienced when two further engines arrived from the Royal Marine barracks. Later, an adequate water supply was established, but because of the inflammable nature of the contents of the workshop, "the whole building was consumed".

A serious fire in Sandgate in 1877 made the people of the town realise how neglectful they had been in not providing adequate fire protection. Although Sandgate's first volunteer fire brigade had been founded in 1859, nobody appears to have taken any interest in it and the brigade had lost most of their buckets (borrowed for pig swill) and other vital equipment. When the 1877 fire broke out, no-one could at first find the key to the engine-house and when it was eventually opened, the engine could not be got out. When at last it was dragged to the fire, it was found to be quite useless. Thanks to a change of wind, the damage, though great, was contained to the building of origin.

Despite great concern amongst the townspeople, nothing was done to change the situation until five years later, when in February 1882, an appeal was launched to provide the town with efficient fire-fighting apparatus. The appeal was headed by Lord and Lady Pelham, and James Morris who was governor of the Bank of England gave £50, and a further £150 was sought from the residents. Six months later, amid the cheers of the townspeople, a new Shand Mason fire engine, equipped with a new set of ladders, was drawn through the streets of the town to temporary quarters in the coach-house of the Royal Kent Hotel. In the records of Chatham, the following laconic note appeared for the year 1877: "No fires of any importance took place in Chatham this year."

However, the brigade was not so lucky in 1878. After a series of major outbreaks in January and March, one of the largest fires the town had experienced for some years destroyed a wooden warehouse on Holborn Wharf on May 4th. The contents were highly inflammable and included 100 quarters of oats, large quantities of beers in barrels, tar, and benzoline. The efforts of the brigade had to be confined to saving the Wharf and a timber yard, and this was achieved with the assistance of the Rochester Brigade and the engines from the Dockyard and the Royal Marines. A fire-party from Chatham Garrison also attended.

"An Act for Leathern Buckets and Latchers", recorded in the Wardmote Book of the Town and Port of Faversham for 1602, gave the town probably the best organisation available in Kent at that time. But nothing is known what happened in the town for over 250 years, although it must be assumed that like other places of importance in the

County, Faversham too, went through the gradual development of having some protection consisting of leather hose, hose-carts, simple manual engines and eventually insurance equipment. By the middle of the 19th century, there were two manuals in the town, one provided by the 'Kent' and the other by the Norwich Union. It was in 1879 that a volunteer brigade was formed by some of the more important citizens. This became later known as "The Gentlemen's Brigade". It is not known whether the 'Gentlemen' also acquired an engine, but a three-man escape squad was active in the town about this time. An old Corporation of Faversham 1880 horse-drawn manual pump was found at the local council yard in 1969 in a terribly dilapidated state, and was restored to its old glory by firemen from the Faversham unit of the Kent Fire Brigade.

The Kent County Fire Brigades Association organised a competition at Ashford in July 1880. Among the many competitions were volunteer brigades from Canterbury, Tunbridge Wells, Bromley, Deal, Wingham, Edenbridge, Tonbridge and Goudhurst, all of which won prizes in the various drills.

Leigh Volunteer Fire Brigade was formed in 1880, through the initiative, as in so many other places of well-to-do people in the parish. The impetus was a big fire in a stabling yard in which two horses were burned to death, and soon after this incident, a Mr Sam Morley (grandfather of the present Lord Holland) got together with a few prominent citizens and formed the brigade. A manual fire engine, bought with Mr Morley's money, was housed at Hall Place where the new brigade also had its headquarters.

Calling-out methods in the 1880's were cumbersome and complicated. When a fire occurred within the area of a brigade, church bells could be used; or maroons (which were unpopular with people because of the noisy explosions they cause); or messengers on horseback or on foot, but if firemen were required in outlying districts or were asked to give assistance to neighbouring towns, telegrams were the usual method of calling the brigade to work. A good example was Bexleyheath whose brigade at that time was the only one in the district. Their engine had to serve as far away as Dartford, Sidcup, Erith, Belvedere and Abbey Wood, and the method of alerting them was to telegraph from the railway station of one of these, to Bexley's where the message would be given to a cabman. He galloped off to Bexleyheath to rouse one member of the brigade who would then rush round to the places of work or houses of the other firemen, until the whole brigade was assembled. Only then would they turn out for their long journey to the fire: quite a difference from today's 30-seconds turn-out from a whole-time fire station in Kent. Amusing details are given in the reminiscences of Captain Charles Corville who retired from the Bexley Heath Brigade in 1930 after 40 years service as a volunteer fireman.

"In 1880 I joined the Brigade and was the youngest fireman. At that time the Brigade had a four-wheeled manual. The first big fire I took part in was at the Crayford Celluloid Factory, which occupied the site where Vickers works now stands. Horses for the use of the Brigade were hired from a local jobmaster in those days. This fire broke out in the morning – a very bad morning. It was raining heavens hard. We went to get the horses from the stable proprietor. But that morning he was in a vile humour and he would not let us have the horses for the fire engine. "You don't think I'm going to take my horses out of the stable on a morning like this, do you?" he said, and nothing would soften him, so we had to go away. We tried several other places and the last place we went to was the Lord Hill, but we were disappointed. In the long run we decided, horses being out of the question, to pull the engine to the fire ourselves, without any brakes on the engine. Bassom and myself took the role, the other firemen hanging on. Just as we got nicely started to go down Crayford Hill, all the others mounted the engine, and we went tearing down, hell for leather. Talk about the dirt track – I can tell you it was a brisk journey. If either of the pair of us who were playing horses had stumbled, there would have been a queer mix-up! However, by keeping the pole straight we managed to keep an even keel, as the sailors say, and eventually arrived to do our duty at the fire. This sort of thing happened on many occasions. I have known some of the men run as far as Horton Kirby."

Herne Bay, although comparatively late in forming its own fire brigade, quickly developed fire protection in a most efficient and even pioneering way. On December 8th 1881, a meeting was held at the Town Hall to form a fire brigade, and a Mr C. W. Courtney became its first captain. Only three weeks later, and still without any equipment, the brigade attended their first fire and helped the Canterbury, the Cathedral and the Phoenix Brigades by using buckets they could obtain. On March 8th 1882, a second meeting officially formed the brigade with 14 men selected from volunteers, and with a small manual pump loaned by the Cathedral Brigade. The volunteer firemen – a much sought after position – had to pay 30 shillings on joining. This went towards their uniforms, equipment and personal insurance; and black leather helmets. Soon, these helmets were replaced by brass ones, at a further cost to the men of 30 shillings each. In January 1883, a large manual pump was purchased from Shand Mason for £300, and in December, the first stone was laid for a fire station in the High Street adjoining the Town Hall. The Fire Station and the Town Hall were later destroyed by fire in June 1925.

Herne Bay Volunteer Brigade was probably the first in Kent to take on the job of life-saving at sea, a task, with modern sophisticated equipment, frequently carried out by the Kent Fire Brigade today. When in 1883, the Herne Bay men realised that the nearest lifeboat station was at Margate, they decided to do something about vessels in difficulties and driven inshore. They acquired a rocket line for off-shore rescue work and often drilled with this at Hampton Pier. Nor were the Herne Bay fire-fighters slow in taking stern measures when they found that the local Water Company failed to supply them with sufficient water for fire-fighting. At a special meeting of the Local Board on Christmas Eve 1883, Captain Courtney reported that "at a fire in East Parade 15 minutes were lost by the Fire Brigade in endeavouring to get water from the mains. The engine had to be backed down to the sea and water was procured therefrom."

The meeting decided that "proceedings be taken against the Herne Bay Water Company for not having a supply of water in their mains on the night of December 20th 1883, when a fire occurred at Nos 3 & 4 East Parade, and that Mr Walter Farley be engaged to conduct the case before the Magistrates". It appears that the Water Company was later fined £5.

It seems strange that little is known about the early fire-fighting provisions in some of the more important towns in Kent. There is no reference to a Sevenoaks Volunteer Brigade until the early 1860's, but some organisation must have been in existence long before, because when the town acquired a new engine in 1882 it was to replace a 60-year old manual. The new engine was purchased by public subscription as the local Board of Guardians had refused to expend the £200 required. A contemporary report noted the delight of the townspeople with their new engine: "The townspeople decided to welcome the new engine with every honour, and on January 3rd 1883, when the purchase arrived in Sevenoaks, the town was gaily decorated and crowds of people thronged the streets. At 3 o'clock, a procession was formed at the South Eastern Railway Station, and the engine, with the men on it, was drawn by four horses up Tubs Hill, being escorted by the Tonbridge Brass Band which played lively airs en route. Opposite the London and County Bank the ceremony of christening the engine was observed, this being done by the little daughter of Mr Stepney (the Superintendent of the Brigade), the name given being the 'Ready'."

A fascinating insight into the working of a Kent Volunteer Fire Brigade in the late 19th century is given in the Minute Books of the Hythe Volunteer Brigade, now preserved in the Kent Fire Brigade Museum. Beautifully bound and written by hand, it records the minutes of meetings between 1883 and 1890. Extracts from these minutes are here reproduced:

6.6.1883

Through illness on the part of the Capt they had not been able to wait upon Mr Wilkes or any other person as arranged with Mr West himself for the acquiring of land for Engine House.

It was proposed and carried that if found necessary the efficient members should wear numbers same as Sandgate, put to the vote five for and four against.

Proposed that we try the same system as that at Sandgate in running the hose out.

It was also decided not to continue our Subscription to the Kent Association until information had been received in reference to the operations of the above.

15.9.1883

Proposed by Mr Worthington seconded by Mr Booth that Mr Lee procure nine Windsor Chairs and one arm chair for Engine House.

That Mr Amos make table, also a Locker 6 ft long with division and seat at top.

Mr Worthington procure the necessary brushes etc for use of Engine etc.

Decided to have drill on following Monday.

Decided to abandon the rest of County outings this year, and on the completion of New Engine House on the night of October 12th have the same formally opened with refreshments for members. Capt Lee to arrange the same.

Question of new uniforms again stands over.

Meeting held December 29th 1886. Present Capt Cobb in the chair. Messrs Amos, Hoad and R. Worthington.

Minutes of previous meeting read and confirmed.

Accounts of supper in September presented and passed £1.11.1½.

Proposed that the Engine House be lent to Snowball Minstrels for about three months on payment of expenses of 1/- per night.

Proposed Mr Hoad that Captain Cobb be caterer for the next six months. Carried.

A letter from the Town Clerk asking the Brigade to take part in the procession on Jubilee day in Hythe on June 22nd was read and decided on the proposition of Mr Lee seconded R. Worthington that the Brigade take part in the same, to be summoned at 10 o'clock.

Drill postponed until 4th Monday in June.

A discussion was raised on an excursion of the Brigade during the summer months. To be settled at a meeting later on.

Committee meeting held at Engine House July 1/87.

Mr Cobb Captain in the chair, H. Vile, H. Manning, R. Booth, N. Amos and Lee.

Minutes of previous meeting read and confirmed.

The Secretary refused to write to Secretary Snowballs Minstrels again because of receiving no reply to two applications.

9.8.1887

The question of charges for attending fire at a shack in Corporation field belonging to Mr B. Edwards was then gone into and to be made out as follows

Use of Engine to non subscribers	£2- 2-0
Services of Brigade 1st hour	£2- 0-0
Services of Brigade 5 hours 10/-	£2-10-0
Refreshments	11-6
32 Pumpers 5 hours	£4-11-6
	£12- 0-0
Reduction	£6- 0-0
	£6- 0-0

That in consequence of the bad supply of water or the same being withheld from the Brigade a deputation wait upon the Corporation in the morning to ascertain whether a better understanding could not be arrived at and why the water was withheld when the surveyor stated it was turned on, that a letter be sent to the Mayor asking him to receive the deputation. Deputation to consist of Captain, two Lieutenants, Secretary and two firemen.

23.9.1887

Proposed by Mr Ashdown seconded by Mr Booth that the members be told of the numbers they are to be for efficiency sake and the part of duties they shall fulfill at a fire or drill.

That Mr Williams be asked to give up his uniform for the present it being given him prematurely.

That the Committee lend the use of the Engine House to the Glee union of which Mr W. Paine Jr. is the Secretary on their paying expenses of 1/- per night.

Mr William's offer of a Lecture on how an ambulance works be accepted.

Committee meeting held November 25th 1889. Present J. W. Cobb in the chair, Messrs Amos, Vile, Booth, C. Capon, E. Manning, W. J. Paine, H. Capon, J. Jeal, G. Wilks, N. Manning, R. Worthington and Secretary.

Minutes previous meeting read and confirmed.

The meeting proceeded to deal with the results of the morning drill in reference to the new hydrants on Seabrook Road after some amount of discussion it was decided to send the following report to the Council.

It has been the unanimous wish of all the members to have adopted one uniform Hydrant throughout the Borough, and that the simplest and most suitable, which wish has often been expressed to the Council at different times and the present ones in the town are such as give satisfaction. The new hydrants that are now fixed on the Seabrook Road (four in number) have been tested by the Brigade on Monday 25th November at a special drill. The desire of the whole of the members is that they should be altered so that they are all of one pattern. Objection is raised to the cap being at the top, most difficult to take off, and requiring three men to support the hose to keep it from bending and so lose pressure. Hoping that you will have the necessary alterations made as they are never likely to give satisfaction. Attention might be given to the position of stop cock to see that they are perfectly perpendicular.

There is also the question of placing a board on the Town Hall for a Fire Notice, as objection is raised to the front of the Hall, will the Council grant permission for placing it underneath.

23.3.1890
Committee meeting held July 18th 1890. Present Mr Cobb in the chair, Messrs Amos, E. Manning, C. Capon, W. Chapman, R. Booth, R. Worthington, H. Vile and Secretary.

Minutes former meeting read and confirmed.

Letter read from Corporation stating that the necessary alterations had been ordered to be done to the Hydrants on Seabrook Road.

It was decided to attend Church Parade on next Sunday with oddfellows at 2.30 it being Hospital Day.

Unfortunately, one of the most interesting items in the Hythe Minute Book gives insufficient evidence of what must have been a major crisis in the near 100-year history of the brigade. It appears that in the spring of 1891, public allegations were made about the management of the Brigade and, in particular, about the purchase of hose, which led to an article in the *Hythe Reporter*, and furious responses from Captain Cobb and the members of the Brigade. To quote the minutes of a special meeting of the Brigade Committee on June 29th 1891: "The Secretary read leading article touching the reputation of the Brigade and then read part of his own letter (which had been sent to the *Hythe Reporter*) which had been cut to pieces." Referring to the allegations of mismanagement which had been made public, the Committee were of the opinion that only a member of the Brigade could have furnished these, as they contained dates and details about hose purchases, holidays and the raising of money for brass helmets, items which had only been discussed in Committee. The meeting put on record that the article was "an insult to the Captain and the Officers who were at the head of the Brigade, and also to all the Members".

The meeting then adjourned until July 7th 1891, when the Captain stated that a deputation had waited upon the Editor of the *Hythe Reporter* and demanded the name of the writer or informant, the result had been that the Editor, Mr Palmer, had stated that Mr A. Williams was the informant, not the writer. Mr A. Williams then spoke at length, trying to justify his action in giving the information which had led to all the present correspondence, and on the subject stated that he also had given his opinion as well as information. The members that spoke were of an opinion adverse to his on the question and the discussion was continued for some time, but no resolution arrived at. The Captain produced a length of hose which had been found evidently cut with a pen knife or some other pointed instrument. The feeling of all the Brigade was one of utter contempt of the guilty party who was mean enough to do such a thing.

A Committee Meeting was held in the Engine House on July 13th 1891 and continued the investigation. "One question arising in reference to the name of the writer of the letter or informant, the letter being signed subscriber and no resolution having come to Mr Cobb, proposing that as the letter was and information given was such an insult to our Captain that Mr Williams either give the name of the Subscriber of the letter in question or resign membership of the Brigade. Mr A. Williams stated that he could not do so as it would be a Breach of Confidence. Mr Williams then wrote out his resignation as follows which was Proposed by Mr Chapman, seconded by R. Worthington. Mr Williams resignation be accepted, he having refused to give the information asked for viz the name of the subscriber on the grounds that by doing so he would commit a breach of confidence and that he entertains no antipathy against the Brigade and that should the Brigade require his services at any time he would be pleased to help them."

In September 1884, Edenbridge experienced the most destructive fire since the formation of its brigade, when the Edenbridge Tannery was completely destroyed. As late as the mid-1880's Northfleet seems to have been badly protected from fire. A local board was not formed until 1874, and it was ten years later that the Clerk had to call attention "to the necessity for measures to extinguish fire". A motion was passed recommending that five hydrants be laid in suitable places, but not before the Surveyor of Nuisances, a Mr Samuel Honeycombe (who incidentally was the great-grandfather of Gordon Honeycombe the broadcaster and author who wrote "Red Watch") "see the Superintendent of Fire Engines at Gravesend and get information on the subject generally".

After prolonged wrangling with the Water Company about the price of installing the hydrants, the Clerk finally reported on January 7th 1885 – three months after the first proposal – that the hydrants had been put in place. By July 1885, the Northfleet Board, still without a brigade, asked Shand Mason and Merryweather to tender for a supply of hose, reel and unions; and one month later, the offer by Shand Mason "to supply the necessaries for fire extinguishing for £92.15.3" was accepted. At the same meeting, a letter from certain Gentlemen "desirous of aiding in forming an efficient fire brigade" was read and the Surveyor was instructed to "ascertain and report as to the best method of forming a brigade or otherwise of working the hose".

The fire appliances were delivered by the beginning of September and the Sarjeant at the Northfleet Police Station was appointed Deputy Superintendent of Fire Appliances. At a meeting of the Board on September 16th, the Surveyor submitted a list of men who were willing to become members of the Volunteer Brigade, and was instructed to arrange a meeting with the Gentlemen who first suggested the formation of such. Finally, on October 21st, the Surveyor reported that a public meeting the day before had passed a resolution that "15 men and two officers should constitute the Brigade, to be managed by three members of the Local Board and four members of the Brigade – the Board to provide all appliances, uniforms and accoutrements and to be responsible for all expenses".

The Board decided that they should provide six helmets and hatchets but no further accoutrements, that no expenses should be incurred by the Board, but that all rules should be made by the Brigade itself. How six helmets and hatchets and no uniforms could equip a Brigade of 17 officers and men was not disclosed. The exact date when the Northfleet Volunteer Brigade came into being is not known, but on November 28th 1885, it was reported that the fire brigade successfully localised a fire at the "Northfleet Tavern" in Dover Road.

The origins of the Tenterden Fire Brigade are also shrouded in the mists of history. No indication of its first formation can be found, but by 1888, the town must have had a flourishing brigade with excellent equipment. Proof can be found in a policy from the Sun Fire Office, dated April 25th 1888, issued to the Treasurer of the Tenterden Volunteer Fire Brigade. In it, it is stated that "a plant consisting of three fire engines with the full complement of hose and appliances in the engine house in High Street, Tenterden, in Kent, brick and slated and a small well-screened stove therein" was insured for £200 at an annual premium of four shillings against loss or damage by fire. About this time, a man who ran horse-buses from Tenterden to Ashford and Appledore, and who kept 60 horses in a yard at West Cross, had a contract with the council "to have at least two horses ready, day and night, for the fire engine".

Bilsington formed its first brigade in 1889, under the name of Bilsington and District Fire Brigade. The district included Aldington, Bonnington, Eastbridge, Hurst, Newchurch, Ruckinge and Snave. Subscriptions were invited, and with the help of donations from the Kent Fire Office, the Norwich Union and the Hand-in-Hand insurance offices, the Brigade was able to buy a horse-drawn manual engine at a cost of £110.10.0. The engine could be worked by 16 men and "was capable of throwing 80 gallons a minute 110 feet high". The engine was housed in a small brick building with a red lamp over the door and the Brigade charged an overall fee of one guinea every time it was called out. "Pump and bucket men" were paid 1/6 for the first hour on duty and 1/- for each succeeding hour".

October 26th 1889 was a day of disaster for the little old-world town of Wye. A small fire, probably caused by a discarded cigarette, started in an old house under renovation next to the King's Head Inn and Brewery, rapidly spread, and by the time it was put out many hours later, damage of more than £10,000 had been incurred and "a huge area of ground which had been covered by buildings for hundreds of years had been cleared of all but a heap of smouldering debris". Wye, at that time, had no brigade of its own, not even a small manual engine; and fire protection, apart from a number of buckets, was provided by the Ashford Brigade. A contemporary record of the conflagration gives a graphic account of the fight to save at least parts of the town and is worth quoting here:

"On Saturday a man named Masterton, who had been at work with others in the renovation of the house, was the last to leave it. He went out of the front door at a quarter to 5 o'clock and lit a cigarette the moment before throwing the match down. He is not certain whether the match fell inside or outside the house, but the inference is that the match caused the fire, probably having set light to some papers or shavings. At half past five Charles Chittenden, the old maltster and brewer, who had been at work in the brewery left it and went to his tea in a house nearly opposite to which he is removed leaving his wife to serve in the bar.

"While Chittenden was at his tea the fire broke out in the front of the house under repair and almost instantly it came through the partition into Mr Clarabut's shop. At the moment Mr Clarabut had his safe open, and his book before him, settling an account with a customer, and he only had time to snatch up and carry off his books and his cash box and Mrs Clarabut made an attempt to go upstairs and fetch some valued articles belonging to a deceased daughter, but she too had to retreat like Mr Clarabut, with no clothing than they were dressed in. In the meantime some persons went and brought Mrs Chittenden out of the back bar where her position was becoming dangerous, for a strong north east wind was driving the flames onward with fearful rapidity and they were taking hold of the King's Head at such a rate that it was found impossible to get more than a few things outside and Mr Spike, manager, had to retreat from behind the bar without being able to clear out the cash, although by wonderful luck he recovered it next day. Mr Clarabut's house and shop was down in 20 minutes, and the fire was raging fiercely behind in the brew house, malt house, hop room, engine house, and other departments of the brewery. A stream of sparks extended fully half a mile from the conflagration and the glare could be seen far and wide.

"The inhabitants of Wye hastened to the scene and rendered what assistance they could, and an attempt was made to check the spread of the fire by means of water thrown from buckets, but the heat was too intense for people to get near. A telegram was despatched to Ashford Fire Brigade at about a quarter to 7 o'clock, and Captain Hart and his men arrived with their steamer and manual about twenty to 8 o'clock. Water could only be procured from the wells and pumps, the fire being some 1,800 feet from the river. Chains of men were formed to pass buckets to and from the town pump and elsewhere, and the engine pumped from tubs. Colonel Hardy arrived on the scene from Chilham, with his fire engine and men soon after the Ashford Brigade, and everyone agrees that the Colonel and his party rendered splendid service, and helped greatly to prevent the fire burning down the entire side of the street. The house adjoining the King's Head, on the south side, and inhabited by Mrs Rossiter, was also taking fire, and had to be partially unroofed, water being poured in from the apertures. The furniture, not only of this house but of all the other houses on that side of the street, was taken out and placed on the other side of the street, and it was proposed to pull down Mr Rossiter's house and the house adjoining to stop the conflagration. A valve of the Ashford steamer broke and stopped it from pumping for a time, and the Charing Fire Brigade was thereupon telegraphed for, but it seems the message was thought to be a hoax, and they did not come. The South Ashford Fire Brigade, however came over, bringing with them a long length of hose, which subsequently enabled the firemen to make water in the river available. Mr George Kennett and Mr A. Amos had their horse drawn water barrels diligently employed bringing water from the stream.

"The fire was not fully mastered until midnight, and the Ashford engines were playing nearly all day on Sunday. Some narrow escapes of terrible accidents occurred from the falling of a ponderous chimney, but only two young men from Mountain Street, Chilham, who had been several times cautioned to keep back, were struck severely. They were knocked down by some bricks on an occasion when a descent of several tons took place.

"As may be imagined, there was an immense influx of people into Wye from Ashford, as well as from surrounding parishes, and Supt. Wenham with Sergt. Bartlett, and a staff of six constables, rendered invaluable service in securing room for the firemen and others who were assisting to work. The ruins were visited on Sunday and subsequent days by great numbers of people."

A series of fires in the late 1880's led to the formation of the Lydd Volunteer Fire Brigade. With only rudimentary fire protection available

70

Fig. 10. Lydd Fire Brigade. Winner of the South-Eastern District Challenge Shield, National Fire Brigade Union. Ramsgate, May 30th, 1898.

in the town, the nearest brigades at the time were at Rye, Hythe and Tenterden, all several miles away. The council decided to establish its own brigade and to supply an engine. A public meeting was held in the Town Hall in April 1890, and a brigade was formed with 12 officers and men, the first captain being Harold Finn, son of the Mayor. A 22-man manual engine with 500 feet of hose was ordered from Merryweathers; and the council bought an old thatched building to which they added an engine room as a fire station. The town was obviously prosperous and the council generous, for apart from all necessary tackle, including 1,100 feet of delivery hose, they also purchased full dress and undress uniforms for all the men. Expenses had to be met from voluntary contributions and from moneys received from the insurance companies for fires attended at insured premises.

Dartford Volunteer Fire Brigade seems to have been left behind in the race for modernisation, for in 1891, when all they had was an old manual pump of many years standing, the local Board of Health set up a fund to purchase a steam fire-engine. Money was also collected for uniforms and other equipment and the target of £455 was soon reached. However, the first mention of the new horse-drawn steamer is not until 11 years later when, at the opening of Dartford's first official fire station on July 16th 1902, the steam fire-engine was christened "King Edward VII".

"A very large and elaborate" mental hospital, established in North Grove, Hawkhurst, by a Dr William Harmer in 1839, was completely destroyed in the early morning of November 16th 1891. Described at the time as the greatest fire in the history of the village, the flames quickly spread through the main building and adjoining summer-houses, whipped by a strong wind. The brigade was quickly on the scene, but with no water pressure available at the site, hoses had to be laid to the High Street. Injured patients were taken to hospital in Ticehurst, and later, the badly burnt body of a Miss Jemmett, a guest at the hospital, was found.

The origins of the Seal Fire Brigade are uncertain, but the opening of a fire station in 1891 proves that the parish had by then a flourishing brigade. The fire station, given to the community and paid for by the then Lord Hillingdon, was a "small but suitable building". The opening, on August 14th 1891, was a red-letter day for the village, with the houses and shops gaily decorated and with neighbouring brigades sending fire-engines and teams to the ceremony. After the opening, the various brigades took part in a number of contests and exhibition drills. In the evening, all the firemen were entertained by Lord Hillingdon in the village hall and the time was devoted to "toasts and harmony".

By 1892, Margate Fire Brigade had grown to 16 officers and men, and their equipment included two manuals, a hose-tender, a hose-truck with scaling ladder, two escapes, three hand-pumps, jumping-sheets and hose. Firemen were still called out by the firing of maroons, a noisy and unpopular method of alarm which, in July 1892, provoked an anonymous chief officer of a volunteer brigade to write a letter of protest to the national magazine "Fire and Water". His letter is given in full:

"Dear Sir – Will you allow me space to express my annoyance at the conduct of the authorities in this town in permitting the use of a maroon to call together the members of the local Fire Brigade? Being here in a visit, with an invalid wife, on two nights when refreshing sleep was just giving relief from pain and weariness, a terrible crash, as of falling rocks, disturbed by dynamite or gun-powder rent the air. To spring out of bed bewildered and terrified was the work of a moment, and when in half-sleepy tones and enquiry was made as to the cause, we were calmly told that it was 'only the Fire Brigade' being called. These two fires were – first, a chimney sweep's chimney on fire! and second, a curtain alight; both all over long before firemen arrived. Thousands of frightened women and children are disturbed and hundreds of tired businessmen upset and disgusted, simply because the town is behind the times. Surely it is time some steps were taken to install electric bells, or a telephone, to call the men together. Anything would be better than this ridiculous and dangerous absurdity.

Yours truly, Chief Officer V.F.B."

The letter seems to have had an effect because, in April 1893, Margate Town Council decided to introduce electric call-bells for their firemen. They accepted a tender for £27.13.6d for the connection of eight houses to the fire station and also employed a runner with a bicycle to call the other firemen when needed.

Erith Fire Brigade must have been formed in the latter part of the 19th century, but no records exist until 1892 when the local Board took out an insurance for its firemen. In 1895, the brigade took part in the Lord Mayor's Show, London. Another brigade with an uncertain date of formation is Chislehurst. In 1892, they held their first annual competition, but whether that meant that the brigade was formed in 1891 or that that was just their first competition, is unclear. About this time, Chislehurst had a manual pump (which was in service until the town bought a steamer in 1910) and in 1894, a new fire station was built, suggesting that, for some years prior to this, a brigade had existed with an engine and a place to put it in. About 1892, volunteer brigades were formed in Westerham, Erith, Penge and Smarden, but no records of fire protection in these places could be found, nor of the organisation and equipment of the brigades.

The time has come to look again at what has happened to the Hythe Volunteer Fire Brigade, founded in 1802, and the oldest in Kent. By 1892, the brigade's strength had been reduced to 20 officers and men under the captaincy of Mr Cobb. They had two horse-drawn appliances, a manual, and a steamer, and 800 feet of hose. The reduction in manpower was probably due to the greater effectiveness of the steam-engine. At their 90th Anniversary Dinner in 1892, the brigade presented a budget for the year of £43.15s and reported that during the past year they had only been called out once to a fire. Money had been raised to buy a new, wheeled-escape and later, members of the Folkestone Brigade, who were "well acquainted with this type of escape", gave the Hythe men drill and other instructions in its use.

A Goudhurst woman carried out a courageous rescue in 1892, while the Weald of Kent (Goudhurst) Brigade was still being summoned. Florrie Excell, who lived in an old farm house at Ladysden with her family, was getting her bridal gown ready for her wedding next day, when fire broke out. Braving the smoke and flames, she ran upstairs to save some of her wedding things, only to find her old grandfather unconscious, lying on the stairs. Ignoring her wedding things, she humped the heavy man onto her back and carried him to safety. The house and all the contents was burnt to the ground, but the wedding must have taken place because a few months later, a certificate together with a wedding gift were presented to Mrs Florrie Bateup (nee Excell) as a "testimonial from various subscribers in the village to commend her bravery and unselfishness in sacrificing her own property set aside for her marriage to rescue her grandfather".

Reference has already been made to the rather uncertain origins of fire-fighting in Tunbridge Wells, but a plaque, dug up in 1898, showed that the town had an engine and fire station in 1794. Accurate dates are scarce, but in the 1880's the brigade's headquarters were in Monson Road. A paddock behind the station was used by cab-drivers to graze their horses, and in case of a fire alarm, the first volunteer to arrive at the station ran into into the paddock, grabbed two horses and harnessed them to the fire-engine.

Edward Westbrook, who later became chief of the Tunbridge Wells Brigade and one of the best known chief officers in the county, joined in 1873 and served in the town's brigade for over 30 years. In 1875, he was appointed escape conductor and seven years later, he was promoted to Chief Officer. By this time, Tunbridge Wells had a large and well-equipped brigade, run by the borough council, with a central station at the Town Hall and district stations at Neville Street, St. John's Road and Lower Green Road. Associated with them was the Rusthall Volunteer Contingent which also came under the command of the Tunbridge Wells chief.

In 1887, a volunteer Salvage Corps was founded in the town. Their main duty was, after the saving of life, to protect and salvage property from the ravages of fire. The Salvage Corps was an auxiliary to the local volunteer brigade under the same chief officer, but differences between the two bodies led to the Salvage Corps being taken over by the Corporation in 1890. Tunbridge Wells was the first in Kent, and probably in the provinces, to recognise the value of having a salvage corps and the amount of property that could be saved by it. The importance of the Corps was emphasised when, on July 11th 1891, they were inspected by Captain Shaw of the Metropolitan Fire Brigade and were reviewed by "His Imperial and Royal Majesty, the German Emperor, on the occasion of the annual meeting of the National Fire Brigades Union at the Crystal Palace".

In January 1897, the council published "Rules for the Regulation of the Fire Brigade and Salvage Corps" together with "Directions for the Preservation of Life and Hints to Inmates and Bystanders". It may be of interest to reproduce extracts of these rules and regulations:

GENERAL

The Fire Brigade shall consist of an Honorary Captain, a Captain, Second Officer, Engineer, Escape Conductor, 18 Men and two Messengers.

Every Member of the Brigade will be provided with a Tunic, Trousers, Helmet, Cap, Belt, Boots, Hatchet, Hose Wrench, Lamp and Life Line, which must be kept in good condition and returned to the Captain for the time being on the Member leaving the Brigade.

That all members of the Brigade shall resign on reaching the age of 55, and on retiring shall be allowed to retain their uniforms during the pleasure of the Watch Committee.

The number of each Member shall be placed upon the house where he resides.

The Engine, Hose Reels, Hose Carts, Fire Escapes, and the whole of the Brigade Apparatus shall be kept in all respects, ready for immediate use.

Every Member shall keep a copy of these Regulations at his residence.

After every Drill or Fire, all the apparatus used shall be thoroughly cleaned, dried and oiled, and stowed away in the appointed place by the Members attending such Drill or Fire.

The Brigade shall not attend fires outside the Borough, except at the property of the Corporation.

Keys to the Engine House and the Fire Escape Stations shall be kept at the Police Station, and at the residences of the Captain and Officers of the Brigade.

FIRES

Every Member of the Brigade shall attend for the performance of his duties whensoever called upon so to do; and if any Member shall neglect to attend when summoned, either by night or by day, he shall, upon being reported to the Watch Committee, be discharged and another appointed in his place.

In all cases of Fire the apparatus from the Central Station shall be taken to the Fire in the following order:

Hose Carts, Fire Queen, Kingston Escape

The Lattice Girder Escape is not to be taken to fires between 8 a.m. and 6 p.m. unless by special order. The Engine is only to be taken by special order. The apparatus from the District Stations shall be taken to the fire in the following order:

Hose Carts, Escapes

The Captain shall have authority to obtain a sufficient number of horses (not exceeding four) for the purpose of taking the Engine to a Fire. When horses are used the Brigade shall place themselves on the Engine in the following order: Officers in front, even numbers on the right side, and odd numbers on the left.

Every Member shall perform his duties as silently as possible, remembering always that order, coolness, promptitude and despatch are indispensable. Any person making inquiries should be referred to the Captain or Officer in charge.

Members shall not leave a Fire without the permission of the Captain or Officer in charge.

In withdrawing the Brigade after a Fire has been extinguished, the Captain – or in his absence, the Officer in charge of the Salvage Corps – must, if necessary, place a sufficient number of the Salvage Corps in charge of the premises.

FIRE BELLS

Electric communication shall be established between the Town Hall and the residence of every Member of the Brigade, and the apparatus shall be tested every Sunday at 9 a.m., and every Wednesday at 7 p.m.

CAPTAIN

The Captain shall have and exercise command and general control over every Member of the Brigade whilst on duty, and shall be responsible to the Watch Committee for the efficiency, discipline and conduct of the Brigade, and also for the maintenance of the apparatus in a good, sound and cleanly condition, and in readiness for immediate use.

He shall within two days after every Fire furnish the Borough Accountant with a Report upon the Fire, stating the owner and occupier of the premises where the Fire occurred, and in what offices and under what policies the building and contents are insured.

FIREMEN AND MESSENGERS

Every Member of the Brigade shall faithfully perform all orders from time to time given to him by his superior Officers, and shall not take or obey orders given to him by any other person whomsoever; and if any Member shall disobey the orders of his superior Officers, or become intoxicated, or otherwise misconduct himself whilst on duty, the Captain or Officer for the time being in charge of the Brigade may at once suspend him.

If any Member of the Brigade shall leave the Borough, he shall give immediate notice thereof to the Captain, so that another may be appointed in his place. In the event of a short absence a substitute may with the Captain's permission, be provided until the Member's return.

In the event of neither of the Officers of the Brigade being present at a fire, the Senior Fireman shall take command; and the Members shall render the same obedience to him whilst in command as they would to their Officers, and he shall be invested with all the powers of the Captain and shall be responsible to the Watch Committee in precisely the same way as the Captain would be if he were present.

The Captain or Officer in charge shall have authority to engage for employment at a fire such number of Labourers as he shall think necessary, not exceeding twenty.

No payment on account of beer, spirits or other refreshments will be allowed.

No Member of the Brigade is permitted to receive money for any service connected with his duty without a written order from the Captain.

If a Member of the Brigade shall not arrive at a fire within half-an-hour of the time when the Brigade is summoned, a deduction shall be made from his pay, of not less than one shilling and not more than five shillings, at the discretion of the Watch Committee.

Instructions for the Salvage Corps are also given:

The Salvage Corps is established with a twofold object, viz:

(i) To tender first help at a fire if they should happen to be there before any Fire Brigade.

(ii) To protect (if necessary remove) the property of any place or house that may be on fire.

To save life, should be the first aim of the Corps when arriving at a fire, before the Fire Brigade is present. After seeing that all the people are out, the Corps should set to work with their apparatus to do their very best to extinguish the fire. When the Corps arrives, the Chief Officer should, as far as possible, hastily make himself somewhat acquainted with the stability of the building with a view to ascertaining how far he may venture to take his men into it, without exposing them to too much risk, always remembering that life is more valuable than property, and that there is no true bravery in risking unduly his own or his men's lives. Caution should therefore be taken that in the event of any portion giving way, the men may be quickly withdrawn.

If the upper part is on fire, the men should be ready as near under the floor burning as possible, and immediately cover or remove anything in danger of being damaged by water, and take such steps to save the ceilings which may be above by making two or three small holes, and collect the water as it falls, as the means at hand will permit.

A Salvage Corps duties are very different to those of a Fire Brigade, they do not leave when the fire is extinguished. It is the duty of the Officer in command to find out in what Office the property is insured. They should take charge of it, handing it over to the care of the Agent of the Insurance Company in which it is insured, if not insured to the owner. Nothing should be done in a great hurry, remembering that very frequently more harm than good is done at a fire because of the rush that is made to move things.

The first ever Motor Show in Britain was held in Tunbridge Wells on October 15th 1895, and it was at that event that the first petrol-driven fire pump in Britain was exhibited and demonstrated. The new appliance, bought by the Hon. Evelyn Ellis for his country house brigade at Datchet, caused much excitement throughout the brigades in the country. A Daimler, built in Germany, it was not self-propelled, and consisted of an engine belt driving a horizontal pump on a carriage designed to be drawn by one horse or a team of men. At the Show, it was pulled into the ring by eight members of the Tunbridge Wells Fire Brigade and got to work from cold in under one minute. However, visiting fire chiefs were not unduly impressed by the new machine, claiming that the jet it produced "was no more than that of a six-man manual".

Returning from a fire at Erith in April 1893, Bexley Heath volunteer firemen were involved in an accident which injured several of them, including their captain. A contemporary newspaper account stated that "one of the horses drawing the manual engine fell, causing the machine to overturn. Several firemen and two or three civilians on the appliance were all flung off and injured or shaken. Captain Jenkins fell on his head under the manual and was, with difficulty, extricated. It was found that his foot was crushed, but the helmet had preserved him from further injury". A few days after the incident, Captain Jenkins stated that the injured men were all progressing favourably and he himself hoped to be back in service soon. In the accident one of the horses was injured, and the manual was damaged. Although the first extant records of a volunteer fire brigade in Birchington-on-Sea is dated 1894, the town must have had a well-developed fire protection organisation long before then. A poster in the Kent Fire Brigade Museum, unfortunately undated but probably from the early 19th century, gives clear warning that the Brigade expects to be paid for its services on the spot (i.e. at the scene of the fire) or it would pack up and go home. The poster reads:

"Fire!

Birchington-on-Sea Fire Brigade
In consequence of the difficulty in
obtaining the Fire Brigade Charges
it has been determined that in case
of Fire the Brigade will proceed to
the scene of Conflagration at once,
but unless the Property Owner will
sign a Guarantee for Expenses Incurred,
the Brigade will Pack Up and return
within half-an-hour

Signed: W. Jones, Secretary"

About 1894 the existing brigade was reorganised, and a balance sheet dated 1896 of the reorganised brigade for the previous two years shows an income of £201 with which an "engine was obtained and all necessary expenses paid", thus leaving a fully equipped organisation with £3 in hand.

The Birchington Brigade was a combined Fire and Life Brigade, a section of the members acting as lifeboatmen. The Local Government Act of 1894 created parish councils and empowered them to maintain a fire brigade. This Act had a strong influence on the development of fire protection in the country and many volunteer brigades, including several in Kent, now came under the control of these parish councils. Such a brigade was Westgate-on-Sea, which, less than a year after its formation or re-formation, or possibly re-organisation, asked the Westgate-on-Sea Parish Council in January 1895 to take over the appliances and equipment of the Brigade. That a brigade existed in Westgate in the 1880's is clear from documents still in existence. A series of public meetings throughout 1894 indicates an early connection with the nearby Birchington-on-Sea Fire Brigade and possibly even a joint captaincy. Records of the meetings also show missing hose, worn-out uniforms, suggestions of mismanagement and financial inaccuracies. Short extracts from the minutes of these meetings are here given, but some of these may add to the confusion rather than clarify what was happening at that time:

"20th February 1894. Public meeting held at Station Hotel to consider what steps should be taken to provide the Town with Fire and Life saving apparatus. A Committee was appointed to arrange for a supply of hose to be kept in the Town and to collect a sufficient sum of money to provide proper appliances, and to report to an adjourned public meeting on 6th March.

6th March 1894. Adjourned public meeting held, there being a very large attendance. The Committee was reappointed, Mr Weston was reappointed Chief Officer. Mr Best asked what had become of the fire appliance belonging to the former Brigade and it was said that £25 had been spent on uniforms etc. Captain Ashton (who was at one point Captain of Birchington Brigade) said that the tunics etc were worn out, and that he had given new tunics to the Brigade five years ago: Two lengths of leather hose were said to have been given by a Mr Parkinson, and Captain Ashton said he left these at Westgate and knew nothing of them now. Mr Day believed the hose had been sold to Broadstairs.

Representatives of Shand Mason and Co and Messrs Rose and Co, produced models of fire escapes, and it was decided to purchase an Escape and hose box combined should funds permit. The meeting was then informed that Mr Cousins would sell the whole of his gear for £75 and this announcement was received with loud applause."

The following resolution was passed:

"That having regard to the fact that the Local Government Extension (Parish Councils) Act will shortly come into operation and that complications respecting ownership may arise, all appliances and accoutrements purchased by the Committee shall be forthwith legally vested in three Trustees, who shall have power to treat with any

Administrative Body that may be created, for the sale of such property, and after payment of expenses to return the money thus realised pro rata to the subscribers."

20th February 1894. First meeting of Fire Brigade Committee held at Station Hotel. It was decided to take immediate steps to provide hose and appliances for the use of the town. Mr Cousins offered to lend the hose, standpipes, etc for a fortnight, with option to purchase. Mr V. Weston was instructed to act as Chief Officer, with power to him in the event of fire to employ one, two or three experienced men in whom he had confidence to assist him. The appliances were placed in his care and was authorised to purchase three maroons. A sub-Committee was appointed to draw up and issue a circular asking for subscriptions to the Brigade. It was also decided to ask Mr Cousins for a detailed statement showing the lowest price at which he would dispose of *all* his appliances, including engine and sundries.

23rd February 1894. The Fire Brigade Committee decided to ask Coast Guards for their co-operation in case of outbreak of fire and to communicate with the C.O. if at any time they saw any indication of a conflagration.

6th March 1894. A Public Meeting appointed the Fire Brigade Committee, consisting of 12 members, including Mr W. Weston, Chief Officer.

6th March 1894. Committee decided to purchase at once the gear belonging to Mr Cousins for £75. Mr Jackson was thanked for undertaking to fetch the Engine and gear from Birchington and to house the same for the present.

8th March 1894. At a special meeting of the Committee evidence was produced, in the form of a receipt, that Mr Cousins had perfect right to dispose of the engine and gear.

> The Haven
> Birchington-on-Sea
> March 23rd 1893

Received of Mr Geo. G. Cousins in payment of above Fire Engine and appliances, Boat and Gear as per schedule, the sum of Two pounds which together with the balance of Account of £79.14 amounting to £18.14 in full purchase of same.

> signed. Alfred Ashton
> 1d stamp
> March 23rd 1893"

15th March 1894. It was decided to order a 40′ Shand Mason Curricle Escape with shoot.

20th March 1894. 11 firemen were elected. Of these, Mr Baigent was appointed Superintendent, Mr J. W. Pemple Foreman and Mr C. Emptage Engineer.

6th April 1894. Arrangement entered into with Mr Jackson to supply horses and driver for the engine. A scale of charges for the use of the engine was adopted.

30th April 1894. Mr Jackson, a member of the Committee, reported that the engine could be housed in the coach house attached to his stables in Station Road and the Escape and hose-cart in the lean-to of his yard: (rent £20 per annum) or, if the Committee wished, the whole of the stable and coach house in the Station Road was at the Committee's disposal. The C.O. promised to paint the engine.

29th May 1984. It was decided that the inaugural turnout of the Brigade be held on 2nd June.

14th January 1895. After considering the financial position, the Secretary was instructed to write to Westgate-on-Sea Parish Council to ask if they would be prepared to take over the appliances and equipment of the Westgate-on-Sea Fire Brigade.

4th April 1895. First meeting of Westgate-on-Sea Parish Council Fire Brigade Committee held at Mr Bessant's."

Canterbury's fire-fighting arrangements (or disarrangements) were the cause of a furious exchange of letters in the national magazine "Fire and Water" in 1895. At that time, the City had several brigades, including a volunteer brigade, two maintained by insurance companies, one by the Cathedral, and one by the Council which was apparently under police control. An anonymous 'Visitor' wrote a letter to the magazine, expressing his disgust at the "defective fire extinguishing arrangements" in the City, and was immediately answered by Captain W. G. Pidduck, the Chief of the County Fire Office Brigade. Captain Pidduck will of course be remembered as the colourful character who, after the fire at the Cathedral in 1872, accused the Sun Insurance Office of cheating him of 2d when the brigade's expenses came to £4.8s.8d and, after a long delay, he received only £4.8s.6d from that office. The reader may appreciate getting the full texts of the letter from 'Visitor' (most likely an officer from some other volunteer brigade) and Captain Pidduck's reply, both of which are given here:

"DEFECTIVE FIRE EXTINGUISHING ARRANGEMENTS
To the Editor of Fire and Water

Dear Sir – The Corporation of the grand old City of Canterbury, with a population of over 23,000, seem to ignore their responsibility in regard to providing efficient and proper protection against loss of life and property by fire. The water supply is good, and the pressure on the mains excellent; but the system is, to my mind, as bad and false as can be; in fact, this city is 50 years behind the world in this respect.

At present the police force consists, including officers, of 26 men, and these are the firemen, so that in case of a fire the city is left to the mercy of any enterprising criminal, and no order exists at the scene of a fire because the police are otherwise employed.

The appliances are as inadequate for the work as the men. There is an antiquated escape ladder on wheels which has stood at the police station exposed to all weather for some years, and if used would more likely increase the danger to life than assist on saving. In the Market Place there are some two or three builders' ladders on a hand truck, both difficult to get at, and far from easy to raise, especially in such a city as Canterbury. At night time these are carefully locked up, and it is doubtful if they are now in a safe state to be relied on in case of an emergency. The hose belonging to the Corporation is of a very limited amount, and its condition does not inspire one with the idea that much care is bestowed upon it, so that whenever it is used there generally is great confusion with burst lengths. Little or no system of drilling takes place, nor can one expect policemen to undertake this extra duty, which should always be distinct from their work. At fires the police are required for special duty in keeping a clear space for the firemen to work in and prevent pillaging.

The County Fire Office and the Kent Fire Office, to minimise their losses, under these circumstances have maintained an engine each in the town, and so, instead of having one good system, there exists a regular muddle of divided interests. The County engine has been looked after by their agent, who has gathered round him a small Brigade of nine men, and for years they have done much service in and out of the town; but there is a want of system to be the best in the town. The Kent engine is of a very ancient pattern, and seems now to be discarded, as the Cathedral authorities, after the fire in the Cathedral roof some few years back, purchased a very large steam fire engine, which is kept in their engine-house, and managed by a Brigade of nine men. This station is a fairly good one, though in a very narrow thoroughfare. The quantity of hose here is very limited, and from want of attention is gradually becoming useless. The system of drilling with this Brigade is of the most rudimentary description, with very long intervals.

Such a thing as a life-line does not, I think, exist there, and scaling ladders are considered useless. The Cathedral and Kent Brigade, I understand have only one engineer, so that if he is absent the steamer cannot be worked. In case of fire it is rare for any of these Brigades to turn out without delays, and, although there are plenty of job-masters in the town, there appears to be no system for supplying horses. Again, the City Surveyor thinks no fireman should open a hydrant without his authority. Thus, often when a fire occurs, there is confusion and unpleasantness in Canterbury, and the Corporation will wake up after some serious calamity to find how much they are to blame for neglecting their duty in providing a proper and efficient Fire Brigade.

Yours, truly,
'VISITOR'

Canterbury, January 2nd 1895"

In the next issue, Captain Pidduck comes thundering back in defence of his brigade, but nevertheless, seems more than unhappy about the City Councillors and police involvement:

"DEFECTIVE FIRE EXTINGUISHING APPARATUS AT CANTERBURY

To the Editor of Fire and Water

Dear Sir – May I crave a little space in your valuable paper to put 'Visitor' right on one or two points in his letter under the head of 'Defective Fire Arrangements'?

He is evidently a stranger, or would know that the County Fire Brigade is regularly drilled once a week during eight months and once a month the remaining portion of the twelve, while the prizes gained in competitions are proof of efficiency and the value of drills. Every man of my Brigade has a life-line. It is part of his equipment. With regard to horses, we have a contract with a job-master whose stables are close to our engine house; so there is no delay, beyond the time occupied by our antiquated system of foot messengers. The police, it is true, call some of my men when a fire is outside the city boundaries.

When the fire is within the city it is quite a different matter. Our rulers make the police do firemen's duty (!) oblivious of the necessity for keeping order and the roads clear, to say nothing of leaving all the rest of the city unprotected. Then 'Visitor' should be here to see the fun. Inspectors and mob, serjeants and police, firemen, rag-tag and bobtail all rushing pell-mell down the streets. We think ourselves lucky when we push through the crowd, and luckier still if our hose is not pricked or cut or burst in the melee.

Such is the charmingly simple (want of) arrangement decreed by our City Councillors, who, therefore, being responsible for the protection of the lives and property of the citizens, ought to be enrolled as special constables and patrol the unprotected parts of the city while the transformation scenes and pantomimes are being enacted at the scene of the fire for the general gratification of the onlookers.

I could give 'Visitor' a few more examples of our splendid organisation, but have already traspassed on your space much too far.

I remain, dear sir,

Yours faithfully, etc.

W. G. Pidduck, Captain, County Fire Brigade"

Canterbury, February 5th 1895.

Although the history of fire-fighting in two of the Thanet towns, Margate and Broadstairs, is well documented, little is known about the third – Ramsgate. There is evidence that a Mr West, a London fireman, came to Ramsgate in 1887 and became chief officer of the brigade in 1895. What is not certain is whether West came to Kent to join an already existing volunteer brigade, or whether he was instrumental in forming one. Whatever organisation existed in the 1880's was under police control until West was promoted chief in 1895. By then, the town's fire protection must have been flourishing with an associated brigade at St Lawrence. This brigade was taken over by the Ramsgate Town Council in 1898. In June 1900, the Ramsgate and Margate brigades took part in a fire brigades' competition and demonstration, in Arras in Normandy; and in a series of contests between the two brigades, Ramsgate won three of the five events.

The method of calling volunteer firemen to the scene of an outbreak had for centuries been a major problem. In the very early days, church bells were reasonably effective in warning the population that fire had broken out and that they should gather to give what help they could with buckets and primitive tools. As more organised fire protection made its appearance in the villages and towns of Kent, messengers on foot or horse were sent to summon volunteers to their duties; but this was a slow and cumbersome method and led to long delays in attending a fire. In the mid-19th century, maroons were introduced but, although effective, they were hated by the population because of the noise they made and the way "they frightened adults, children and animals alike". About 1890, electric call-bells in the houses of officers and men began to make their appearance, but difficulties arose immediately when the G.P.O. claimed that this constituted "an infringement of the exclusive telegraphic rights conferred on the Postmaster General".

Ashford firemen, who for many years had been in the forefront of new developments in the County, seemed to have been well behind in their methods of calling out volunteers; and in 1892, they were severely criticised in the magazine "Fire and Water" for using maroons for the first time on October 23rd, and claiming that "the promptness shown by members of the brigade in assembling demonstrated the great advantage of the new system".

Commented the magazine: "Surely the world is going too fast for our contemporary. We had thought that the maroon as a fire call was discarded by the most sensible authorities long since on account of its disadvantages. To have the system paraded as a new and advantageous one must be most painful to the few fire brigades who are compelled, against their will, to continue this antiquated method." Ashford was apparently deeply hurt by this attack in the national magazine and started to investigate the installation of electric call-bells. But, like several other Kent brigades, they came up against the G.P.O. and its rights. Much of the time of the Ashford Brigade during the whole of 1896 is taken up with a battle with the G.P.O. to retain their electric call-bells. Letters were going back and forth between the brigade secretary, the G.P.O., the local Member of Parliament, and several unidentified gentlemen from whom advice was sought.

A selection of these letters, preserved in the correspondence book of the Ashford Brigade for 1896 (now in the Kent Fire Brigade Museum), are here given:

7th March 1896

F. E. Stuart Esq. C.E.
Ealing, London
Dear Sir

We have this day received a communication from the G.P.O. re our Electric Bells intimating an infringement of the exclusive telegraphic rights conferred on the Postmaster-General and asking us to furnish any observations which we may desire to offer in the matter.

We fail to see how we infringe these rights being a public body, but possibly you could enlighten us, and if any infringement point out where or otherwise.

If you will kindly favour me with reply at an early date it would be esteemed by
        Yours faithfully
              C. W. Savage, Secretary.

A copy of this letter was sent on the same day to a Mr H. Folker at Guildford, probably a member of the National Fire Brigades Union, asking for advice:

Dear Sir
    Capt Hart having received the enclosed from the G.P.O. this morning thought it advisable before calling a meeting to write and ask your advice, as probably other Brigades have been   in similar way and you would be acquainted with the manner in which they have acted.
    We fail to see how we infringe the act as we are a public body and merely use an electric bell. As regards the bell to the Police Station this seems most essential as by this means the Police are enabled to get to the scene of a Fire as early as ourselves and thus render material assistance. In fact we consider them a part of the Brigade and the Chief Constable of Kent sanctioned the Bell.
    Should the Union consider this a matter for them to take up, we shall be pleased to confer with our M.P.
    Kindly favour with reply and return of G.P.O. letter as early as convenient and oblige.
        Yours faithfully
              C. W. Savage, Secretary.

                                  23rd March 1896
The Secretary
General Post Office
Dear Sir
    In reply to yours of 6th inst. we were not aware that we were infringing the right of the Postmaster-General in any way by Electric Bell communication between the Fire Station Ashford and (1) the residences of the Officers and members of the Brigade.
    We understand Telegraph as defined in the act to mean any apparatus for transmitting message or other communication by means of electric signals. The communication must be "ejusdem generis" with message and this is simply ringing a bell. Sub sec 2 of Sec 5 being telegrams transmitted by a telegraph maintained for the private use of a corporation, company or person in respect of which no charge is made and we make no charge.
    (2) The Police Station. We have considered the Police a part of the

Brigade, and have called them to all Fires for many years, with the consent of the Chief Constable of Kent.

      Yours faithfully
          C. W. Savage, Secretary.

A month later came the reply from an 'obedient' but unsigned civil servant:

                               G.P.O. London
                             29th April 1896

Sir – With reference to your further letter of the 23rd ultimo, I am directed to inform you that, as the Postmaster-General is advised, it is to be educed from the Telegraph Act of 1869, together with the decision in reference to the Attorney General and the Edison Telephone Company, that signals transmitted by means of Electric Bells constitute telegraphic communication, and that such signals between premises which are not both in the occupation of one and the same person, firm or public body constitute an infringement of the Postmaster-General's exclusive telegraphic rights. The Ashford Police and the Fire Brigade being under the control of different authorities, the use of electric bell communication between the Fire Station and the Police Station infringes the rights referred to; as does also the use of such circuits between the Fire Station and the private residences of Officers and members of the Volunteer Fire Brigade.

      I am Sir
          Your obedient Servant.

                                2nd May 1896

H. Folker Esq
Trinity Chambers
Guildford
Dear Sir

      Herewith I beg to hand you copy of reply from G.P.O. as per request re Electric Bells.

      This seems a matter for the Union to take up most strongly as it appears to be an absurd thing to interfere with what is of so great a benefit to the public at large and for which we receive no compensation. Surely we should be considered a public body. They term us as a Volunteer Fire Brigade, but we have ceased to use the word Volunteer for many years.

      You will observe they make no suggestions neither intimate their intentions. Will you kindly advise before I reply and oblige.

      Yours respectfully
          C. W. Savage, Secretary.

By July the local M.P. had been approached to help Ashford in their battle to keep their call-bells.

4th July 1896

L. Hardy Esq M.P.
Sandling Park
Dear Sir

Having had 2 or 3 letters from the Secretary of the G.P.O. charging us with infringing the exclusive telegraphic rights of the Postmaster-General by the use of electric bells to the firemen's houses we feel it a matter that should be brought before the House, as neither the members or the brigade derive any benefit from it. It is merely the ringing of a bell which summons the whole of the members in an instant in the case of an outbreak of Fire, and where Life is in danger, delay of any kind is a serious matter.

Knowing the deep interest you take in our welfare, if you could possibly spare a few minutes of your valuable time when in Ashford on Wednesday next to meet a small deputation of the Brigade at the Fire Station at any time you might name, and confer with them on this matter it would be greatly esteemed. Trusting to receive a favourable reply, I am

Yours faithfully
C. W. Savage, Secretary.

A week later the Duke of Norfolk had become involved and Laurence Hardy M.P. was going to ask a question in the House of Commons.

H. Folker Esq
Trinity Chambers
Guildford
Dear Sir
Re: Electric Bells

I fear you have been too busy lately to give my former letter any attention, but thought you might be glad to know Laurence Hardy Esq M.P. for this division has written to the Duke of Norfolk respecting same. He also wrote me on Saturday for the correspondence from G.P.O. that he might have the actual words before him when putting a question in the House. Probably you might have means of supporting him on this.

Yours faithfully
C. W. Savage, Secretary.

By August 28th 1896 some progress seems to have been made with a draft agreement from the G.P.O. being discussed by the Ashford Brigade.

The Secretary
General Post Office
London
Dear Sir

In reply to your favour of 21st inst. re our Electric Bells. Your letter with Draft Agreement has been brought before a full meeting of the members, who are willing to accept your terms but suggest slight alteration, you say the existing electric bell circuits, our full strength is 20 members, but occasionally one removes his place of residence or a member leaves the brigade and a new member is elected. Will you please make provision for these necessary alterations and oblige.

Yours faithfully
C. W. Savage, Secretary.

In a letter to Captain Westbrook, chief of the Tunbridge Wells Brigade and secretary of the south-east area of the National Fire Brigades Union, the Ashford Brigade Secretary mentions again the vexed question of the call-bells:

"I would however suggest that something should be done re 'Electric Call-Bells', as I hear from good authority that several 'Volunteer' Fire Brigades have been prohibited from having them fixed by G.P.O. We have however come to an amicable arrangement with them by paying a royalty of 2/- per year."

The question of the Ashford call bells at least having apparently been settled, the Brigade now turned to the need of a new steamer. A letter to the Chairman of Ashford Urban District Council, dated March 10th 1897, stated: "At a meeting of the Brigade held on Monday the 8th inst. it was resolved in consideration of the present Steamer having been in use upwards of twenty-five years and that in a very short time it would require a considerable sum of money to be spent on it to make it reliable that immediate steps be taken to make a public appeal to the inhabitants of Ashford and the surrounding districts towards securing funds to purchase a new quick steaming Engine in place of the old one in celebration of the Diamond Jubilee of the reign of her Most Gracious Majesty the Queen."

In April 1896, Folkestone Town Council granted permission for the town fire brigade to be represented at the French Fire Federation International Competition at Rouen, during May. With Captain White in charge, men with a manual travelled across the Channel and won second prize in the competitions against all-comers for which they received 250 francs and a medal.

The curious fact that the fire protection organisations in some of the bigger towns in Kent in the early 19th century remain obscure, has

Fig. 11. Tonbridge Brigade at the opening of their fire station in 1902.

already been mentioned. Tonbridge, for example, must have had a thriving volunteer brigade by the 1850's, but no records of dates, equipment or personnel have come to light. That the Tonbridge volunteers, like several other brigades, had difficulty in obtaining payments for their services is clear from the minutes of a meeting of subscribers in September 1896, which proposed a complete reorganisation of the brigade because of financial difficulties. During the meeting "The Chairman (Mr W. Blair) gave as a reason for the reorganisation the difficulty of obtaining payment for services rendered while a volunteer Brigade. The Committee, he said, desired to drop the title 'Volunteer' and make the Brigade one in which the members should be paid a reasonable sum for their services. Under the new system, the members who joined, being the paid servants of the institution, would sign an agreement as to duties and payment. The "Tonbridge and District Fire Brigade", as it would be called, would consist of an honorary Captain, a sub captain, engineer, sub-engineer, and not less than 14 firemen, the officers being appointed by the Committee, and the men by the Captain. The property of the Brigade would be vested in three trustees, and in case of fire a Committee meeting would be held within seven days. The charges for the Brigade's services would be in

90

accordance with a scale suggested by the National Fire Brigades' Union, and the payment to members as follows: – Officers 3s.6d. for each monthly drill attended, for the first three hours at fires 7s.6d., and each additional hour 1s.6d.; firemen 2s.6d. per drill, 5s. for first three hours at a fire, and 1s. per hour afterwards. When called to a fire and not required to work, each man would be entitled to 2s.6d., and every member detailed for station duty in the absence of the Brigade would be paid at the same rate as workers. After some discussion the reorganisation scheme and rules were passed without alteration, and it was agreed that the reorganisation should take effect from September 29th. The Tonbridge Brigade is at present supported mainly by subscribers, the Town Council contributing £20 annually, which sum is now to be increased to £40."

About this time, several new brigades were formed, some probably in conjunction with the parish council, but no detailed records seem to have survived. New brigades included Snodland, Milton, Horton Kirby and Bayham Abbey.

While the Ashford volunteers were fighting the G.P.O. over their electric call-bells, their Captain, Frank Hart, issued an interesting report on the equipment of the brigade. The following appliances, he states, are the property of the brigade and are in excellent working order: one 350-gallon direct acting steam fire-engine, one 6-inch manual, one patent telescoping escape, one jump-sheet, 1,450 feet of canvas hose, 170 feet of leather hose, five rubber suctions (steam), three leather suctions (manual), one set double harness, four spare traces, one small hand pump and hose, seven copper handlamps, 24 leather buckets, three hay cutters and coil wire rope. Captain Hart (who in 1897 dropped the title of captain and from then on called himself Chief Fire Officer), reported that in September 1896 a telegram was received from the Tenterden brigade asking for assistance at a very large fire in their town, their own engine having broken down. The Ashford brigade "although the distance was very considerable" was able to render valuable assistance to their colleagues at Tenterden.

Many volunteer brigades in those days used part of their income for an annual outing or dinner, or other festivity. These seemed to have been fairly grand occasions, with much eating, drinking, and general revelry. The Ashford volunteers kept a small, private account book, still in the Kent Brigade Museum, entitled "Members Private Outing Fund", and one entry, dated August 1899, showed not only initiative in the choice of venue, but also the small cost of a trip abroad in those days. The annual outing was to be to France and 11 volunteers went to Boulogne and back for 7/6 per ticket. With meals and drinks, it is believed that the 11 men had a very enjoyable day abroad for well under £10. Other outings from Ashford included "to Margate by water from Folkestone", and to the White City in London.

Two fire brigades, Eynsford and Horton Kirby, seem to have been formed about 1895, but the first factual mention of both brigades is in November 1899 with Horton Kirby going to the aid of Eynsford when the four-storey Eynsford Paper Mill was ablaze from top to bottom. In an issue of "The Papermaker", the following account appeared shortly after the fire:

"A good deal of damage was done by a fire at the Eynsford Paper Mills, owned by Messrs Arnold and Foster. A furious gale prevailed at the time, and in a few minutes the whole of the four-storey building, comprising rag store, boiling house, drying loft, engineers' shop, carpenters' shop, coach-house, and storerooms, was a mass of flame, the reflection of which could be seen for miles round. The Eynsford Fire Brigade, of which Mr Foster is captain, was soon got to work, and a steady stream of water from two deliveries was so directed that the flames were confined to the building first attacked. In this work the Horton Kirby engine and brigade, arriving soon after the outbreak, rendered valuable aid. The most important part of the mill and the stock of manufactured paper were saved. Every credit is due to the firemen for their excellent work, but, according to the report of the captain of the fire brigade, they were 'considerably hampered by discreditable conduct of some of the pumpers, who desisted at times from work to secure promise of drink'. From the suddenness and strength of the outbreak, it is supposed that the fire must have been smouldering for some time. As about a month must elapse before the mill can be put in full working order, many families suffer from being out of employment."

During the 1880's and 1890's, Maidstone was a hive of activity in the fire protection field. Apart from the 'official' brigades, (those run by the insurance companies and the volunteers), there were nearly 20 'private' brigades operating in the town and district during that period. These consisted of 'Country House' brigades, paid for by the owners of these houses for their protection (the firemen made up of their staff), and a variety of brigades organised by mill-owners, tradesmen, and the owners of large farms. In many ways these private brigades were the forerunners of today's works fire brigades. Some records of the time also refer to a Maidstone Police fire brigade but it is doubtful whether this was a proper fire-fighting force. The police seem to have assisted at some fires with "a cart and hose", but their main duties seemed to have been in crowd control.

The Maidstone Volunteer Brigade founded in 1873 continued to flourish, and in 1881, their strength was given as: one captain, two lieutenants, two sergeants, one engineer and 20 firemen. The Volunteers, or the Maidstone Fire Brigade as they were affectionately called, were popular in the town and frequently took part in official functions and celebrations. By 1883, the brigade's finances, never very strong, were again in difficulties and regular appeals for subscriptions "towards this excellent and deserving institution" were issued. Uniforms, too, which the original members had to buy for £10 of their own money, were becoming "tattered and torn" after ten years use, and did not add to the prestige of the men at official functions. The brigade left their headquarters at "The Bell" in 1890, and moved to a new and more central headquarters in King Street. During most of the 1890's, fire alarms were still given by the ringing of the town hall bell, but by 1897, all members of the brigade had been connected by telephone to the police station, and two fire alarms had been installed in the town.

In 1899, the Royal Show was held in Maidstone, and for its duration the Volunteer Brigade set up a temporary fire station at the show ground in Mote Park. For these duties the Corporation increased their annual grant to the brigade from £40 to £58.17s.2d.

The end of the century also meant the end of the Maidstone Volunteer Brigade. Long discussions took place throughout 1900 about the formation of a new Maidstone Borough Fire Brigade. The Kent Fire Office Brigade was taken over by the Royal Insurance, and their steamer was presented to the Corporation. The Volunteers, who had not been included in the proposals of the Council, felt that they had been treated shabbily, and when, as individuals, they were asked to apply to join the new brigade, all declined. At the end of March 1901, the Maidstone Borough Brigade was in existence and all the Volunteers' appliances and engines became the property of the Corporation.

The efficiency and speed of Post Office telegrams in 1899 is well illustrated by a telegraphic alarm received by the Hawkhurst Brigade to a fire in Ticehurst. Handed in at Ticehurst Post Office at 1.27 p.m. on August 27th 1899, it arrived at Hawkhurst Post Office two minutes later at 1.29 p.m. One wonders how long such a telegram would take today, if the service had not been abolished altogether.

Not until 1900 did Eastry acquire its first volunteer brigade. No records exist how the area was protected against fire before then, but it appears that little or no organised fire-fighting was in existence. An interesting poster, dated January 13th 1834, promises a £300 reward following a fire at Eastry Court which "was the diabolical act of some person or persons". The owners of the property offered a reward of £200 for the conviction of the offender or offenders, and H.M. Government offered a further £100 to anyone who could give information to lead to "the discovery and conviction of the Offender or Offenders and a Free Pardon, except to the person who actually committed the offence". (See illustration on page 22.) Such a huge reward and such generous contribution from the Government indicates not only a very heavy fire loss, but also a non-existing fire brigade. The new Eastry fire brigade received a valuable present of a steamer from the then Lord Northbourne. This appliance remained in service until 1937 when it was finally replaced by a chain-driven pump escape purchased from Margate.

Criticism of the fire brigade by people who should know better (not entirely unknown today), was fairly common in earlier days. In January 1900, some Margate Councillors accused their brigade of "too much show-off" especially as they felt "they must dash along, whether it was a large fire or a small one". The criticism followed an accident when the engine, on the way to a fire, was involved in a crash with the carriage of a local doctor, and the council had to find £50 for damages. How the poor firemen were to know, on receiving a call, whether it was a large fire or a small one, and more important, whether any lives were in danger, is usually not explained by these critics.

However, life in the brigades also had a brighter side. In June of that year, Margate joined with Ramsgate to send 20 firemen across the Channel to Arras in Normandy, on the invitation of the Mayor of that town, to take part in the Fire Brigade demonstrations there. During their visit, the English fire-fighters were royally entertained by their French colleagues, took part in parades and competitions, and arrived back home with several valuable prizes they had won.

As late as the beginning of this century, some country districts in Kent had to rely for their fire protection on brigades in neighbouring towns. In the 1880's for example, Rainham had to call on Chatham for help in any but the most minor outbreaks. Chatham naturally expected to be paid for their services and a notice to this effect, dated 1888, stated: "the summons for the Brigade must be sent by the owner of the property or a responsible agent, otherwise the call cannot be responded to. The Borough of Chatham Fire Brigade holds itself ready day and night to attend fires in country districts, but notice is hereby given that the members can only give their services on condition that the person sending for the engine holds himself responsible for the under mentioned charges: Firemen – no charge, engine working £1.10s. per hour, horsing engine (four horses) three guineas, hose in use, per yard, 2 pence, damage to gear-actual and refreshments (for firemen) actual." By 1900, however, neighbouring brigades felt that Rainham should have its own brigade, and Sittingbourne Brigade generously presented a horse-drawn fire-pump to Rainham which brought in a number of volunteers. The engine was housed in a shed in the recreation ground and two horses for it were stabled at the "White Horse". The men were called by maroon and the firemen than had to run or cycle to the "White Horse", prepare the horses, gallop to the engine shed, hitch up the pump and rush to the fire.

Sittingbourne's Shand Mason Double-Vertical Steamer 'Victoria', built for the brigade in 1898, came into its own and received much praise during a very serious fire at Lloyds Paper Mills in May 1900. An article in the *East Kent Gazette* at the time reported that:

"The call was received by the Sittingbourne Fire Brigade at 9.40 p.m.

94

and the discharge of the maroon from the fire station, coupled with the fact that the mill whistle had been blowing, at once announced the fact that the works were on fire. With marvellous celerity the Fire Brigade had their Steamer out, fully manned, and the men were upon the scene of action in five minutes ... Other local hose cart ... followed shortly afterwards by Murston Brigade with its fire-extinguishing appliances. By 10 o'clock, however, the fire had secured a firm hold of the whole range of the manufacturing rooms ... It was apparent that the whole block was doomed. All that could be done was to endeavour to prevent the flames spreading to adjacent parts of the mill.

There was work here for a dozen steamers, let alone Sittingbourne's 'Victoria'. But gallantly the engine responded to the call made upon her ... the Sittingbourne firemen directed their efforts to the protection of the finishing room and paper store, behind which is a magnificent 1,000 horse-power steam engine, which was in great jeopardy, for if the fire reached the paper store nothing could have prevented the destruction of the engine and that section of the mill. The Sittingbourne firemen accordingly got a splendid stream of water to bear upon the wall of the finishing room nearest No. 5 machine; and they were none too soon, for great tongues of flame were shooting through the aperture at the top at the time when the hose was brought into play. Four branches were got to work with two deliveries, and while one was in use on the finishing room, checking the advance of the flames in that direction, the other delivery was in operation at the junction of the old and new mills. At these two points there were tremendous quantities of water thrown in to the buildings, and it is gratifying to know that in these particular efforts the firemen were successful, entirely beating back any invasion of the fire at these points ... In two hours after the fire broke out, all danger of its further spreading had passed and the fire was confined to the range of machine rooms in which it originated.

If ever anything justified its existence it is the Steam Fire Engine 'Victoria', possessed by the Sittingbourne Fire Brigade. The salvation of the finishing room and large paper store – in fact the main section of the new mill – is attributed to this gallant little steamer.... She was run down to the fire by hand, and under the charge of her engineers was pumping for four hours without a break, during which time she raised 50,000 gallons of water and at this rate did her work beautifully, to the admiration of everyone."

Mystery surrounds an item in the minutes of the Annual General Meeting of the Hythe Fire Brigade in February 1900. During the meeting it was resolved to send a telegram to Ambulance Fireman Wilmore at Southampton where he was awaiting to join a ship for the Cape of Good Hope. The telegram wished him "a prosperous journey and a safe return" but unfortunately, no later record shows what happened to the man, why he went and whether he safely returned. Nor is the question answered why he was asked to volunteer or whether it had something to do with the Boer War.

Three Kent volunteer brigades which seemed very much alive and thriving in 1903, but for which no information prior to that date could be found, are Pembury, Footscray and Upchurch. The Annual Dinner of the Footscray Brigade in Sidcup in March 1903 seems to have been a very splendid affair with visitors and guests from the Metropolitan (London) Fire Brigade, and from the Chislehurst, Lamorbey, Bexley Heath, Bexley and St Mary Cray fire brigades.

Pembury at that time had a most unusual captain for their volunteer brigade – the Rev. H. S. Brooke, vicar of the parish. A photograph, published in 1903, shows Mr Brooke in his full captain's uniform with brass helmet and medals, and which he fondly referred to as "his fire-fighting vestments". He had ten firemen under his command and it was stated at the time that "it was appropriate that a gentleman who has the care of the souls of the parish should also be at the head of a body of men whose business it is to save the lives and property of the inhabitants".

In September 1902, the coachman of the Dartford Brigade was seriously injured when, proceeding to a fire, he turned a street corner too sharply and was thrown head-first onto the pavement. The coachman, a Mr Curd, had his helmet smashed in which probably saved his life, but he sustained a broken jaw and leg when the engine wheels passed over him. A contemporary report stated that "as so often in case of serious accidents, the fire was but a slight one and was extinguished without the aid of the steam fire engine".

After Sevenoaks received its fine new steamer called the 'Ready' in 1883, the town's volunteer brigade became known as the 'Ready Brigade'. It consisted of 12 officers and men and, according to records, did much good work in the district and won many prizes at competitions. Unfortunately, nothing is known about troubles that started brewing between the brigade and the council at the turn of the century, and which led in 1902 to the disbandment of the Ready Brigade. The immediate cause seems to have been the secret sale of the steamer to the council, apparently organised by the officers of the brigade without the knowledge of the men. A row blew up, the town's people were divided, letters went to the local paper and one, giving a summary of the situation, is worth giving here: "Sir, we the superintendent, engineer and firemen of the 'Ready' Volunteer Brigade, having heard indirectly that our engine has been sold to the Sevenoaks U.D.C., and not having heard anything from our captain, decided to have a meeting in the engine house. Greatly to our disappointment and sorrow we found a new padlock on the door which prevented us from entering. As we are all still willing to volunteer our services, we think we are justified in asking for an explanation." How the row was resolved, and whether the volunteers ever received an explanation, is not recorded, but from then on the 'Ready' Brigade disappeared.

Beckenham is another town in Kent where records of early fire-fighting organisations and volunteer brigades are lost. There is some evidence that a volunteer brigade existed by 1869 and one must assume that fire protection before then was carried out probably by some insurance office and possibly by brigades from nearby towns. However, by 1903, Beckenham had a well-established brigade and in some ways were even innovators. Up to that year the Brigade was called out by the now old-fashioned maroon, but because of objections from the people of the town, and because on at least one occasion the maroon damaged the roof of the parish church, it was decided to abandon this method and to purchase "a patent horn at a cost of £10 to call together the members of the Brigade in case of fire". The 'patent horn' was probably a type of klaxon, but in no way a forerunner of today's two-tone horn.

The Bromley Volunteer Brigade, in existence since 1868, had grown together with the town. In 1887, their famous captain, Mr Nickalls, retired and his post was taken by a Mr J. Hopton. Ten years later, the brigade was taken over by Bromley Urban District Council and a new fire station was established in West Street. A new steamer was purchased in 1897, and in 1900 a new captain, Mr J. Ingles, was appointed. Bromley continued to grow and by 1904, with about 30,000 inhabitants, it became an incorporated town. Most of the volunteers were now getting on in age and under the new circumstances the town council felt it was time to abolish the voluntary system and to place the brigade on a more professional basis under the command of a qualified expert. A new brigade was created with a member of the London Fire Brigade, a Mr Samual Manning, as its first Chief Officer.

Four people had to die in a fire before Cliffe got its own fire brigade in 1904. When the outbreak was discovered, a man had to ride many miles on horseback to Rochester to alarm the nearest brigade and by the time they were in attendance, both people and property had perished. Immediately after the disaster, the Cliffe parishioners held a protest meeting demanding their own fire protection, and in the same year a fire station at the Buttway was opened. At first the new brigade seems not to have distinguished themselves, because the first fire they were called to was at the Manor Farm, the home of their chief officer, Mr J. Robertson; according to the records, it was "a complete burn-out".

In the 1890's, the Right Hon J. G. Talbot of Falconhurst formed a fire brigade for the protection of his own residence and estate but in 1900, at his suggestion, the organisation of the brigade was improved and it became the Falconhurst and District Fire Brigade, with Mr Talbot as president. He also provided the brigade with its appliances and organised voluntary subscriptions for the support of the brigade. By 1904 the brigade consisted of eight uniformed men and were equipped with a manual engine, ladders and other appliances.

It took nearly 13 years, after a committee to look into the establishment of a volunteer fire brigade for Halling which was set up in 1892, before the town had some sort of organised fire protection. In 1905, a brigade of two officers and five men was finally formed, but no record exists as to their appliances, although this volunteer force existed in the parish right up until the second World War when it became part of the National Fire Service. Also in 1905, a volunteer brigade was at work in Otford, but nothing is known about their origins or first formation. The Queenborough Fire Brigade started its life sometime towards the end of the 19th century in the old Cement Works. Whether it was originally a works brigade is unclear, but in 1906 it came under the jurisdiction of the town council, and the new brigade took over as its only appliance the old Cement Works manual. The first chief officer was a publican, Captain George Arnold, the licensee of the old Queen Phillipa Hotel, a strict disciplinarian who trained his men mercilessly but soon achieved standards which won the brigade many competitions. A disastrous fire at Eynsford Paper Mill on March 16th 1906, nearly overwhelmed the Eynsford Fire Brigade, caused heavy damage and the loss of work for 80 employees, and involved assistance from several fire brigades over a wide area. A report in a local newspaper at the time gives a good description of fire-fighting at the beginning of the 20th century: "A disastrous fire broke out at the Eynsford Paper Mill, owned by Messrs Arnold and Foster, on Saturday night, which resulted in the partial destruction of the mill, and all the valuable paper-making machines being totally destroyed. But this is not all. The most serious outcome of the conflagration is that between 70 and 80 employees are thrown out of work, and it will be at least six months before the machinery can be re-constructed. This enforced idleness for so long a period is no trifling matter for those concerned, and must of necessity seriously affect trade both at Eynsford and Farningham, where the employees reside. Another very grave problem is that the paper-making industry in this locality will be in a state of stagnation for months hence. The firm has several big contacts in hand, including the manufacture of a certain kind of paper which can only be made at Eynsford, as the firm, it is stated, had a machine specially constructed for its manufacture.

The outbreak was first discovered by an employee at the mill, named S. Hussey, jun., who was out for a walk at about 7.30 p.m. He noticed smoke and flames, and instantly gave the alarm to the watchman, and the mill whistle was sounded. Owing to the gale which was blowing, the flames spread with alarming rapidity, and it appeared that the whole of the buildings were involved. In less than a minute and a half, tongues of fire burst out from all quarters, and some of the structures being composed of wood and other inflammable material, it seemed almost a matter of impossibility to save any of the property. The reflection of the fire was seen for many miles around, even as far as Erith, and hundreds of people rushed to the scene.

The Eynsford Fire Brigade, under Captain W. A. Foster, was on the spot with the manual at work within three minutes of the receipt of the call. It is fortunate that the engine is kept close to the mill. Had the firemen been a couple of minutes later, the whole of the paper store and offices must have been gutted. The Horton Kirby Fire Brigade, under Captain French, arrived shortly afterwards with the manual, and in the nick of time to assist in saving the paper store and offices. It would have been impossible for the Eynsford brigade to have accomplished this feat alone, as it was quite apparent that the one manual engine was unequal to the task, in face of the strong wind which fanned the flames, although the brigade had at its disposal a good supply of water from the river.

The Sutton-at-Hone Fire Brigade, under Captain A. Hewett, left Swanley Junction at about 7.35 with the steam fire engine and ten officers and men. By the time the brigade reached the top of Farningham Hill full steam was up. When the Sutton-at-Hone firemen arrived they received a hearty welcome from the other two brigades, for the manuals seemed to have little effect on the flames, in face of the fact already stated that the firemen did their duty in every shape and form. But they had the honour of saving the paper store and offices.

However, there were several buildings to the left of the mill, including a drying room, etc, that was absolutely at the mercy of the flames when the steam engine arrived. There was a bountiful supply of water, and the steam fire engine soon had a visible effect upon the fire, the great advantage of steam pumping being indisputable. Mr Foster in conversation with our representative, expressed great admiration for the work done by the steam engine. A large portion of the mill, he said, was saved by the efforts of the Sutton Brigade and they extinguished the fire in an uncommonly short space of time. The Eynsford firemen were very thankful to everyone, both firemen and private persons, who assisted, and especially commend the police for the tactical way they kept the crowd in order.

The chief officer of the Sidcup Fire Brigade, and half a dozen members, journeyed to Eynsford by motor car, and offered their services, but they were not required. The Orpington contingent of the Crays and Orpington District Fire Brigade also put in an appearance with the hose cart, but their services were likewise not considered necessary.

The damage amounts to quite £7,000, but the property is covered by insurance in several fire offices."

Much activity took place in Kent fire brigades in the year 1907. Several new brigades were formed, major fires caused great damage and an entire brigade was asked by the Council to resign. Some brigades, such as Orpington and Swanscombe, seem to have been in existence in that year, but the only reference to be found is the mention of assistance given by them to other brigades. As so often, no historical facts seem to have survived. The beginning of the Swanley Fire Brigade certainly goes back before 1907, because in that year, the town already had a steamer and a fire station, as well as a captain, a Mr Hewitt, who operated the Basket Works in Swanley Lane and where the engine was housed. The engine was pulled by two cab-horses, normally employed in carrying passengers to and from Swanley Railway Station and stabled at the rear of Lullingstone Castle Hotel. The firemen were called out by maroon or by the sounding of the whistle at the local jam factory. The first two men to respond to the alarm had to fetch the horses from the stables and take them about half a mile to the fire station. Meanwhile, the fire in the boiler of the steamer had been lit and eventually the brigade was ready for their turn-out.

Headcorn formed its first brigade in 1907 with ten men, soon to be increased to 15, under Captain C. P. Kingsland who remained chief until 1928. Their appliances consisted of a handcart, hoses, connectors, standpipe and hydrant key, and were kept in a store room at the 'Chequers'. Payment to the brigade was at the rate of 2s. for the first hour and 6d. for subsequent hours.

Disagreement between Whitstable Urban Council and its fire brigade led to a council meeting in May 1907 when by three votes to two, it was resolved "to request the whole of the members of the fire brigade to hand in their resignation". The council considered this step necessary because of disagreements between it and the brigade, and decided to re-organise the fire protection of the town. Thus the old brigade which had been in existence for at least 40 years, disappeared.

Comparatively little is known about fire-fighting activities in the important town and port of Dover. Although, as already mentioned, the town had one of the earliest fire engines in Kent, presented by the Mayor in 1700, records are few about activities in the next 200 years. That such an important port should have been left unprotected is obviously inconceivable, and one must surmise that records were either lost or are buried in some archive. It is most likely that over the years, Dover went through a similar process to other towns of having a volunteer brigade, manuals and steamers. By the beginning of the 20th century, the brigade was under police control, a fact documented in the minutes of the town council on October 2nd 1907, following a big fire in the town the month before.

"The work of the Dover Police Fire Brigade at a serious fire in the High Street was the subject of a discussion at the meeting of the Town Council on October 2nd. Alderman Pepper, the owner of the warehouse in which the fire occured, expressed his gratitude to the Brigade for the smart stop effected. Owing chiefly to the efforts of Chief Constable Knott and his men, the damage was only one-tenth of the amount at risk

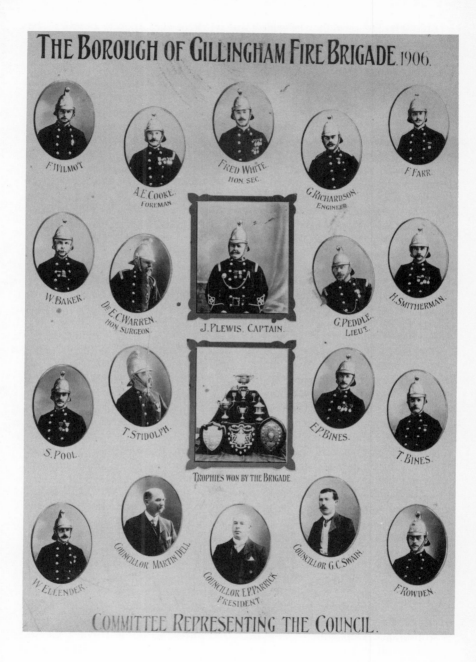

THE BOROUGH OF GILLINGHAM FIRE BRIGADE. 1906.

F. WILMOT

A. E. COOKE.
FOREMAN

FRED WHITE.
HON. SEC.

G. RICHARDSON.
ENGINEER

F. FARR.

W. BAKER.

Dr. E. C. WARREN.
HON. SURGEON.

J. PLEWIS. CAPTAIN.

G. PEDDLE.
LIEUT.

H. SMITHERMAN.

S. POOL.

T. STIDOLPH.

TROPHIES WON BY THE BRIGADE.

E. P. BINES.

T. BINES.

W. ELLENDER.

COUNCILLOR MARTIN DELL.

COUNCILLOR E. P. PARRICK.
PRESIDENT.

COUNCILLOR G. C. SWAIN.

F. ROWDEN.

COMMITTEE REPRESENTING THE COUNCIL.

(£10,000). He thought the successful work of the Brigade ought to be notified to the Insurance Companies. They well deserved special remuneration for the service they rendered at great risk to themselves. Replying to a question, the Chief Constable stated that the men received half-a-crown for each fire attended, whether large or small. No compensation had been allowed for damage to clothing sustained by members of the Brigade who, though off duty, voluntarily assisted at the fire in their own clothes. The matter of placing the case of the police firemen before the Insurance Companies was left to Alderman Pepper." The following year Chief Constable Knott resigned as chief of the Brigade after 30 years service, which shows that a police brigade was in existence in 1878.

On August 1st 1906, Captain Edward Westbrook, chief of the Tunbridge Wells Fire Brigade and Salvage Corps, died after a long illness. Only 53 years old when he died, Captain Westbrook during his 33 years service in Tunbridge Wells had become one of the country's most respected and honoured chief fire officers. Under the heading "Captain Westbrook responds to his last call", the national magazine "Fire and Water" described his career, his achievements and his funeral, and one can do no better than to quote from its pages at length: "With deep regret that will be shared by every one of his numerous friends in the British Fire Service, we record the death of Mr Edward Westbrook, the widely known and respected Chief Officer of the Tunbridge Wells Fire Brigade. The sad event took place on August 1st, at the Nursing Home, where for the latter part of his long and painful illness he had been staying in the hope of benefiting by the skilled care and attention available. Although it was known for some months past that his illness was of a serious character, it was hoped that he would pull through, and favourable reports of his condition were made up to within a short time of the end. The news of his death therefore came as an unexpected blow to his fellow workers in the Service. Captain Westbrook, who was 53 years of age, leaves a widow and two sons, one of whom is secretary of the Tunbridge Wells Brigade.

The funeral of the deceased officer, on August 4th, was of a public character, the imposing cortege including the Mayor and members of the Tunbridge Wells Borough Council, Officers and men from the Fire Brigades of Eynsford, Sidcup, Sevenoaks, Bayham Abbey, Seal, Lydd, Southborough, Sutton-at-Hone, Horton Kirby, Crowborough, Faversham, Gillingham, Rochester, Whyteleafe, Windsor, Burgess Hill, Caterham, Tonbridge, Sittingbourne, Tonbridge Union, Falconhurst, Bournemouth, Milton, Folkestone, Hampton, Hastings, Sandgate, Bexhill, Pembury, Northfleet and East Grinstead, together with representatives of the French, Belgian and Italian Federations, N.F.B.U. Ambulance Department, N.F.B.U. Executive, London Salvage Corps, and a full muster of the Tunbridge Wells Borough and Steam Fire Brigades and Salvage Corps.

In Fire Brigade circles the name of Westbrook is a household word. No name figures more prominently in the annals of the Volunteer Fire Service, and no name is more deservedly honoured, nor less likely to be forgotten. To the readers of this journal his prowess and capabilities come as no revelation. They have watched his career from small beginnings, through every grade of the Service until he enjoyed the proud distinction of being the only provincial officer to share with Sir Eyre Massey Shaw, C.B. and Second Officer Gamble the life membership of the N.F.B.U., conferred upon them by the Central Council. His reputation in the Service had long since extended beyond the borders of his county, and had brought him international honours and recognition, all testimonies to his excellent work and worthiness.

Mr Westbrook joined the Tunbridge Wells Borough Fire Brigade in 1873, and was appointed Escape Conductor in 1875. Seven years later, in 1882, he was promoted to Chief Officer of the Brigade, and assumed entire control of the local Salvage Corps when that body became affiliated with the Brigade in 1887. At the time of his appointment the organisation was in urgent need of improvement, and to this purpose he devoted his best efforts, until the whole force, Salvage Corps included, underwent a complete transformation, and became, as it is today, one of the most efficient and best equipped Brigades (for a town of its size) in the United Kingdom.

Prior to Captain Westbrook's appointment as Chief of the Borough Fire Brigade, there was considerable ill-feeling existing between the two sections in the Borough especially at fires, but the new Captain did his best to promote a better understanding between them, and for many years past the two Brigades have worked well together. It may be interesting to note that since Captain Westbrook took over the command of the Brigade, the Station itself has increased to six times its original size, not including a very convenient muster room, a horse hose van station, and six sub-stations. Great additions have also been made to the appliances and plant. At first they practically consisted of a manual engine and fly-ladder fire escape. They now consist of a steam fire engine, manual, horse hose van, horse fire escape, six fire escapes, hose carts, chemical machines, etc., etc.

In everything connected with the Fire Service, Captain Westbrook had large and progressive ideas. It may be said that he applied locally what he thought nationally. His contention was that all towns and districts should be properly served and equipped in order to safeguard life and property against 'the devouring element'. He was no 'superior' officer who issued his orders from some interior sanctum, and left his subordinates to see that they were duly carried out. 'I never ask my men to do what I cannot do myself', he once said and so through the long period of his command he shared the risks and perils of the fireman's calling, his impulsive zeal often taking him into the 'danger zone' in which his coolness and courage were the admiration of his men.

And so he passes from our ken
In answer to the final call
The Captain Chief had need of him
Beyond the outer wall."

Only a year after Captain Westbrook's death, brigade affairs in Tunbridge Wells began to go wrong. Jealousies over the appointment of a new captain led to disagreements between the brigade and the committee and the resignation of the Salvage Corps. In February 1907 "Fire and Water" stated: "Much regret will be felt at the decision of the members of the Tunbridge Wells Salvage Corps to terminate a long and useful career by resignation en bloc. The fact that so well-established and popular a body should take this extreme step, together with the apparent absence of any effort to induce the members to reconsider their action, suggests that there is more in the business than has yet been made public.

It is not fair to judge the action of either the Corps or the Committee without the full details of the case, but it is the greatest pity that the difference between the two could not have been settled in an amicable manner, if only in the interests of the town. For the Committee, it must be admitted their position in the selection of a successor to the late Captain Westbrook was made exceptionally difficult by the rival claims of the three Brigade and Salvage Corps officers, and they adopted what they considered to be the best solution – the appointment of the Chief Constable as head of the Fire Brigade Service. On the other hand, it would seem that the Committee, though doubtless unintentionally, were somewhat lacking in courtesy in their treatment of the Chief Officer of the Salvage Corps. Whether this alone would be sufficient justification for depriving the town of the services of the Corps we are not inclined to say."

Until 1908, fire protection in Wye was supplied by the Ashford Brigade. Probably following the Great Fire of Wye in 1889, the townspeople must have felt the need for some fire-fighting equipment of their own but no records are extant other than the announcement in 1908 that Ashford had relinquished their duties in Wye and that the town had formed its own brigade. What this new brigade consisted of and what equipment they had is not known.

The keenness of Broadstairs firemen to get as quickly as possible to a fire led to the death of one of the men. A contemporary record recalls: "In July 1908 Fireman Temple was killed when the fire engine, which was being pulled, got out of control and ran over him. The Brigade was called by maroon at 6.30 p.m. to a small fire at the Old Fish Market, and following their usual custom when the fire was near the station the first three or four men to arrive dragged out the pair-horse manual engine and, without waiting for horses, proceeded to draw it by hand to the fire. Running down the hill leading from the fire station to the railway bridge the engine attained a rapid pace and the sudden jerking of the pole, which Firemen Temple and Mond were guiding the machine with, when it hit a channel, threw Temple off his feet and both wheels passed over him. He died on Sunday. Supt. Ferrier, at the inquest, thought drag ropes would be dangerous. Jury returned verdict of Accidental Death, with rider recommending that the engine should not be taken out without horses or with larger number of firemen in charge. Foreman of Jury expressed entire satisfaction with the efficiency and working of the Brigade. Funeral on 9th July was attended by 50 officers and men from Margate, Ramsgate, Westgate, Broadstairs, Sandwich and Birchington Brigades."

Several new brigades were formed between 1900 and 1910 but, as in so many cases, no records exist except an occasional mention in connection with another brigade. Included in these places with 'ghost' fire brigades are St Margaret's, Hildenborough, Crayford, Chevening and Staplehurst.

Folkestone experienced one of its biggest fires for many years in April 1909, when fire broke out in an oil store in the High Street. A plumber was repairing a pipe leading from the oil store to an adjoining shop with a blow lamp when the pipe broke and the oil was set alight. The flames rapidly spread through the wooden two-storey building. The town fire brigade quickly arrived on the scene under the command of their Captain Nicholls and, with their powerful steamer, managed to confine the blaze to the place of origin in a built-up area. After five hours of "fire-fighting, damping-down and turning over" the brigade left; but early next morning they were recalled when an adjoining shop was found to be on fire. It took the brigade two more hours before they could finally leave the scene.

The speed and efficiency of the Lydd Fire Brigade soon became known and they were called upon to fight fires all over Romney Marsh. Until June 1909, when the telephone came to Lydd, the firemen were called out by telegraph, but with the arrival of the new and quicker method of alarming his men, Captain Finn decided to form small contingents of men at New Romney, Brookland and Brenzett. Although these men had no proper equipment, they were trained to contain a fire as best as they could, carry out rescues and assist the brigade on arrival. If the brigade was wanted at Dymchurch or in the Brookland area, arrangements were made with carriers to have fresh horses ready half-way, and when the engine arrived from Lydd, the new horses were hitched in seconds and the brigade proceeded at full gallop to the fire.

After only seven years in existence, the Farnborough Fire Brigade resigned 'en bloc' in July 1909. The reason seems to have been a trivial one – a quarrel between Captain Ferris and the parish council over who should be responsible for the "lighting and care" of the fire station lamp! First the captain resigned and by the apparently old motto "one out, all out", all the firemen resigned in support. During a special parish meeting, a resolution requesting the council to reinstate the brigade was defeated by 63 votes to 15, and after thanking the old brigade for their past services, a new one was formed by the council under a Mr Owen. Nor does this seem to have been the end of troubles in Farnborough. In 1912, an item appeared in a newspaper reporting that the Farnborough brigade had lost five of its active members through resignation and that "the assistance of the local troop of Boy Scouts (sic) has been accepted, who will in future turn out with the brigade".

Little is known about the origins of the Chislehurst Volunteer Fire Brigade. Probably formed in 1891, the first definite clue to their existence comes not until 1910 when the Urban District Council exchanged their manual, in service for many years, for a new steamer. It was a day of much rejoicing for the town when, on September 3rd, "the new engine arrived at Prickend Pond with a clattering of hooves and flashing of polished brass". With most of the townspeople present, the horses were withdrawn, the fire stoked up, and within minutes, jets of water were rising over the pond. However, this much admired engine did not last long, for only a year later, the council (no doubt to show their progressive attitude to the firemen) exchanged the steamer for a chain-driven motor pump.

Maroons as a system for calling out volunteer firemen had always been unpopular with the people because of the noise and occasional damage they caused. Still in use in many brigades during the early 20th century, they were only slowly replaced by electric call-bells and the telephone. Bridge Fire Brigade, formed in 1891, were still using maroons in 1910, when they were directly responsible for the death of their engineer, a Mr John Fenn. When fire broke out in the town, Mr Fenn was the first to arrive at the fire station and attempted to fire the signal. When other members of the brigade arrived, they found their engineer unconscious "with the left side of his face completely fractured". A doctor was called but Mr Fenn died shortly afterwards. The alarm was to a fire in Bridge at four cottages which were completely burnt out. Shortly after his funeral, carried out with full brigade honours and attended by many other brigades, the Captain of the Bridge brigade, Commander Guy Gamble, opened a subscription list "on behalf of the widow and two children of the late J. Fenn, who lost his life under such tragic circumstances whilst in the execution of his duty as a member of the Brigade, and whose wife and children are without means of support".

A grand display by Beckenham Fire Brigade in 1911 to celebrate Coronation Day nearly ended in tragedy and in some respects is very similar to the disaster at Gillingham in 1929 when, during a display, 15 people were burnt to death. The Beckenham accident was described in a newspaper at the time: "The Brigade arranged to complete a capital series of drills with a house-on-fire scene. For this purpose a temporary wooden structure was erected to represent a shop, and inside was placed a plentiful supply of highly inflammable materials. It was proposed to ignite these, and then, after rescuing two men from the top of the building, to extinguish the fire. But the Fire Brigade had counted without the wind and the crowd. The former sent the flames swirling through the house; the crowd prevented the rapid progress of the Brigade with escape and jumping sheet. The two firemen were speedily in peril of their lives. Both made a rush for the life-line, slipped and fell 20 feet to the ground. Each sustained painful burns, and one, Fireman Cray, in addition, had one of his wrists badly strained by the fall."

Lamorbey Fire Brigade which was formed in about 1903 had a short life. In 1911 the brigade was disbanded, and their appliances and equipment were distributed between the Bexley and Bexley Heath brigades which then protected Lamorbey and district. The first chief officer of the Sturry Fire Brigade was a Mr L. Ashenden who was also the chief officer of the Kent Insurance Fire Brigade at Canterbury. Founded in 1913, Sturry was one of the most poorly-equipped brigades in the County, a situation which lasted for many years. Their fire station was a shed in the 'Rose Inn' yard, their 'engine' was a hand-truck with only six lengths of hose, a standpipe, key, bar and branch. Turn-out was by a messenger on foot and the number of firemen or fires attended is not recorded.

While in 1913 Sturry still seemed to be in the dark ages as far as fire protection was concerned, 'go-ahead' Sittingbourne acquired in the same year what was described as "the very last word in motor ambulances". The gift of a Mr and Mrs Dean, it was handed over by them to the town and then passed over to the fire brigade for service.

An extract from the Gravesend Municipal Corporation Year Book and Diary for 1913 suggests that the brigade was at that stage run by the police. Under the heading 'Fire Brigade', it stated: "all members of the police force (under their Captain A. G. Martin) are drilled in fire brigade work and there are (in addition) six auxiliary firemen, namely two waterworks turncocks and four fitters. In the event of fire, alarm should be given at the Police Station or at three sub-fire stations. There are two fire engines, one steamer and one manual and two fire escapes."

Monday January 6th 1913, was a black day for Beckenham and in some ways for its brigade. About 7.30 p.m., fire broke out in the 15th century Park Langley Manor, destroying valuable frescoes, old paintings, and rare Italian marble pieces, as well as most of the historic buildings. After the blaze was put out – and it took 14 hours of pumping and another three days before the brigade could leave – allegations of brigade incompetence were made, counter claims published, the Council drawn into the affair, and fire-fighting operations criticised in letters to the papers. Long reports in the *Beckenham Journal* gave a graphic account of what happened: "The fire originated on Monday evening in the fine old dining room, which formerly served as the ballroom and is some 40 ft by 50 ft, and contained some 15 to 20 exquisite frescoes representing the various arts and sciences. In addition, the room possessed a rare and handsome marble mantelpiece of Italian workmanship, which was said to be valued at something like £150 to £200, and valuable paintings adorned the walls. Unfortunately, not a stick or thread, to use a metaphorical phrase, remains of these valuable and magnificent works of art.

At 7.30 p.m. on Monday the steward's boy, Lane, was engaged in washing up when his attention was aroused by a crash. Having in mind the fact that several attempts had been made to burgle the place, he promptly shouted to Mr W. Brett, the steward, who was upstairs. Mr Brett immediately proceeded to go downstairs, but was called back by his wife, who implored him not to go unarmed and gave him a revolver. He and the boy Lane, who had armed himself with an Indian club, then proceeded to the dining room where the noise had come from, and on opening the door were met and half-blinded with a rush of smoke which poured out from the large room.

Just as they arrived a large portion of the ceiling fell with a crash, and it was no doubt a similar occurrence which had attracted Lane's attention. Seeing that the ceiling was well alight in the centre, Mr Brett rushed to the telephone box and called up the Beckenham and Bromley Fire Brigades. The building was lighted by gas, and the steward's next act was to turn the gas off at the meter. He then saw that Mrs Brett and the three children who, together with the maid, had come downstairs, were placed in safety. Owing to the dense smoke the steward had great difficulty in remaining at the telephone while sending out the calls, and while he and the lad were engaged in trying to put out the flames they had a narrow escape from being struck by a wheel from a lift which fell near them. When the steward went to the telephone he left the lad at the dining room, and returned there for him in about 15 minutes but found him gone. After a search, he discovered the lad in the upper rooms apparently making for the roof, and together they quickly left the now blazing building.

It is extremely fortunate for the lad that he didn't succeed in getting to the roof as it was not long before it fell in with a crash, sending sparks and flames high into the air. At the time they discovered the fire it had got a firm hold of the dining room, and by the time the Beckenham Brigade arrived at 8.00 p.m. the whole was blazing fiercely, and in the words of the steward "it burnt like matchwood".

The Beckenham Fire Brigade received the call over the telephone at 7.50 p.m., and in a little over a minute, Supt. Gear, with four men, had turned out with the motor engine. They arrived at the scene of the fire about 8 o'clock. Here they were faced with a most difficult task as they

108

had to get through two narrow gateways in order to reach the lake, which lies 200 or 300 yards to the front of the building. The ground was extremely soft and difficult to negotiate, and it says much for the skill of the Superintendent, who was at the wheel, that the engine was moved into position without any hitch except when the engine stuck for a minute or two in the soft mud. While the engine was being got into position the Superintendent despatched a couple of men into the building with a hand pump for the purpose of ascertaining the nature of the fire. They were not long in seeing that the job in hand was a big one, and handing over the pump to the steward and his boy, they hastened to give assistance at the engine. In a very short time the hose was out and the turbines pumping at full pressure. At the commencement, one hose was worked with a pressure of 175-lbs., but later a second hose was added, and the pressure was naturally slightly reduced. At 9 o'clock, Supt. Gear telephoned from the seat of the fire to the station for additional hose, and that was quickly brought up by the horsed engine. Breeching pieces were utilised, and four jets played on the flames, which at this time had engulfed the whole of the building, and fanned by a fairly strong wind, were driving far and high to the north. At this time, some 14 men of the Beckenham Brigade were in attendance, and at 10.00 p.m. a telephone message was sent to the Bromley Brigade, who arrived with their motor and firemen. Three men from the West Wickham Volunteer Fire Brigade were also present to assist.

The four jets were maintained at full pressure till 6 a.m. on Tuesday when the number was reduced to two for the purpose of cooling down the ruins. When the Beckenham men arrived, the whole of the old part of the building which included the large dining room was blazing fiercely, and the flames had begun to spread to the newer portion. Supt. Gear and his men at once took a jet upstairs to the upper floors which, with the exception of the ladies' dressing rooms and the committee room, that were in the newer portion of the building, were practically empty and very seldom used. The flames and smoke, however, were too much for them and they were beaten back to the ground floor, where they stuck to their task amid blinding smoke and falling debris. Several of the men received the usual minor cuts and injuries, but Firemen Bokes and Pope were struck on the head by falling debris and knocked down, both sustaining bad cuts.

All attempts to check the flames proved unavailing, and the main building was completely burnt to the ground. Nothing remained standing on Tuesday morning but the blackened walls with gaunt gaping windows and a heap of charred timber on the ground. Not a single thing was saved from the dining room, but all the club's books, the majority of the furniture from the committee room, and a small quantity of members' property were got out and taken in hand on Tuesday by the Salvage Corps men, who arrived on the scene.''

109

Soon after the fire, criticisms of the brigade, its equipment, and delays, were being published in the local paper:

WHAT WAS WRONG WITH THE TELEPHONE?
The Editor of the *Beckenham Journal*

Dear Sir – In your otherwise excellent comments on the Langley Park fire in Friday's Journal, I was rather surprised that you had nothing to say on the fact that the telephone message took just under an hour to get from the burning building to the fire station. The instructions given in every telephone Directory, are that in the case of fire all that is necessary is to call 'fire', and the operator does the rest. Had the call been put through to the Beckenham brigade immediately after it had been given, it seems probable that the major portion of the mansion would have been saved. I doubt if a dozen engines could have done much with an old structure like that if they were not called till the fire had an hour's start.

Yours faithfully,
"HELLO".

AN ADVERSE CRITICISM.
THE FIRE.
The Editor of the *Beckenham Journal*

Sir – Your valued paper frequently applaud our Fire Brigade. Will you permit adverse criticism?

I was one of the first dozen to reach the scene of Monday's disastrous fire at Langley Park, and for nearly three hours witnessed the abortive attempts of the Brigade. While appreciating the distance of the water supply I would enquire whether the motor could not have worked another hose, and whether other Brigades could not have been earlier summoned to assist. It was not apparent that any official was in active command of the whole scene of operation.

A combined attack from the South by three or more hoses properly disposed would have localised the fire, and with greater celerity in getting to work might have saved the dining room portion of the building from being burnt out.

In the practices, which, the brigade presumably holds, are conditions ever assumed in which no hydrant is available within a few score feet?

Does not the possession by Beckenham of "the last word in fire engines", and of up-to-date appliances, demand that dexterity and resourcefulness of crew and captain should be thoroughly developed? Else is the ratepayers' money, but ill-invested.

Yours faithfully,
L. G. Paxon.

The following week, at a special meeting, the Beckenham Council investigated the fire and sprang to the defence of their brigade. Mr

110

Dykes, Chairman of the Beckenham Fire Brigade Committee, made a full statement on the investigations into the fire and exonerated the brigade. He said that: "The Council and the inhabitants of the district had every reason to be perfectly satisfied with the steps taken. The Council had placed at the disposal of the Fire Brigade, the very latest and most up-to-date appliances for fighting fire, and after careful investigation and consideration, he thought everybody would agree that the Superintendent and the firemen showed themselves worthy of the confidence reposed in them, and that they did everything that could possibly be expected of them to deal with the situation.

Of course, some people made remarks and there had been adverse reports. People might be asking why was not the fire put out? He thought that when they knew the true facts of the case everyone would be perfectly satisfied with the reply. There was very little doubt that the fire was started in one of the beams of the ceiling of the first floor projecting into one of the flues, and that that beam had been smouldering for hours, probably for days. It then set alight to the ceiling, and with the ceiling well alight, flaming pieces dropped to the floor below, to set fire to that. It was not until the ceiling on the ground floor was actually in flames that the boy gave the alarm at 7.30. The caretaker got on the telephone for the Fire Brigade, but the call was not received until 7.59, but the Brigade turned out immediately with the motor fire engine, and arrived on the scene somewhere about ten past eight.

The men immediately went into the building with instructions to close doors and windows to prevent a draught, and the Superintendent took the heavy fire engine round by way of the farm buildings to the pond some 300 yards away, which was the only source of water supply. That proceeding was not an easy one owing to the soft state of the road or want of road and the darkness. When he got to the pond the water was as much mud as water, and time had to be taken to dig a pit into which to put the strainer of suction hose.

At 15 minutes past eight the engine was at work, and did not stop till 11.30 the following day. At one part of the time it was pumping through two lengths of hose, and at another through four lengths. He wanted them to realise that it would have been impossible for that work to have been done by their old fire engine. In the first place the valves would have been clogged with such water, and in the second place the boiler would not have worked with muddy water. When the engine arrived and had started pumping, the roof was well alight, and had begun to fall in, and personally he did not believe if the London Fire Brigade, with the resources at its command, had arrived, they could have saved the building. What the men did was to take steps to prevent the fire spreading to the other portion of the building, and in that they succeeded to a very great extent, as shown by the fact that part of the

111

Fig. 12. An early motor fire engine.

steward's quarters and also the sheds were not burnt. The old building itself burnt like tinder, and nothing could be done to put it out.

He also heard reports that they were short of petrol, but that was disproved by the fact that the engine worked throughout without a stop, and before the supply taken grew short more was sent for.

Mr Dykes added that the Superintendent attempted to telephone for the Bromley Fire Brigade, and a message was got through at 10 o'clock, and they came and rendered valuable assistance, and he was sure all the members of the Council would thank them for the assistance they rendered."

The outbreak of the Great War in 1914 brought new problems to Britain's fire services and, in particular, to fire-fighting organisations in the counties and rural areas. With the Government discounting any dangers from fire-raids, and later refusing firemen exemption from call-up, brigades throughout the country, especially those of non-professional or volunteer status, lost many of their men who, in the first enthusiasm to fight, joined the Navy and Army in their thousands. Although the raids by German planes and Zeppelins were sporadic, fires were caused, and often the desperately under-manned brigades found it difficult to cope. Of far greater danger than enemy action were the frequent explosions in the munition factories which claimed many lives and created major conflagrations.

While the position of the fire service in the big cities and towns during 1914/18 is well documented, comparatively little is known about the council and volunteer brigades in the more rural areas which, nevertheless, constituted the biggest fire-fighting force in the country. Kent, although not in the immediate front line as in the last war, had well over 100 volunteer brigades providing fire cover in the County; most of these within months of the outbreak of war lost as many as half of their members. As the air-raids increased, professional firemen secured exemption from the Conscription Act, but such a privilege was not thought necessary in the case of volunteers in the semi-urban and rural areas. With heavy casualties in the big battles in Europe, more and more men were drafted into the forces, and rural brigades had to rely on very young men and the older ones (but even they had to be of a low medical grade) to provide what fire protection they could.

Following some especially heavy raids on London in 1917, the Government introduced compulsory measures for the co-ordination of fire brigades under the Defence of the Realm Act. This meant that the Home Secretary could, at his discretion, arrange that "the fire brigades and fire appliances in the area should be employed under single control to constitute a special fire brigade area, acting under the chief officer of one of the brigades". At first only the London Metropolitan Police district was so designated, but included a town in Kent – Dartford.

It was in Kent that the first German bomb of the war fell. On Christmas Eve 1914, it was dropped on Dover and exploded near the castle. Little damage was done, except a few broken windows, and no fires were started. With their undermanned brigades and uncertain future, other towns and parishes in the County tried to re-organise their fire-protection as well as they could. Hythe, with over half their members gone into the Armed Forces asked, and received, a grant of £200 per annum from the Municipal Corporation. Several of the Hythe firemen who had joined up, were killed on active service and a brass plaque recording their names is now in the Kent Fire Brigade Museum.

The two villages of Teynham and Lynstead, which relied for their fire protection on a steamer from Sittingbourne, decided in 1916, in view of the war, to set up their own volunteer brigade. Under the leadership of a former fireman, Mr A. E. Ferris, who had taken up residence in the district, £100 was raised and a hose-cart, hose, and some other equipment were purchased. Gradually, a fire station was erected in the yard of the 'George Inn' and a manual pump bought.

Shortly after noon on April 2nd 1916, one of the biggest disasters in the history of the British explosives industry occurred in Faversham, killing 105 people, including many fire-fighters, and injuring scores of others. Several munition factories were situated in Faversham which was for several centuries a centre of explosives production, and was fully involved in the war effort. The Explosive Loading Company, situated at Uplees Marches, was one of the biggest of them and it was in their premises that the disaster developed from very small beginnings.

Strict censorship at the time prevented any full contemporary accounts, and it was not until after the war that the story could be pieced together. The fire was fought by the works fire brigade, (all of whom were killed): by the Kent and Norwich Insurance brigades, by the Borough Volunteer Brigade, and by several brigades from the surrounding area, and other works brigades; units from the Armed Forces, including the Kent Royal Garrison Artillery; engineers from the anti-aircraft battery at Oare, and men from the Lancashire Battery and West Lancashire Brigade. Extracts from a post-war report give some of the details of the disaster:

"At approximately 12.10 p.m. on 2nd April 1916, it was noticed that sparks from a boiler house had set fire to some empty sacks which were piled against the matchboard wall of a shed being used as a TNT store. By an unhappy chance, the same building was also being used to store ammonium nitrate, which when mixed with TNT produces a more powerful and less stable explosive known as amatol. Reports of the quantity of explosive vary, but it seems probable that the store may have held as much as 200 tons, while the total distributed around the factory site may well have exceeded 500 tons. The staff formed a bucket chain, and the factory fire brigade got to work with their manual fire engine in an attempt to extinguish the fire. Despite their efforts for over an hour, the fire obtained a good hold, and the factory manager, Mr G. Evetts, ordered the attempt to be abandoned and the area to be cleared. Very shortly afterwards, at approximately 1.20 p.m., the building blew up and there were two large sympathetic explosions in the nitro-glycerine washing-plant some 150 yards away. All the buildings in the immediate vicinity of the first explosion, which caused a crater more than 40 yards across and 20 feet deep, were destroyed or seriously damaged; fires were started through the factory site, and dead and injured lay everywhere, often covered in mud or debris and with their clothes alight.

Rescue work and fire-fighting continued for many hours after the explosion in conditions of very great danger. Two further TNT stores blew up, some 20 minutes and 40 minutes respectively after the first explosion, and there were numerous smaller explosions as individual munitions, particularly mines, caught fire. Many of those engaged in the original fire-fighting attempts were killed and later rescue work and fire-fighting were largely carried out by four separately identifiable groups – factory staff, including factory fire brigades, from the Explosive Loading Company and the Cotton Powder Company whose premises were immediately adjacent, and under considerable threat; fire brigades from the surrounding district; and parties of troops who rushed to the scene."

Many medals and commendations in connection with the explosion were won by firemen, soldiers and civilians alike, although most of them were not published until after the war. The Mayor of Faversham submitted the names of 29 members of the three Faversham brigades present, and others honoured were firemen from the Cotton Powder Company's Works Fire Brigade. The three officers of the Faversham brigades and three firemen from Cotton Powder Company brigade received their awards for "conspicuous courage and devotion to duty on the occasion of a fire at an explosive factory". They were:

Chief Officer James Goode, Norwich Union Fire Brigade, Faversham

Chief Officer Charles Henry Semark, Kent Fire Office Brigade, Faversham

Captain Guy Tassell, Faversham Volunteer Fire Brigade

Fireman Stephen Epps, Cotton Powder Company's Fire Brigade

Fireman Herbert Foley, Cotton Powder Company's Fire Brigade

Fireman Stephen Vidgeon Sayewell, Cotton Powder Company's Fire Brigade.

Their citation further stated: "Mr Tassell with his brigade worked all day in the danger zone, many explosions occurring near him. Mr Semark was also present with his brigade. He rolled filled shells already hot into the dyke, removed cases of TNT from threatened buildings and stood close to a magazine filled with explosives and with sparks flying around it handing up buckets of water to a man on the roof. Chief Officer Goode also worked untiringly in the danger zone and was specially distinguished by his successful efforts to prevent the fire spreading to a full magazine of TNT. He also rolled hot shells into a dyke."

Eventually, the Government realised that their original contention of "no fire or bombing raids" on Britain could no longer be sustained, and exemptions from call-up of fire service personnel were gradually increased. Wealthy local benefactors, too, were presenting engines and equipment to their fire brigades, and in Ramsgate (the coastal towns of Kent were particularly vulnerable to enemy attack), Councillor Dame Janet Stancomb-Wills gave the brigade two motor fire engines. Indeed, the gift was just in time, for on June 17th 1917, a Zeppelin bomb meant for Dover hit the Royal Navy ammunition store at the Fish Market, Ramsgate, causing a huge explosion and fire, and wrecking 700 homes in the town. Over 10,000 windows were shattered, and shells, ammunition and mines continued to explode for a long time in the fierce heat of the fire. First on the scene were personnel of the Ramsgate Naval Base who tried to tackle the blaze under highly dangerous conditions. They were quickly followed by the Ramsgate Fire Brigade and then by the brigades of the neighbouring towns of Margate and Broadstairs. The raid, during which eight bombs fell, killed three people and injured 16. Again, many awards followed this major incident. Chief Officer A. Johnson of Ramsgate Fire Brigade and Chief Officer H. Hammond of Margate Fire Brigade received the King's Police Medal, and the B.E.M. was awarded to 16 men of the Ramsgate Brigade, to eight of the Margate Brigade, and to six of the Broadstairs Brigade.

Chief Officer Johnson's recommendation covered all his war service with Ramsgate Fire Brigade but noted especially for the Fish Market Fire: "For conspicuous gallantry on several occasions and for continued meritorious service during the War. During the War 119 enemy air raids and bombardments have occurred at Ramsgate and the services of the Fire Brigade under the able command of Chief Officer Johnson have been of great value. On three occasions, during a fire and explosion on board a torpedo boat, during the explosion of an ammunition dump caused by a bomb from an airship, and during a fire in a gas holder caused by a bomb from an aeroplane, Chief Officer Johnson has displayed conspicuous gallantry in circumstances of the gravest danger."

Chief Officer Hammond's recommendation stated: "He has entirely reorganised the Fire Brigade and done extremely good work in connection with air raids. The Brigade has turned out 117 times in connection with air raids and bombardments, 25 times while the raid was in progress. On one occasion assisted the Ramsgate Brigade all night to extinguish fires caused by bombs."

Awards to firemen of the Ramsgate, Margate and Broadstairs Brigades were made with the citation "for conspicuous courage and devotion to duty on the occasion of a fire at an ammunition store" as follows:

Ramsgate Fire Brigade: Second Officer G. H. Watson; Firemen W. Andrews, A. W. Attwell, W. E. Brewer, W. W. Castle, F. A. Coleman, A. W. E. Goodwin, C. G. H. Hammon, H. G. Holdbrook, C. Larkins, J. E. Palmer, M. L. Prinkham, J. Solly, G. Waller; Motorman F. R. Goodbourn; Coachman A. F. Nairne.

Margate Fire Brigade: Superintendent E. J. Bryant; First Officer S. W. Stiff; Firemen E. Harper, E. Testa, F. Watson, W. Yeomans; Engineer H. Dixon; Sub-Engineer D. Malpas.

Broadstairs Fire Brigade: Superintendent G. B. Austin; Firemen A. S. Jarman, A. E. Temple, H. Turner; Engineer A. E. Brisley.

In addition to their medals the Ramsgate firemen each received a five pound note and were entertained to dinner at the Granville Hotel, Ramsgate, through the generosity of Dame Janet Stancomb-Wills D.B.E. Dame Janet was a distinguished local councillor and benefactor of the Borough Fire Brigade.

There is little doubt that many other places in Kent must have suffered during the Great War, but records still available naturally concentrate on the biggest and most spectacular incidents. In 1919, a war-weary nation slowly drifted back to normality. Fire brigades, who had lost many of their men in the war, tried to re-organise with more modern appliances, and younger men were brought onto their strength. Nationally, too, changes took place. The National Fire Brigades Union, which had a very strong membership in Kent, changed its name to the National Fire Brigades Association' to avoid confusion, as the Association was not a trades union. Another change of name was that of

Fig. 13. Victory celebrations, Herne Bay 1918.

117

the Association of Professional Fire Brigade Officers to the 'Professional Fire Brigades Association' as many of their members were now made up of rank and file. At the end of 1918, the Institution of Fire Engineers was formed – an organisation solely concerned with the technical and educational advance of the fire service.

Back in rural Kent, the village of Cuxton decided that, now the war was over, it wanted its own fire brigade. Before and during the war, Cuxton had to rely on Rochester for their fire protection, and by the time the horse-drawn engine arrived, it was often too late. The new brigade acquired a handcart, hose and a standpipe, which were kept in a small hut on some wasteland. Their first captain was a Mr Sparrow and their standpipe man was a one-legged school caretaker, Ted Murphy. Alarm was by maroon, and training was given to the Cuxton men by the regulars at Rochester. Rochester's brigade would attend all major fires in the village, but sometimes the Rochester engine would be driven, unmanned, to Cuxton, and the local men relied upon to cope.

During the war, more and more horses were requisitioned by the army for active duty; and brigades in rural areas and indeed in many towns, who had relied on these animals to pull their steamers and in many cases their big manuals as well, found themselves without adequate pulling power. Instances have been recorded where brigades could not respond to a fire call because the men could not drag the heavy engines to the fire.

The result was a gradual motorisation of the Service with a number of motor-pumps being provided in the bigger places in Kent. After the war, for example, Maidstone received three more motor-engines and Rochester, one. Tenterden, too, became motorised when the council bought a second-hand chain-driven Daimler which, with a hand-made iron towing-bar, pulled their engine at speed to fires. Not satisfied with a Daimler, the town soon acquired a Rolls-Royce (presented to the brigade by a Mr Tubbs), which was in use until the beginning of the last war in 1939. Sturry Fire Brigade, which started life in 1921 with a hose-cart pulled by two firemen, soon acquired a horse-drawn manual and later bought a steamer from Bedford. A vehicle was needed to tow this heavy engine and the brigade purchased a Hotchkiss Tender which had started life as a taxi and had been converted by a Canterbury coachbuilder into a fire engine. In 1923, Northfleet Fire Brigade purchased a Ford Model 'T' fire appliance and a photograph of the machine with its brass-helmeted crew is now in the Kent Fire Brigade Museum.

With the many changes that took place in the nation's fire services during and after the 1914/18 war, with the increase in population and industrialisation, and with the new status, techniques and equipment of the Service, demands were made by the professional associations, by the local authorities, and by the brigades themselves for an inquiry into the

Fig. 14. Folkestone Fire Brigade 1919, with early breathing apparatus and wheeled stretcher.

whole set-up of the country's fire protection. The Royal Commission on Fire Brigades and Fire Prevention was set up in 1921, and sat for over two years. Suggestions were made – and strongly opposed – that the fire service should come under some sort of government control, or that county councils should co-ordinate the brigades in their areas. The question of charging the owners of premises requiring the services of a brigade was raised, as was the renewed demand by local authorities for contributions from the insurance companies towards the cost of the service. Attacks were made on the fire brigade system, under which it was not necessarily the duty of a local authority to maintain a fire brigade, thus resulting in inadequate fire cover and appliances.

A suggestion by a member of the Commission that "Chatham, Rochester and Gillingham, might with very great advantage have one really efficient fire brigade for the whole area" brought a reply from a Kent member: "if that were attempted you would have the town councils of those three towns up in arms against such a suggestion". On the same theme, a councillor from Folkestone said: "so far as we are concerned, we can look after ourselves. We think no grouping should result in suffering to Folkestone by an increase in the existing cost". Finally, the Commission published a report of some 60,000 words and containing 142 recommendations and conclusions.

As with so many Royal Commissions, little immediate action resulted from it. Most of the service in Kent continued in the same way, modernising its equipment, purchasing motor appliances, and still heavily relying on its volunteers to protect the population from the worst ravages of fire.

In 1925, Herne Bay Town Hall caught fire, and despite all the efforts of the brigade, the building was so badly damaged that it had to be demolished, together with the fire station which formed part of the Town Hall. The strength of the Herne Bay Brigade at that time was one captain, two lieutenants and 16 men. During the next two years, the brigade purchased two motor appliances – a Leyland with a 30 foot Ajax ladder, and another vehicle with a wheeled escape. Their steamer remained in service and could be towed behind a motor vehicle, especially in the case of rural fires.

During 1926, an important year in the annals of the Faversham Fire Service, the town acquired a brand-new brigade, disbanded three existing ones, bought a new motor-pump, fought an unusual fire at an ice-rink, and quarrelled with the neighbouring volunteer Brigades of Teynham and Lynstead. It all began when the Town Council decided to buy a new motor pump to replace their horse-drawn manual in service since 1880. The council then formed a fire brigade consisting of a chief officer, second officer and 12 firemen, and disbanded the three existing town brigades: the 'Kent', the Norwich Union, and the volunteer 'Gentlemen's Brigade'. This was accomplished with goodwill all round, the two insurance brigades and the 'Gentlemen' handing over all their equipment

120

and the Insurance Offices each contributing £100 to the new brigade. The existing fire station, a small building, had to be altered to accommodate the new motor pump. In order to lighten the burden on the local rates, the town council invited Faversham R.D.C. to share in the cost of the brigade and receive, in return, fire cover for the rural district. This was accepted, but it sowed the seeds of the quarrel with neighbouring Teynham. Meanwhile, the members of the old and now disbanded brigades were made honorary members of the new brigade, and since the town had only one engine, which might be out at night at a rural fire, the honorary members were equipped with a hose-cart for use in such an emergency. Little is known about the fire at the Faversham Ice Rink in that year, but the new brigade apparently acquitted itself well, and although the Rink was destroyed, they were praised for their efforts. Incidentally, this was the last fire at which the 1880 manual was in use.

With fire cover in the rural district, and therefore in Teynham (now the responsibility of the Faversham Brigade), bad feelings between the two brigades quickly developed. The Teynham postmaster was instructed to call the Faversham brigade as soon as the Teynham maroon went off, with the result that Faversham came rushing over to Teynham or Lynstead for chimney fires or other small jobs which the Teynham men claimed they had successfully dealt with for many years. The situation became worse, and finally, the Faversham Council sacked their chief officer because he had moved to Canterbury and was not available at night, and appointed a Mr Stuart Holmes their new chief. Mr Holmes appears to have been a remarkable man, for "through his tact and good humour" he quickly resolved all difficulties, and the Teynham brigade was allowed to play its part unhindered in its own area, but calling in Faversham when fires were too big for their own resources.

By 1928, the Lydd Fire Brigade had found a better way of getting their steamer to a fire than by live horse-power. They had an arrangement that one of the Style and Winch Brewery lorries should always be available in case of fire to tow the engine, and it must have been a jolly turn-out with the firemen sitting in the back of the lorry, presumably on empty beer crates.

The first street fire alarms were installed in Bexley Heath in 1929. At first, there were only five heads but these were rapidly increased, so that five years later, the whole of the town was covered by 75 installations. It was an open-circuit system, with the control boards in the council electricity station, where a 24-hour watch had to be kept by council employees. The system was connected to the firemen's call-bells and to the fire stations which recorded the number of the head pulled. In the same year, all hoses and branches of the Bexley Heath Brigade were fitted with instantaneous couplings, well ahead of London whose fire brigade kept their slow and heavy, round thread couplings until 1942. Also, in 1929, Rainham Fire Brigade was taken over by the Gillingham

Borough Council and the former's chief officer became officer-in-charge of the Rainham Fire Station.

One of the last volunteer fire brigades to be formed in Kent was in 1929, when the little village of Matfield decided it needed some fire protection of its own. Although the initiative was taken by the Brenchley Parish Council, who had already bought some fire appliances for Matfield (before even a brigade existed), the Matfield Brigade, under the leadership of a most remarkable man, achieved within 18 months of its formation a leading position in that part of the County. In July 1929, the Brenchley Council approached Mr E. W. Hubbard of Matfield House, asking "if he would undertake, in conjunction with the Council, to raise a fire brigade in Matfield, to handle the fire extinguishing appliances which had been bought for the village some two months previously". Mr Hubbard accepted the proposal and on July 25th, the inaugural meeting of the brigade was held at his home. The meeting was attended by 20 parishioners who were addressed by Mr Hubbard "who outlined the position of the district and the village as regards fire protection". He mentioned the disbandment of the Tunbridge Wells Steam Volunteer Fire Brigade four months previously (this is a new name as far as Tunbridge Wells Fire Brigade history is concerned, but if the Corporation Fire Brigade and Salvage Corps was meant, there is certainly no record of its disbandment).

Mr Hubbard who, before coming to Matfield, was for some time a member of the Shanghai (China) fire brigade, was a man of vision and a strong believer in the value of an effective fire service. During the first meeting he spoke about public service and "the high record of the British Fire Service and the necessity of cultivating the spirit of keenness in the work if the brigade was not to be allowed to die out in a year or so, as so many similar efforts had done in the past". Within one week, the first drill took place, attended by 17 volunteers and from then on weekly wet-and-dry drills were held. A few months later, the brigade received the gift of a motor-tender, had telephone links with all brigade members, and equipment well in advance of those kept by brigades in similar small places. Chief Officer Hubbard produced a nicely printed annual report at the end of 1930, recording the first 17 months of the brigade and its activities. Perhaps the best way to show the full achievements of the Matfield brigade is to reproduce extracts from this annual report here:

MATFIELD FIRE BRIGADE

Committee:

E. Dadson, E. W. Hubbard, H. Larkin, R. Larkin,
Sir Amberson Marten.

Chief Officer & Secretary:
E. W. Hubbard, Matfield House

2nd Officer:
E. Dadson, Matfield Green

ANNUAL REPORT

This being our first Annual Report, it covers the period of 17 months during which the Brigade has been in existence up to the close of 1930.

The Brigade was inaugurated on the 25th July 1929, and in the following March what may be described as an Interim Report was issued, in the form of a letter to the Brenchley and Matfield householders, in which a brief history of the Brigade up to date was given and an appeal was made for donations and subscriptions towards its upkeep.

Since that Report was issued, the Brigade has received a magnificent gift in the shape of a Motor Tender, capable of carrying the whole of the fire-fighting appliances – comprising portable motor-driven turbine fire pump, one thousand feet of hose with nozzles and accessories, chemical extinguishers for use against both ordinary and oil fires and London pattern hand-pump – as well as six or seven men.

This Tender, which is a 30/40 h.p. Wolseley car, the touring body of which has been replaced by a Tender body specially designed for fire purposes, was publicly presented to the Brigade by the Chief Officer's father-in-law on the 24th June last, when some two hundred people collected on the Green to witness the presentation. It is interesting to note that the new body was built by Mr Baldock of Matfield Green.

It is safe to say that our gear and equipment now compares very favourably with that of any other small village in the country.

During the past fifteen months the services of the Brigade have been called upon on six occasions and in each instance the members have acquitted themselves smartly and efficiently.

In one case the occupier of the property which the Brigade, by very prompt turn-out, saved from certain destruction has presented us with a silver trophy as a token of his gratitude and this is to be competed for annually by members of the Brigade, This year, in a two-man drill, it was won by R. Larkin and S. Johnson.

We made our first appearance in the National Fire Brigades Association, South Eastern District, Spring Tournament, held at Faversham on Whit Monday, entering teams for two events, in one of which we secured third prize.

The Brigade gave displays on the occasion of the Matfield Peace

Commemoration Sports and the Brenchley and Matfield Horticultural Society's Show, when collections were made for the benefit of the N.F.B.A. Widows, Orphans and Benevolent Fund.

A weekly meeting of the members is held. In the summer evenings the tender is usually taken out and pump or other drill is carried out in different parts of the parish. During the winter we are receiving a course of lectures on First Aid from Police Sargeant Reeve, to whom we are extremely grateful for giving up his evenings for our benefit.

As opportunity affords, small parties of members are being taken privately to London to witness the weekly demonstration carried out by the L.C.C. Fire Brigade at their headquarters at Southwark.

The Gear and Uniform rooms at the Fire Station have now been fitted with a hot water heating installation, at no expense to Brigade funds.

In arranging for the transmission of fire calls by telephone I should like to acknowledge the ready co-operation of Mr Hodges and his family at the Brenchley telephone exchange and also the public spirited assistance of Mr Newbold, at Matfield Post Office, who, at his own expense, maintains a telephone extension bell in his bedroom and is thus able at any time of the night to receive fire calls, which he has undertaken to pass on to the proper quarter.

We thank all those who are assisting the Brigade financially and we ask for support also from those who are not yet subscribers. Annual expenses have to be met and it is most desirable to build up a reserve fund against the time when appliances become obsolete and require to be renewed.

> Eric W. Hubbard,
> Chief Officer.

By 1933, the Matfield Brigade was an example to every village in the County. Well equipped with motor tender, hose, hook ladders, scaling ladders and automatic fire escapes, they fought fires successfully over a wide area. But the final seal of approval for the brigade came on July 3rd 1933, when Captain Gordon Dyson M.I.Fire E., Chief Officer of the Shanghai Fire Brigade, on leave in this country, inspected the Matfield Brigade. A contemporary account in the *Courier* described the event as a "red letter day" for Matfield:

"In introducing Captain Dyson to the members of the Brigade, Captain Hubbard said that this was the first occasion on which they had been honoured by an inspection by an eminent professional Fire Officer. In holding the position of Chief Officer of the Shanghai Fire Department, Captain Dyson occupied one of the most important posts in the British Fire Service.

He had under his command a force of over six hundred officers and men, with nine fire stations and more than eighty pieces of motor gear. He was responsible for the safety of a million persons and for the protection of property valued at thirty million pounds sterling.

Captain Hubbard took it as a very high compliment indeed that such a responsible Fire Officer was willing to give up a day of his well-earned leave to come and inspect a little village Fire Brigade in Kent.

Captain Dyson then inspected the members of the Matfield Brigade, who were drawn up with their appliances outside the Fire Station. After the inspection a demonstration drill was carried out, the fire pump being set to work from the Matfield Green pond and two lines of hose were worked through the upper floor of the Matfield House stables, both scaling and hook ladders were brought into use, and two targets were struck. This was followed by a pumping display on the Green and by an exhibition of descent by automatic fire escape from the roof of Matfield House by several members of the Brigade.

Forming up once more the members were addressed by Captain Dyson, who laid stress on the valuable public service which was being rendered by volunteer firemen, and urged them all to keep up their keenness to the highest pitch. He said that a good fireman had no secrets, no politics and no frontiers, and instanced the case of Shanghai, in which the International Settlement, the French Concession and Chinese Territory adjoined one another, and fires occurring on the boundaries were dealt with by the Brigades of whichever authority arrived first on the scene, all working in perfect co-operation with one another.

The Brigade was then dismissed, and refreshments were served in the courtyard, when the health of Captain Dyson was enthusiastically drunk by everyone present.

Interest was also added to the occasion by the presence of Mr Porter and Mr Bowman, two old members of the 'Deluge' Company of the former Volunteer Shanghai Fire Brigade, of which Captain Hubbard was also formerly a member. These two gentlemen were responsible with other old members, for presenting Captain Hubbard with a Chinese silver cup, which is known as the 'Deluge' Cup, and is competed for annually by members of the Matfield Brigade."

It is now necessary to go back a little in time to 1929 and an event which shook not only the people of Kent, but also the nation. On Thursday July 11th, darkness was falling over the park in Gillingham on the final day of the annual fete in aid of the St Bartholomew's Hospital Fund. For the past 20 years, the final display and the star attraction of the programme had been the exciting rescue by the Gillingham Fire Brigade of a "wedding party" who took part in a mock marriage in a large and specially constructed house. Never before had an accident occurred during this display, but in 1929, things went tragically wrong and within minutes 15 people (firemen, sea scouts and naval cadets) had been burnt to death, many beyond recognition, in front of the horrified relatives and spectators. The cause of the disaster remains unsolved to this day as the person who committed the fatal mistake himself died in the flames. Details of the tragedy have been compiled from contemporary reports in local and national newspapers, from the transcript of the inquest, and from a booklet by John Langdon in the Local History Series published by the Kent County Library.

The display house was of three floors, covered on the front in match-boarding, with internal wells giving access by ladder from floor to floor. Empty windows were on each floor and on the ground a door gave access to the building. Before the display, two firemen dressed as groom and bride, walked around the park amusing the spectators, and were joined by a naval Petty Officer dressed as a female and known as 'Auntie'. Eventually these three would go to the 'House' where a reception was to be held, and to join the other wedding guests impersonated by other firemen, sea scouts and naval cadets.

At a pre-arranged signal, a fire was to be simulated by the lighting of red flares inside the house, and the guests, screaming for help, would be rescued by Gillingham Fire Brigade which would be standing by a short distance away. Only then should a real fire have been lit in flammable materials stored on each floor to destroy the structure. A man was stationed on the ground floor, whose duty it was, on the word of command, and when all 'guests' were safely away, to light these fires on his way down the building.

But on that fatal evening, something went horribly wrong. With all the "wedding party" still in the house, flames suddenly shot out of the ground floor, mushroomed upwards and within seconds enveloped the whole structure in a roaring inferno. Most of the spectators still thought it was an especially realistic display, but when figures appeared in the roof enveloped in flames and started to leap to their deaths, the full horror of the tragedy became apparent. As soon as the first flames were seen, Chief Officer Frederick White of the Gillingham Brigade ordered the two motor pumps standing nearby into action. Water was pumped from a special dam holding 1,200 gallons, and rescue attempts were made with ladders and escapes. Chief Officer White and First Lieutenant Edwin Bines made several attempts to enter the burning building, and when White tried to climb an already burning escape, the rungs crumpled under him into ashes. Although the fire was put out within minutes, none of the 15 in the building escaped with his life. Firemen, police, and members of the St John Ambulance Brigade, too, tried in vain to rescue the doomed 'guests' and several received severe burns in the attempt.

These rescue attempts were only possible on the lower floors, but because of the intense heat, those brought out were already either dead or were to die soon. Two days after the disaster, the Mayor of Gillingham received a telegram from Buckingham Palace. It read: "The King and Queen are shocked and distressed at the terrible disaster at

Gillingham, resulting in the loss of so many lives, the majority of them being boys of promise. Their Majesties ask that you will be good enough to convey their expression of warmest sympathy to the relatives of the sufferers." The inquest was opened on Monday July 15th, for identification, and adjourned until July 23rd.

The massed funeral was held on Wednesday July 17th. In the morning there was a special service at St Augustine's church, a church with which some of the young victims had been associated. The afternoon saw the streets of Gillingham packed with thousands of people. There were townspeople and official representatives from the Medway Towns, as well as many men and women from all parts of the country. The procession to the cemetery followed a two mile route which began at the old Council Chambers. Ten draped coffins were carried on fire appliances, which were covered in wreaths and had had their bells muffled with crepe; five more draped coffins were borne on gun carriages. Thousands of representatives of public bodies and institutions followed the coffins on their last journey. All the shops in Gillingham were shut, flags were flown at half-mast. Members of the St John Ambulance Brigade were kept busy, mainly with cases of fainting. Many householders along the funeral route, particularly in Livingstone Road, were also kept busy handing out glasses of water to bystanders and marchers, a gesture particularly appreciated by the several hundred firemen suffering under their brass helmets. After the funeral, the bells of Gillingham parish church were rung half muffled.

The second part of the inquest into the disaster was resumed on Tuesday July 23rd and was concluded on Thursday July 25th. Mr Harris, the County Coroner, was in charge, and was assisted by Colonel Guy Simmonds, D.S.O., a Home Office fire expert. Various official representatives were also in attendance, and included people from the Admiralty, the National Fire Brigades Association, Gillingham Corporation, Gillingham Volunteer Fire Brigade, Gillingham Fete Entertainment Committee, the Police, the St John Ambulance Brigade, the St John Nursing Division, amongst others.

The first witness to be called was Frederick White, Chief Officer of the Gillingham Fire Brigade. He stated that he was in charge of the demonstration, which should have consisted of a number of people in a dummy house, that the number was determined by the officer in charge, and the selection of individuals was made by him. The performers were to remain on the second floor where life lines and life-saving slings and hooks had been placed in readiness. Also on each floor were iron vessels containing material for lighting a fire for illuminating and display purposes. There was a man stationed on the ground floor whose duty, on receiving the word of command, was to light these fires on his way up the building. These orders were given by Lieutenant Bines, and the man who was to have lit the fires was Fireman Cockayne. White instructed

Cockayne, he continued, to carry on, and was satisfied that everything was correct at that moment. He then sent a fireman up the building to see that everybody was in his place and knew what to do. The fireman returned and reported that everyone was ready.

Cockayne should then have gone up the ladder to the first floor and lit the smoke fires which were to give illumination, then make his way to the top of the building and give the alarm, when a maroon would be sounded and two motor pumps, 30 yards and 50 yards away respectively, were to be rushed in, one from the front and one from the rear of the structure. The escapes would be unshipped immediately. The curricle escape – the one with wheels – was to be used by Fireman Tabrett to rescue Worrall, dressed as the bride, and would then be used to effect other escapes. On the opposite side of the building, a telescopic escape was pitched at the spot where a davy line had been previously secured, and where other rescues would have taken place. The motor pumps also carried pompier ladders for rescue purposes. All firemen had been detailed for their particular duties, and were equipped with belts and hooks. About 20 yards from the house, a dam to hold water had been erected, measuring 8 feet by 4 feet by 4 feet high, and holding 1,200 gallons. A length of hose had also been rigged, leading from a nearby hydrant to the dam, to give further supplies of water.

White told the inquest that he left immediately after he told Cockayne to carry on, and "could not possibly see what he did". He first realised that something was wrong when he was about 10 or 12 paces away from the building when his First Lieutenant told him that the shavings on the ground floor were alight. They both then ran back and saw the shavings all alight, and a steady light at the window. White said he then ran to the demonstrating van and told the man on duty there: "That fire's gone wrong, put everything you have got on it, at once". He then went to the motor pump by the dam and assisted in getting the hose to work, bringing two branches to play on the fire. He then thought he could use the curricle escape to reach the window as the fire had got well down and was well under. He was halfway up the escape ladder when the charred rungs gave way. The second escape ladder was already burnt beyond use, too. On this floor, White saw a number of bodies lying across one another; the floor which was substantially made, had not yet burned through although the flames were fierce. Nine bodies had been recovered, one of them a fireman. The position of the bodies on the second floor was at the correct place for rescue in the mock fire. In White's opinion, all would have been rescued in another three minutes, but the heat had been too intense.

Answering the Coroner, White said that fire spread was so rapid that all the victims had been suffocated by the intense heat, and that they had all succumbed inside two minutes. He had ordered the motor pump back as it was scorching in a position only 12 feet from the building.

Firemen who had run forward to pick up bodies of those victims who had jumped, were seriously burned.

Fireman Cockayne, White repeated, had been on the ground floor when ordered to carry on, and wouldn't have had time to light the fires in the building. In any case, White didn't know what Cockayne would use to ignite the fires. Twenty-four firemen were at the demonstration, apart from those in the house. To a series of repeat questions, White re-affirmed that the fire should not have been started until the maroon had sounded and everybody had left; that all the boys except one had been found on the second floor; and that the last time he had seen Cockayne, he had been on the ground floor.

Lieutenant Bines said that he had instructed the men in their duties at the demonstration, both in the house and outside. He had told Cockayne to light the flares on the first, second and top floors, and to report to him at the front door when the building was clear. That was all he had told Cockayne to do. He then waited for the alarm which Cockayne was to have given by shouting from the top of the building. Bines had seen that all his men were in position, when he heard someone say: "They are lighting up"; he looked and saw a small flame on the ground floor. He immediately ran to the house and called to Station-Engineer Daniels to bring the hand extinguishers. When he went inside he saw that the shavings were alight, although he was positive that they were not all over the floor. He immediately shouted to Fireman Nicholls, who was on the second floor, to throw out the life-lines, but he heard no response. He had not waited, but had left immediately to bring up one of the motor pumps, as they were not having much success with the hand extinguishers. The fire was eventually put out in 3 to 4 minutes with the help of the two motor pumps.

The Coroner, in his summing up, said: "We have come to the end of this very painful enquiry, and I don't propose to go in detail through the evidence, because a good deal of it would be quite unnecessary. In the first place, the jury are perfectly familiar as to the nature of the demonstration which was being carried out. It had been done on many occasions previously, and never before had there been any mishap. This form of demonstration, I understand, is very popular, and one which is carried out all over the country; and the most important result of that enquiry would be the possible prevention of any such fatality happening again. The jury have heard that the demonstration took place just about 10 o'clock on the night of July 11th. Lieutenant Bines has told how the combustibles were placed in the building, and how he gave detailed duties to various firemen – all of whom, unfortunately, have since died – and, finally, how he detailed Fireman Cockayne to light flares on the first, second and top floors, and then report to him at the front door when the building was clear – that is, when those who had been taking part in the mock rescue should have got quite away from the building.

Then, and not till then, were the shavings to be set alight, and the whole building demolished. Well, that is what should have happened. If that had happened, we should not be here today. I am perfectly sure that those orders were not carried out, and the question is: why were they miscarried?"

Evidence had been given, went on the Coroner, to show that the orders were not carried out as had been laid down. The fires had been lit in the wrong order. That order was top floor, second floor and then first floor, but they had actually been lit in reverse order and, almost at the same time, a flare had broken out on the ground floor.

After retiring for three-quarters of an hour the jury returned, and when asked if they agreed on a verdict the Foreman answered that they were agreed. The verdict must be Misadventure. The jury were also of the opinion, he continued, that the occurrence had arisen from the premature lighting of a fire on the ground floor by some person unknown. The jury then agreed to the Coroner's re-wording of their verdict to read: "Death from misadventure, due to shock from burns received while taking part in a fire brigade life-saving demonstration, due to a fire being prematurely started by a person or persons unknown".

Those who died in the disaster were:
Scout Reginald Henry Lewis Barrett (13)
Cadet David Stanley Brunning (12)
Cadet Eric Edward Cheeseman (12)
Leslie George Neale (13)
Cadet Leonard Charles Searles (10)
Cadet Ivor Douglas Weston Sinden (11)
Scout William Herbert Jack Spinks (13)
   Robert Dennis Usher (14)
Scout Leonard Gordon Winn (13)
Fireman Francis Bull Cockayne (53)
Ronald George Mitchell (37)
Fireman Albert Joseph Nicholls (56) – secretary of fire brigade
Petty Officer John Thomas Nutton (37) – 'Auntie'
Fireman Arthur John Tabrett (40) – 'Bridegroom'
Frederick Arthur Worrall (30) – 'Bride'

The early 1930's saw more and more Kent brigades raising money to buy motor pumps and to dispense with their old steamers. Many people had always assumed, myself included, that soon after the Great War, fire protection services – even outside the great cities – were rapidly being equipped with modern appliances incorporating the latest technical developments and inventions. It was therefore surprising to find in the records, that many steamers and even manuals, some having been in service since the turn of the century, were still being used up to the Second War, and in a few instances, up to the introduction of the

National Fire Service. Motor pumps, too, were often bought second-hand from wealthier brigades and some were not self-propelled, but were motorised pumps mounted on vehicles still often drawn by horses. Reading between the lines, it appears that many local authorities and councils, some not even convinced of the value of their brigade, were unwilling to spend sufficient money on the conditions and equipment of their fire-fighting services – a situation not entirely unknown today.

Queenborough Fire Brigade purchased a Morris motor fire engine in 1930 for £635, and in the same year, a "motorised unit" was delivered to Cliffe Fire Brigade, which served them up to and during the war years. It was only in 1932 that Cranbrook sold their large Merryweather manual (which they had used since 1896) and replaced it with a new Dennis turbine trailer pump, towed by a specially adapted Rolls-Royce.

That these motor pumps, perhaps in the hands of untrained mechanics, were not always very effective, is shown in a rather sarcastic and anonymous letter to the editor of the *Kent and Sussex Post*, dated November 1930, and referring to a fire in the parish of Hawkhurst.

"Dear Sir – On Sunday evening, about 9 p.m., the tolling of the fire bell was heard in the parish. Almost immediately a large crowd (including two or three firemen) assembled in front of the engine house. The engine was loaded, hot water put into the radiator, etc. After a quarter of an hour had passed the erratic tolling of the bell could still be heard. The crowd increased and one onlooker was heard to say "Don't she shine, I bet she would look alright in a church parade". At the end of 25 minutes we were treated to a splendid sight – that magnificent piece of engineering, spat and splattered into life, and as the crowd cleared from its path, one was reminded of a racecourse at the start of a race for the crowd with one accord murmured "They're off" – and so they were. With the gallant driver at the wheel that huge mass of energy shot forward three feet, stopped, raised her haughty head, and pranced out of the building.

With her front wheels on the road and back part in the gutter, she hesitated, then jumped forward but changed her mind and slid back. This manoeuvre was repeated about six times. At last, with the help of a dozen or more willing hands, she staggered on to the crown of the road. After a brief rest she continued (with her extra man-power) on her way, tearing over the Highgate at the terrific rate of about four miles an hour, her bell clanging to warn all of the approach of this speed demon.

On reaching Marlborough House, the sudden thought must have dawned upon her "It's Sunday, why should I work on a day of rest?" So she came to a sudden stop. Her works were examined and just as she was about to have her "flues swept" the brush was dropped and could not be found, so she was gently led down a bye-road and left to rest and meditate upon all things in general.

Meanwhile, three cottages at Lamberhurst were being destroyed by the flames, and Hawkhurst, with its up-to-date engine, was unable to respond to their S.O.S.

I understand that a member of the brigade is paid a small sum per week to keep the engine in going order. It would be interesting to know when the fire engine was last taken out and tried. In days gone by it was no rare sight to pass Sir Thomas Dunk's and see our firemen at drill; but who sees it now? How many drills have our new men put in? It is a pity the Parish Council do not see into these things a bit more instead of bickering with the church council.

Could not the engine be taken for a run each weekend and a few fire drills indulged in by the men? We have a splendid fire engine (thanks to the generosity and public spirit of a local gentleman) housed in an ideal building, yet when the dire need arises, it proves a heart-breaking failure.

      Yours truly,
        Enquirer."

West Malling firemen, too, found themselves in 1932 with nothing more than a manual pump and nothing to pull it to a fire. When a motor tender came up for sale in Chatham, the West Malling Brigade was keen to buy it, but the Parish Council considered the cost more than it could afford and rejected the whole scheme. The brigade now took matters into their own hands, organised raffles and other events, hired a barrel organ which was played by firemen in surrounding villages and greatly helped to raise the required cash. So, with a tow bar fixed to their manual, West Malling became mobile. In 1933 the then editor of the *Daily Express* happened to be passing when he observed the brigade working under a great handicap at a fire, directly led to West Malling acquiring its first self-propelled motor pump in 1934. The editor, a Mr Blumenfeld, offered to start a fund with a contribution of £35. Once again the brigade held raffles, dances and whist drives, and raised the amount required to purchase a second-hand motor fire engine which was displayed for sale in a Maidstone garage.

Hythe also purchased a Merryweather 400 g.p.m. motor pump in 1936 at a cost of £1,138, together with searchlights and an additional 400 feet of hose; while Eastry, in 1937, replaced their 30-year-old steamer with a chain-driven pump escape appliance, bought second-hand from Margate Fire Brigade. The great city of Canterbury did not have a motor fire engine until about 1933 when they acquired a Morris fire pump. Until then, Canterbury had to rely on help from much smaller brigades, including the steamer, drawn by a Hotchkiss motor tender from Sturry. In 1935, Sturry Brigade bought their own self-propelled Merryweather pump from Sevenoaks and raised the money by public subscription. It was chain-driven and had a reciprocating Hatfield pump of 1920 vintage.

Changes took place in 1931 in the Dartford area, when five

Fig. 15. Dressed in "Ye olde style" at an annual display.

independent brigades were taken over into a new Dartford Rural Fire Brigade. The former Eynsford, Horton Kirby, Swanley, Stone and Wilmington brigades from then on formed sections of the rural brigade, each with its own officers and coming under the management of the fire brigade committee of the Council.

For many years a curious position regarding fire protection must have obtained in the parish of Cobham. Some sort of volunteer brigade must have existed in the early 1900's, but there is no record of any equipment, fires attended, nor even any mention of firemen. However, in 1932, only seven years before the outbreak of the war, a public meeting was held in Cobham School, to 're-form' the volunteer fire brigade and to elect a committee and a chief officer. Recommendations at this meeting included that "a suitable way should be found to giving an alarm signal in the event of fire" and to "obtain a map of the parish showing the positions of the hydrants". Approaches were to be made to the parish council to "provide a suitable apparatus for drying the fire hose, to obtain information as to the payment for water used in practice and during drills and to ask other fire brigades about payment to firemen, hiring of vehicles for the conveyance of apparatus to and from fires and payments for any firemen's clothing or boots damaged at a fire".

One of Canterbury's biggest pre-war fires occurred on October 17th

1933, when the old Denne's Water Mill was completely destroyed by fire. Used as a corn-grinding water mill, the huge six-storey building near the Cathedral was originally erected in 1792 as a city granary in case of a Napoleonic invasion. The fire was first discovered at about 8.30 a.m. and was immediately attacked by employees with buckets of water. The fire spread rapidly, and when the Canterbury Brigade arrived, the whole of the upper part of the mill was well alight. Assistance was requested from Sturry and Bridge Fire Brigades and later Herne Bay Brigade also arrived to help. Houses in the surrounding congested area were evacuated but many residents lost possessions and indeed their homes in the disaster. Soon the whole of the building was ablaze, the roof crashed in, and burning beams fell onto neighbouring houses. Burning debris set the roof of the "Miller's Arms" inn alight, and with the mill doomed, firemen concentrated on fighting secondary outbreaks caused by flying embers. One whole side of the mill structure fell blazing into the river, causing a blast of heat which drove away watchers on the other bank over 20 yards away. When the fire was finally brought under control about three hours later, little of the building remained.

In 1934, two volunteer brigades, probably the last in Kent before the outbreak of war, were formed at Borough Green and Dymchurch. In that year, the local Chamber of Trade decided that the time had come for the district of Borough Green, Wrotham, Ightham and Seal to have a fire brigade of its own. Before then, the district had to call on Maidstone or Sevenoaks brigades to fight their fires. Long delays because of the distances involved were experienced, and little fires often grew large. Although Seal is mentioned in the records as one of the places needing a fire brigade, it had, in fact, a good brigade since 1891 and it was one of the Seal firemen who trained the Borough Green Brigade when it was formed.

At the suggestion of Mr R. Cloke, a Fire Brigade Committee was set up under the Chairmanship of Mr A. W. Wilkins with Mr L. Daniels as Secretary and Mr H. Williams as Treasurer. Funds were raised by local collections, dances and whist drives. At first the equipment, a standpipe bar and key, a few lengths of hose and two extinguishers, were loaded into Bob Cloke's delivery van and water was obtained direct from the mains. This equipment was often augmented by using a branch and hose which was kept in a locker outside the National Provincial Bank. Later, news came of a pump for sale but if they wanted to buy it, the deal had to be concluded within a week. Appeals and collections raised a lot of money in a very short time, but nothing like enough to buy the pump, and time was running out. At the last moment a local benefactor loaned them the balance of the money and the pump was obtained and proudly put on display outside Bob's shop.

At that time, the Brigade numbered about 13 men, with Bob Cloke in charge. What was needed, however, was a proper fire appliance and when

Lord Kemsley's 1921 Rolls-Royce Silver Ghost was offered for sale, Bob and Bill Kennett, the second in command, travelled to Slough to inspect it. The car was offered to them for £26 but they had only £25 of Brigade funds with them. Pockets were turned out and the money was found. On their return to Borough Green the Rolls-Royce was handed over to a local coach-builder for conversion into a fire tender.

Although Dymchurch Fire Brigade was first formed in 1929 when Romney Marsh R.D.C. handed over to the Parish Council a fire truck, five lengths of hose, a standpipe and two branches, lack of enthusiasm forced the disbandment of the brigade in 1934. Almost immediately, a new brigade was formed, with the limited assets of £1 4s 5d in the bank and two branches and standpipes, the rest of the equipment having disappeared. A new subscription list was started, and under the captaincy of Mr S. Checksfield, keenness was revived, and in November 1934, a solid-tyre Leyland fire appliance was purchased from the Ashford Brigade for £50. Not enough money was in the brigade funds, so the engine was bought on the "never-never", with a down-payment of £10 and the rest over a period of two years. A year later, a Mrs Shorter donated a plot of land for a fire station and with money from subscriptions, the station was built and opened on October 16th 1935. Dymchurch personnel were trained by Folkestone Fire Brigade under their Captain, the late Divisional Officer Woods.

During one night in February 1935, several stores and shops were destroyed by fire in Lenham, the town's biggest blaze for over 20 years. Lenham, which did not seem to have had its own brigade, telephoned for assistance to the Maidstone and Ashford brigades minutes before the telephone wires were burnt through in the intense heat. These brigades sent four appliances, but water from the hydrants was insufficient and the pumps had to be set in at a large pond at Court Lodge. The post office itself was damaged by water and smoke and at least two families were made homeless and lost all their possessions. It took the two brigades, hampered by snow and ice, over three hours to bring the blaze under control.

An unusual fire service recruit – a stray mongrel dog – was brought into Canterbury Police Station in 1939, smelling to high heaven, and after a thorough hosing down by the Fire Service, was christened 'Stinker' and adopted by the men at the Canterbury Fire Station. The dog quickly developed a liking for jets of water, and it was his habit to run to the end of the jet and keep jumping up and biting the water as it fell. During a procession at the beginning of the war, Stinker rode on the head of the ladder, and later demonstrated his prowess at climbing one in front of the Duke of Kent.

Like a true fire-fighter, Stinker met his death in action when a call was received in 1941 to the South Eastern Tar Distillery, Broad Oak, Canterbury. Stinker was held back in the station as was usually done when the appliances turned out to a fire. Several minutes after the appliances had turned out, Stinker was released. He went straight out into the road and seemed to sense the direction that the appliances had taken and left at full speed for the fire, which was about three-quarters of a mile from the Station.

When the appliances arrived at the fire, it was found that flaming tar in large quantities had run out of the compound of the Distillery across a rural road about 18 feet wide, forming a river somewhere about 30–34 feet across, which was filling the ditches on both sides of the road, and was well alight.

While some of the firemen gained access to the compound to get foam on to the seat of the fire, another foam jet was got to work in the road to smother the flames across the road and in the ditches. At this same time Stinker arrived. He quickly sized up the position, and before anyone could stop him, he ran forward into the flaming tar, obviously with the intention of jumping to bite the end of the foam jet. Then Stinker gave an agonising cry, and the tar, still running across the roadway, carried his body into the far side ditch, where later, all that was left of him was carefully dug out of the tar which by this time had set; he was later buried with all the honours due to a good fireman and friend.

Part III

The War, AFS and NFS

1936–1947

With the rapidly deteriorating international situation during 1937/38, the Government began to look seriously at the fire defence of the country. Prompted by the threat of war, rather than (as a Labour M.P. put it in the Commons) "a genuine desire for the improvement of the fire services, which are in drastic need of improvements", a Fire Brigades Bill was drafted in consultation with local authority associations. This Bill, known as the Fire Brigades Act 1938, became law in July and provided that "every borough, urban district and rural district in England and Wales and every burgh and county in Scotland must make provisions for fire extinction by providing and training a fire brigade or by making arrangements with a neighbouring authority. Every authority must, as far as practicable, enter into agreements with neighbouring authorities to secure assistance at large fires". Other provisions in the Act included: that no fire authority after two years following the passing of the Bill charge for the attendance of the brigade at fires (now a rate-borne charge); that the Secretary of State be empowered to appoint inspectors to prescribe standards of efficiency; to establish training centres; and to require uniformity of equipment and appliances.

The Act created 1,440 separate fire authorities in England and Wales and 228 in Scotland, a total of 1,668 fire brigades. Although the Act was soon to be described as insufficient for peace-time needs and worse during a war, every district council from then on had to provide fire protection, and the population was entitled to receive the services of a fire brigade without charge.

The passing of the Act had an immediate effect on the fire brigades in Kent. New local authorities were set up, with parish and voluntary brigades being absorbed into new units, or disbanded. Matfield Volunteer Fire Brigade, already mentioned as one of the most progressive in the County, sent a circular letter to all their subscribers explaining the new Act and their new position. It gives a good summary of what was happening in many areas, and is worth reproduction:

MATFIELD FIRE BRIGADE, KENT
Fire Brigades Act, 1938

Ladies and Gentlemen,

Under the provisions of the above Act, which became law on the 29th July last, the protection of Rural Districts from fire is now the direct responsibility of the Local Authorities and thus becomes a rate-borne charge.

The protection of this District, therefore, is now the duty of the Tonbridge Rural District Council and a rate will be levied over the whole District to provide the necessary appliances and personnel.

Parish Fire Brigades, which are maintained by Parish rates, have to be transferred to the District Council before the 29th January next, but this does not apply to the Matfield Fire Brigade which receives no assistance from Parish rates.

A further section of the new Act provides that in the future no charge may be made on householders by Fire Brigades attending fires on their premises, it being held that, the Fire Brigade being now a rate-provided service, no further payment is due from the householder ratepayer.

The position of the Matfield Fire Brigade is peculiar inasmuch as it is independent of any rate assistance and exists entirely on (a) Subscriptions from Householders, (b) Payments received for attendances at fires.

As regards (b), these payments will now cease and with regard to (a), since all residents will in future have to pay the Rural District Council's Fire Brigade Rate, it is unreasonable to expect that subscriptions to an individual Brigade should still be forthcoming.

It follows, therefore, that the Matfield Fire Brigade will be unable to continue in its present form.

What arrangements will be made by the Rural District Council for the protection of this Parish and of the Rural District as a whole I cannot yet say. The problem is a difficult one and extends beyond the borders of our own District, and collaboration with neighbouring District Authorities will be required.

The main purpose of this letter, which is being sent to all existing subscribers to the Brigade, is to inform them that I can accept no more subscriptions towards Brigade Funds in future and I especially ask those who have signed bankers' orders for their annual subscriptions to instruct their bankers forthwith to cancel the orders.

In the meantime, pending the completion of the Rural District Council's scheme of fire protection, this Brigade will continue to serve the public to the best of its ability, as it has always done in the past.

Eric W. Hubbard
Chief Officer

Cranbrook R.D.C. took over the fire-fighting functions of the Parish Council, as did Eastry R.D.C. from the old volunteer brigade first founded in 1900. Also in 1938, Faversham R.D.C. and Sittingbourne R.D.C. were re-organised as Swale R.D.C. Faversham had to buy another pump, a Dennis, for the protection of the rural district, and on the insistence of the Home Office, Teynham Brigade had to remain in existence as a sub-station of the Faversham Brigade and was supplied with a large Dennis trailer and a Bedford towing vehicle.

In West Malling, the transfer of the brigade from the parish to the rural district council, made great improvements in conditions for personnel and equipment. The strength was increased to ten men and a 'retainer' was paid when 'Volunteer' was dropped from the brigade title.

New uniforms were supplied to the men to replace those in use for over 30 years.

Even before the Fire Brigades Act, a separate Fire Brigades Division of the Home Office had been set up, and in 1937, this Division issued a memorandum on Emergency Fire Brigade Organisation. The memorandum, which was sent to fire authorities throughout the country, asked them to consider the war-time fire risks and draw up fire precaution schemes. The local authorities were asked to submit suggestions for auxiliary fire stations, recruitment of auxiliary firemen, increased water supplies and better communications. They were also told that Central Government would provide pumps and equipment on free loan. The Air Raid Precautions Act 1937 also settled the financial problem of the A.F.S. because, although the pumps and gear were to be supplied on free loan, the cost of training and equipping the A.F.S. was at first to be paid for locally. The A.R.P. Act stipulated a grant of 75% on expenditure which was to be increased to 90% if the cost was not covered by a penny rate.

The first emergency pumps the service received were not to their liking as they constituted a departure from the peace-time machines, and consisted mainly of trailer pumps or pumps which could be mounted on a self-propelled chassis.

By April 1938, 30,000 auxiliary firemen had joined and were being trained in the evenings and at weekends by regular members of fire brigades. The organisation of the new volunteer service varied from area to area and when, following the Munich crisis, thousands of men and women joined the A.F.S., the regulars were quickly outnumbered by the auxiliaries. With fewer than 2,000 of the A.F.S. pumps delivered, there were far more men than appliances. By the beginning of 1939, 140,000 auxiliaries out of the 350,000 the Home Office thought necessary, had been recruited. By the outbreak of war, about 96,000 A.F.S. men and women had been incorporated as full-time members in the professional fire service, and apart from part-time auxiliaries there was a service of about 50,000 from voluntary and retained brigades.

It is impossible to describe the progress and recruitment of the A.F.S. in Kent during that period. With well over 100 local authority and volunteer brigades in the County, it must be assumed that the pattern was similar to that in other rural or semi-urban areas throughout Britain. Local Authorities were obliged, under the Fire Brigades Act 1937 and the Air Raid Precautions Act 1937, to provide not only adequate fire cover in peace-time but also to set up and recruit an emergency organisation in the event of war. It is clear that in 1938/39 much confusion existed about the provision of auxiliary fire stations, supply of uniforms and equipment, and the change-over from old habits to new.

Aldington which, from 1889 until 1939, had no brigade of its own but was covered by the Bilsington Volunteer Brigade, was a good example of this confusion. With the threat of impending war, several local men met and decided to form an "Auxiliary Fire Service Group", most likely outside the official A.F.S. This group of enthusiasts had no equipment, but they managed to obtain a manual pump and some hose from the old Bilsington Volunteers, begged some more equipment from Ashford, and borrowed a trailer from a Mr Hooker which was towed together with a ladder behind his van. Fire calls were received by Mrs Hooker on the telephone, who then called one member who, in turn, called the others. Later, it appears that the Aldington group became members of the proper A.F.S. organisation and were issued with a trailer pump, uniforms, steel helmets and axes.

An anonymous letter in the 1939 April issue of the national journal *Fire* reads:

"In Rural Kent

I am one of a number of A.F.S. volunteers living in a Kentish rural district, of 17 parishes, with a population of about 10,000. So far, 36 men have enrolled, 12 from each of the three largest villages. The rural district council has arranged for us to be trained by an urban neighbour, which has Home Office trailer pumps and equipment.

This training is proceeding very satisfactorily, but we feel we are not receiving the attention and support of the rural council, that we deserve. The council gives us the impression that having started us in training its work is done. Some of us have been enrolled in the A.F.S. for a year or more but when we ask for our uniforms, we are told this matter will receive the council's most sympathetic consideration on completion of training. To reach our training headquarters we have one hour's travelling by bus. Nobody knows who, or what we are, in fact most times we are taken for some dart team. What an advertisement for National Service.

To add to our chagrin we see all round us auxiliaries, who have just joined, fully equipped with uniform.

Disappointed"

By and large, areas in Kent nearest to London, achieved a better emergency organisation more quickly than those further from the metropolis or other large towns. Bexley, for example, engaged two more full-time firemen in 1939 to recruit and train auxiliaries. Four sub-stations were set up and a make-shift control room was built in the main fire station. Each sub-station had from four to six appliances, ranging from light trailer pumps of 260 gallons per minute to heavy pumps of 800 g.p.m. Later on, there were some extra heavy pumps of 1,100 g.p.m.

In complete contrast, a rural village like Marden started its auxiliary fire service with a two-man manual pump of the type which was in use in volunteer brigades nearly 200 years before. This was supplied to them in December 1939 by the Maidstone R.D.C. which was then the local fire authority. With the war in its first year, the Marden A.F.S. unit was loaned an Austin vehicle, which was converted to carry an eight-man manual, long ago used by the Staplehurst Fire Brigade. It was not until 1942, under the National Fire Service, that the Marden unit was issued with a Coventry Climax trailer pump.

When war finally broke out, the fire defence of the Country was still inadequate and badly organised. Had the expected bombing raids taken place from the beginning, and on the scale of the later Blitz, it seems unlikely that the established brigades and their A.F.S. colleagues could have coped with the vast conflagrations yet to come. Many members of the A.F.S. were still without proper uniforms and had to make do with steel helmets, dungarees and rubber boots; their sub-stations which were hastily erected in any building or shed that was available, were mostly of a very poor standard, and the continuous duty-system, later to be abandoned, kept men and women for long periods in dank and insanitary conditions. Although published records are few, it must be assumed that conditions in Kent, later to earn the name of "bomb alley", were similar to those in the rest of the country. For several weeks after the outbreak of war, the brigades and the A.F.S. in Kent stood ready for the attacks which did not come. Children were evacuated to safer areas, stations were gradually improved, training of the new-comers continued, and large-scale exercises were held.

Keen volunteers, ready to get to grips with the enemy and contribute their part to the war effort, the members of the A.F.S. slowly became dispirited. Day after day they trained and perfected their technique or improved their stations and machines. Night after night they sat in their stations waiting for the sound of the sirens. But nothing happened. This was the time of the so-called 'phoney' war, when men and women joined the forces to do their bit, and when the public began to think of the A.F.S. as "draft dodgers" and the "darts brigade". Morale was low and many were leaving the Service, either to join the Forces or to return to their peace-time occupations. By the beginning of 1940, most people believed that the phoney war would continue. Many of the evacuees returned to the target areas, schools that had been taken over as fire stations had to be returned to the local authority, and the public, at first proud of the A.F.S., were now openly hostile. Firemen in uniform were openly insulted, and letters began to appear in local newspapers condemning them as loafers and even cowards.

But soon the public was to realise its foolishness in criticising its fire-fighters. The invasion of France and the Low Countries by the Germans in May 1940, changed the situation almost overnight. Preparations for fire raids were intensified, and on the very day that the German forces entered Holland and Belgium, the first bomb of the war was dropped by a single German plane near Canterbury. At last the phoney war had turned into a real one, and by the end of the month, the Germans had reached the Channel ports and the evacuation from Dunkirk had begun.

Two more months passed in relative quiet before the main attack on London and the Southern Eastern counties began. When the Battle of Britain started and the "First of the Few" joined dog fight after dog fight with the German raiders over the fields and hop gardens of Kent, the County with its important Channel ports and big areas directly adjoining London, was truly placed in the front line of the battle. From August 1940 onwards several famous Kent fighter aerodromes were under constant attack, and towns and villages nearby suffered from fires and civilian casualties. From August 1940 to May 1941, almost nightly bomb and incendiary raids on the Capital brought death and destruction to the neighbouring areas of Kent. Bromley, Bexley, Chislehurst, Westerham, Orpington, Chelsfield, Penge and Sidcup were all attacked directly or suffered as a result of damaged planes dropping their bomb load. Big fires, often requiring scores of pumps, were started, and the previously despised fire-fighters now became the heroes of the people.

Nor was the rest of Kent free from attack. The whole of the County's eastern seaboard, its ports, fighter aerodromes and industry were constantly bombed, strafed and set alight by incendiaries. Even purely rural inland areas suffered, and large fires had to be dealt with by men often using equipment over 50 years old. A hand-written record of the Matfield Fire Brigade, now in the Kent Fire Museum, shows that in just nine weeks of 1940, the Brigade had to deal with 107 red alerts and 32 actual raids of the area. During that time, from June 26th 1940 to September 2nd 1940, the brigade had to deal with fires caused by enemy action; crashed aircraft; farm and woodland fires; and lost one of their best appliances while assisting at an enemy-caused fire at Pembury. Railway lines and junctions in the County were frequently hit and traffic from the coast to London was disrupted for long periods. Here, too, A.F.S. crews had to help with fighting the fires, with rescues and with clearing the lines.

During the afternoon of August 16th 1940, several damaged German bombers dropped over 180 bombs on a small village near Tunbridge Wells (the name, as with so many locations of incidents, had been withheld for security reasons). Missiles hit a local farm, damaging the house, killing the farmer's two sons, 16 cows, and injuring many more farm animals. Later on the same day, another farmer in the village had 53 bombs dropped on his property; 13 cows and bullocks were killed, and his house and farm buildings severely damaged. A major attack on Biggin Hill fighter station at the end of August 1940, killed over 40 people and started a series of major fires on the airfield. Appliances from Bromley, Chislehurst, Bexley and Westerham, were drafted into the area and brought the fires under control shortly before the airfield was again attacked and huge ammunition and petrol stores set alight.

Then on September 7th 1940, 600 German planes raided London and what was to be known as the 'Blitz' had begun. During that night, large areas of the docks of the city, ships, sheds and warehouses were a mass of flames and fire-fighters with hundreds of pumps could make little impact on the conflagration. For many months, saturation raids on London continued. Kent and the south-eastern counties, too, suffered from bombing raids on war-time airports, railway junctions and ports. Other cities and industrial centres in the country, too, were frequently bombed (the City of Coventry was 'coventrated' in a 12-hour raid during the night of November 14th 1940), and the fire services in some areas became stretched to breaking point. Reinforcement schemes within the London area quickly became exhausted, and hundreds of men and pumps were drafted in from neighbouring areas to assist and relieve the tired and often injured fire-fighters. At first, Kent was the major reinforcing pool. Night after night, columns of regulars and A.F.S. crews with their motley appliances of trailer-pumps, open-bodied appliances and old solid-tyred pumps (some with hay knives in their lockers used for cutting into burning stacks), made their way over cratered roads and debris towards the Capital. From miles away, they saw the angry red glow in the sky and heard the explosions which told them that some of them may never see their homes again.

For many members of the Kent A.F.S., who, during the long months of inactivity, had never fought a fire before, it was a terrible baptism. But in the battle with the flames, the men quickly adapted and stood their ground. Arriving in the blazing city, they often could find no officer to report to and frequently a leading fireman had to take charge of a conflagration which, in peace-time, would have brought every senior officer to the scene. Water supplies were always a problem, with mains shattered by high-explosive bombs, and hoses vulnerable from splinters and sparks. It was common for the reinforcing crews to stop at the first unattended fire, find a water supply, and do their best to bring the flames under control. Many were killed or injured as more and more bombs and incendiaries rained down on them from continuous waves of enemy planes which were guided by the sea of flames beneath them.

On September 10th, during one of the heaviest raids on London, a Margate man and a full-time member of the A.F.S., won the George Medal for outstanding courage during a fire at the Royal Arsenal, Woolwich. He was Mr Harry Kinlan, and the citation of the award stated that he and another fireman "remained at their post in face of flying debris and exploding shells of various calibres, and by their action set an example of courage to their comrades. They insisted on remaining even when reminded of the imminent danger, and saved four buildings containing high explosives". Raids, causing serious fire situations, continued in Kent during that period, but because of wartime restrictions, records are few, and incidents so frequent, that it is impossible to give more than a very general picture of the situation at the time. Most affected were the districts nearest to London and the coastal towns of Kent. For example, during the four nights between November 7th and 11th 1940, 52 high-explosive bombs fell on Beckenham; 51 on Bromley; 112 on Chislehurst and Sidcup; 152 on Orpington; and 7 on Penge. The towns suffered damage, deaths and injuries, and incendiaries caused massive fires.

Of the Kent coastal towns, Dover and its emergency services suffered the most and the longest. Even before serious and sustained bombing of Britain began, Dover's firemen had to deal with the many battered and blazing ships, which had sought shelter in its harbours from enemy attacks in the Channel. Bombing, shelling, and 'tip-and-run' raiders, reduced large parts of the port to rubble and caused many casualties amongst its population and its fire-fighters. An official document of the time shows the effect of these attacks on five Kent coastal towns, from September 1940 until October 1941. During that period, Dover experienced 53 air raids with 92 civilians killed (excluding casualties of the emergency services), and 9,000 houses severely damaged. At Margate, the list read: 47 raids, 19 killed, 8,000 buildings damaged; at Ramsgate, 41 raids, 71 killed, 8,500 houses damaged; at Deal, 17 raids, 12 killed, damage to 2,000 buildings; and at Folkestone, 42 raids, 52 dead and 7,000 houses damaged. It is interesting to note that the document states that the numbers are "in round figures" and that "many smaller places are omitted from the list". By the end of 1940, conditions in the A.F.S. had somewhat improved. Most men and women had been issued with proper uniforms; the derelict sub-stations had been improved by the crews themselves; and many of the unsuitable towing vehicles (taxis, vans and private cars) had been replaced by specially designed two-ton vans which became known as "Auxiliary Towing Vehicles" (A.T.V.'s).

Kent fire-fighters continued to be sent on reinforcement duties, not only to London and within the County itself, but also to heavily-raided regions farther afield. But many problems still beset the Service. There were difficulties between the regulars and the A.F.S. crews; at calls away from their home grounds, the men would find different standards, rank markings and equipment. Local authorities, which had to bear a proportion of the cost of the emergency fire brigades from the rates, sometimes refused adequate funds, and volunteers and retained men lost a day's work and pay when they returned exhausted after a night's fire-fighting. And in some rural areas of Kent, 50- and 60-year-old steamers were still in use, fighting modern war-time fires.

With air raids of increasing ferocity and duration all over the country, resulting in huge conflagrations and fire-storms, in the destruction of homes, industry and essential services, and with casualties mounting everywhere, it became obvious that the fire defence of Britain was not adequate. As early as April 1940, voices had been raised by M.P.s and others, asking the Government for a re-organisation of the fire services and the provision of sufficient water supplies, appliances, and better co-operation between neighbouring authorities. Articles and letters began to appear in the press, praising the fire-fighters, but condemning the system as obsolete and dangerous, and unworthy of a great nation. Although the first suggestions for a national fire service were made then, the Government feared an outcry from well over 1,000 local authorities still running the Service, and apart from a series of memoranda sent by the Home Office urging "better planning and more thorough preparation", (frequently ignored by the local authorities), little was done to improve the situation.

A short period of lesser enemy activity over London and the south-east during March 1941 was followed by a major assault on April 16th and 17th. Although London remained the main target, a wide area of Kent was singled out for heavy bombing. Incendiaries, landmines, and bombs rained down on Bromley, Beckenham, Orpington and Penge; huge fires were started; houses, churches and hospitals were destroyed; and hundreds of men, women and children were killed or seriously injured. In Bromley, the bus garage, churches, stores, homes, hospitals and public houses were destroyed by fire and blast. One hour after the start of the raid at 9.30 p.m. on April 16th, most of the town seemed to be ablaze from end to end. Water mains had been fractured by the bombing, and fire-fighters who had fought their way through falling bombs and over rubble-strewn streets from all over north Kent, could do little to prevent the flames from spreading. The signal box at Shortlands railway station received a direct hit and all lines into Kent were blocked for many hours.

As the night proceeded, the raid spread across Beckenham, West Wickham, Orpington and Penge. In Beckenham, three members of the A.F.S. were killed when a bomb fell near their towing vehicle and trailer-pump. The driver of the towing vehicle, Carl Taylor, although badly wounded himself, managed to drag a seriously hurt fireman from the fiercely blazing vehicle to safety before collapsing, himself.

For his heroic action, Fireman Taylor was awarded the George Medal. Bombs, mines and incendiaries caused fires, deaths and injuries in St Mary Cray, Orpington and Mottingham. A direct hit on the Queen Mary's Hospital at Sidcup, killed 18 patients and seriously injured another 30. Altogether, about 150 people were killed and hundreds seriously injured during that night's raids on the Bromley/Orpington region.

Two nights later on April 19th 1941, when London and the south-east region were still clearing up, the sirens sounded for what was to be the heaviest raid of the war. Although the raid was concentrated on the

Thames-side districts of the Capital, damage and casualties were caused again in Bromley, Sidcup and Chislehurst. As assistance messages from London arrived in Kent, A.F.S. men and appliances from Beckenham were sent to London's East End. Soon after the men reported to the station at Bromley-by-Bow, a direct hit demolished most of the building, killing 34 fire-fighters. Twenty-one of those came from the Beckenham A.F.S. Used as they were to sudden war-time deaths, this tragedy stunned the people of Beckenham. Thousands of men turned out for the funeral procession; units of Kent and London A.F.S. lined the route for the service at the Parish Church; and at the cemetery, where the fire-fighters were buried together in one grave, a memorial stone was erected to their memory.

The raids of April and May 1941 on London and parts of Kent were the last serious ones for nearly two years. The raids on Britain during the 'Blitz' had shown where the weaknesses of the Fire Service lay, and steps were taken on a national basis to remedy them before the next series of heavy raids started. There was still insufficient standardisation of ranks and equipment; the reinforcement system did not always work well, since neighbouring authorities often discouraged full co-operation; and equipment was still what the local Town Clerk or Chief Constable thought best.

A conference to discuss the future of the fire service was convened in London on April 28th 1941. There, the whole position was reviewed, and the following day, the Home Secretary (Mr Herbert Morrison) announced his decision to nationalise the Service. As Commander Firebrace, then Chief of Fire Staff at the Home Office, said in his book of memories:

"The Home Secretary had to accept the heavy risk of swapping horses whilst crossing a stream. To put the whole fire service of the country into a melting pot and to fashion it anew at a time when the country was severely hammered by the enemy, and when heavier blows might be expected, demanded great political courage." The Home Secretary announced his nationalisation plan to Parliament on May 13th, and within a week, the Fire Services (Emergency Provisions) Bill 1941, had become law. On August 18th, the independent fire authorities were swept away and the new National Fire Service came into being.

A Fire Service Department was set up at the Home Office and it was decided to divide the new Service into 39 Fire Forces. Most of Kent came under 30 Fire Force, but Tunbridge Wells, Tonbridge, Sevenoaks, Tenterden, Southborough and Cranbrook were incorporated into 31 Fire Force. In Kent, as in the rest of the country, it meant changes, upheavals and difficulties. To re-organise the whole-time fire-fighters, the part-timers, the volunteers and A.F.S. into a national fire force was not easy. Some local authorities, reluctant to give up control over their own

Fig. 16. Headquarters Staff, No. 30 Fire Force.

brigades, were less than co-operative. Everyone who had held rank in a brigade was in effect reduced to the lowest rank, and then re-assessed by a board for the new Service. The law stipulated that he could not be paid less in the N.F.S. than he had received before, but it was possible for a former Chief Officer to find himself serving as a fireman. But, by and large, the grading boards did their work well and provided the N.F.S. with officers best fitted for those responsible posts. The A.F.S., which had proved their abilities during the heavy raids, was also incorporated into the new organisation, and many of their officers now held ranks in the N.F.S. Despite the early difficulties, the new Service quickly settled down. Standardisation of uniforms and rank markings were introduced; assistance, sometimes only grudgingly given, could now be moved freely to wherever it was needed.

By the end of 1941, the N.F.S. was ready to deal with the fire raids which were expected to be even heavier than those during the 'Blitz', but the Luftwaffe had been considerably weakened, and apart from "tip and run" attacks, mainly on Kent coastal towns, and what had become known as the "little Blitz", they never came. Once again, the fickle public began to criticise its fire forces and skilled men were discharged into industry to help with the war effort. Then, in the early summer of 1942, came what were to be known as the 'Baedeker' raids (so called after a famous German guide book to beautiful and historic places), which devastated such non-military, non-industrial cities as Canterbury, Bath, Exeter, York and Norwich.

Canterbury was attacked in the early hours of June 1st 1942. For one and a half hours, wave after wave of bombers flew over the historic city dropping thousands of bombs and incendiaries. Huge fires were started, homes and historic buildings alike were reduced to rubble, and casualties were high. The flames from the burning city could be seen many miles away and N.F.S. crews from all over Kent and as far away as London were rushed to Canterbury to help the city's own fire-fighters. The Cathedral itself was saved from destruction by firemen and fire guards, who risked their lives crawling over the roofs and parapets, throwing incendiaries onto the ground below. By the time the "all clear" sounded, large parts of the city had been flattened, 45 people had been killed and many seriously injured. Destruction was heaviest in the Burgate, Watling Street, St Margaret's Street, St George's Place and St Dunstan's areas, and a total of nearly 4,000 buildings were either destroyed or badly damaged by fire and high explosives. During the next seven days, on June 3rd and 7th, two smaller raids added to the dead, injured and to the destruction. Nor was this the end of Canterbury's ordeal. In the afternoon of October 31st, a low-level attack by 30 German bombers killed 32 people and wrecked more buildings in the congested city centre.

Although the pattern of bombing raids on this country had shifted, they were smaller in size and less frequent. Short, but concentrated fire raids, in which thousands of incendiaries were dropped, kept the N.F.S. busy in the affected areas. War-time censorship and the frequency of incidents makes it difficult to give any kind of detailed picture, but Kent, with its coastline nearest to occupied Europe and in the direct path to the Capital, was very much in the front line. When they were not involved in actual fire-fighting duties, Kent firemen helped in other ways. Squads assisted farmers in the fields and gardens of Kent while others assisted civil defence workers in heavy rescue. The N.F.S. also took part in "Operation Mulberry", the construction of a prefabricated harbour, which later played an important part in the invasion of France. Huge concrete sections of the harbour were constructed in Sandwich and at several points along the Medway, and it was the task of the fire service to use powerful jets to wash away the mud and silt from the construction basins, so that the sections could be floated away. It was cold, wet and sometimes dangerous work.

There were isolated, but often very destructive raids on towns and even villages in Kent, especially in the areas nearest London and the Medway towns. Fire-fighters in the Dover and Folkestone areas had the added hazard of frequent shelling from Cap Gris Nez, and although these did not usually cause serious fire situations, rescue work was carried out by the N.F.S. which itself sustained some casualties in its ranks. In Kent ports, as in other important harbours in the country, N.F.S. Port Officers were appointed to co-ordinate fire-fighting on ships brought damaged into harbour; pumps, breathing apparatus and foam-making equipment were inspected and serviced by N.F.S. personnel; and Merchant Navy crews were instructed in the techniques of fire-fighting and the proper use of equipment. In Dover, Folkestone and other Kent ports, local fire stations stood-by and hoses were laid out whenever ships arrived with, or were loaded with dangerous cargoes such as explosives, oil or chemicals. Some small fires were thus quickly extinguished before a disaster could cause many casualties and great destruction.

During 1943, the tide of the war began to swing gradually in favour of the Allies, and by the end of the year, plans for the invasion of the Continent were progressing. Supply dumps of petrol and ammunition were concentrated round ports of the south and south-east. Expecting heavy raids on these areas and the destruction of vital supplies and ammunition by fire, plans were put into operation to re-inforce the fire forces in the areas with men and machines, mainly from the north.

Large-scale exercises were held, often in close conjunction with the Army. In Folkestone and along the Kent coast, the military imposed a ban excluding the general public from areas under control. In August, the biggest exercise ever organised by the N.F.S. was held in Kent. Code-named 'Harlequin', and carried out in conjunction with the Army, it was to test the fire-fighters' readiness for action before and during the invasion. Mobile columns from many areas converged on Kent.

Hundreds of men and their vehicles had to be accommodated in the danger areas, fuel stores were opened up and reserve water tanks filled to augment drinking supplies. Six schools were put at the disposal of the fire service by the Kent Education Authority for the accommodation and feeding of reinforcements and as emergency control centres.

Emergency fire stations were set up in military camps and naval establishments, and fire crews lived with the military and came under their code of discipline. They carried out inspections of stores, ammunition and petrol dumps, and made detailed records of potential fire risks in their areas, men and equipment available, and the availability of emergency water supplies.

When, after several months, "Exercise Harlequin" came to an end, much valuable experience had been gained and No. 30 Fire Force Commander received a message of thanks and congratulations from the General Officer commanding South-Eastern Command.

The lessons learned from 'Harlequin' were soon put into operation. By the end of 1943, the Fire Service Department at the Home Office divided the country into Red, Brown and Green areas. The Brown areas were those thought to be least likely to be attacked by the enemy, and provided the bulk of the re-inforcements to the coastal areas designated Red. In between, were the Green areas where the fire force was neither reduced nor increased. This movement, of crews and appliances (altogether over 9,000 firemen, 2,000 firewomen and 1,250 appliances), became known as "Operation Colour Scheme", and was carried out under the strictest security. Frequent, highly dangerous fires in ammunition dumps, mostly located in inaccessible places with poor water supplies, kept the fire-fighters busy. A request to the N.F.S. from the Admiralty brought all sea-going fire boats to the south coast, and naval auxiliary boats (N.A.B.'s) were fitted with fire pumps and manned by the N.F.S.

Fire boats were particularly busy in the Dover area where they went to the assistance of damaged naval craft, often with the additional hazard of cross-Channel shelling. At the beginning of 1944, Kent was ready to receive the vast number of crews and appliances to be drafted into 30 Fire Force under the Colour Scheme. A Regional Reserve Station had been set up at Linton, near Maidstone, to act as a reception centre for re-inforcements. Senior Officers attached to Fire Force HQ were put in charge of the Linton Camp, and two Assistant Group Officers were co-opted to look after the interests of the firewomen. By the end of January 1944, the first reinforcements began to arrive at Linton. The majority of the personel were taken by train to Maidstone East Station, while their appliances, stripped of every marking showing their area of origin, for security reasons, were driven, in long convoys, to Kent. Strict security was also enforced on the firemen and firewomen alike, but once in Kent, it quickly became obvious from their accents where they had come from

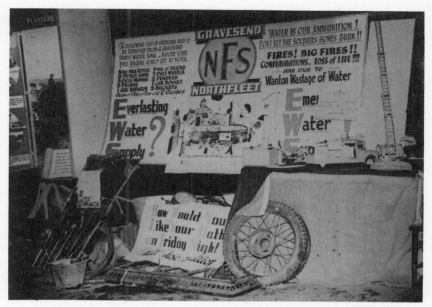

Fig. 17. N.F.S. Exhibition: Save water and keep emergency supplies free of rubbish.

– Yorkshire, Lancashire and the North.

Twenty-four hours after the arrival of the reinforcements at the reception centres, and after their appliances and equipment had been checked, the fire-fighters had been moved to their new stations, ready for the attacks which were expected on D Day. But although the heavy raids never happened, a new menace, the Fly Bomb or "Doodle Bug" brought death and destruction to the south-east and in particular to Kent. When D Day came on June 6th, the invasion was launched from the south coast and not, as had been anticipated, from the Channel ports. The emergency services and the people of Kent heaved a sigh of relief. But not for long. Exactly seven days after D Day, they were in the front line once again.

During the early hours of June 13th, particularly heavy cross-Channel shelling hit the Folkestone area. Soon afterwards, the shelling had extended inland and was hitting Maidstone. Then, a single, fast-flying aircraft, apparently in flames, was seen over the area heading for London. Soon afterwards, the 'aircraft' crashed at Swanscombe, and the first "doodle bug" had hit England and Kent. A second fly bomb crashed at Crouch about one hour later. This was the beginning of an ordeal for the people of Kent which lasted well into the autumn of 1944 and then was replaced by the even more dangerous rockets.

From the beginning, it was obvious that the flying bombs were intended for the Capital. The authorities quickly decided that as many as possible must be shot down over open countryside in the south east and particularly over Kent. "Ack-ack" batteries were re-inforced along the coast and inland, fighter planes would try to explode the bombs with machine gun fire or fly alongside them and with their wings tip them so that, hopefully, they would be returned to sender. Many of the flying bombs were badly aimed and fell short of their target, crashing on the areas of Kent adjoining London. During the week following the crash of the first doodle bug at Swanscombe, hundreds more crossed over the Kent countryside, sounding like squadrons of super-charged motorcycles. During those first seven days, over 100 were shot down by fighter planes and guns. And still they came over. An arc of massed anti-aircraft guns, stretching from Dungeness to Dover, accounted for many of them, but others crashed all over the County, causing very heavy casualties and much destruction.

Fig. 18. Convoy during "Operation Colour Scheme".

Compared with the high explosive, and especially the incendiary raids, the flying bombs caused much more destruction than fires. Those that occurred were usually localised and rarely grew into conflagrations affecting whole districts as happened during the Blitz. The N.F.S., too, by then had excellent communications, great mobility, good equipment and, with the reduction of major fires, had been specially trained in rescue work. Wherever flying bombs, and later rockets fell, they joined civil defence workers in digging out trapped people, sheeting over damaged homes and making safe potential fire risks. Much heroism was displayed by these fire-fighters who often risked their own lives in shattered and crumbling buildings to assist the victims.

In the middle of September 1944, an excellent summary of Kent's ordeal by the flying bombs was published by the *Kent Messenger*. This showed that of 8,000 bombs launched, 2,400 fell, or were destroyed, over Kent – 200 more than in London. Over 1,000 were shot down into the sea off her coast, mainly between Lydd and Folkestone, and around Dover. A detailed map of Kent, showed that bombs crashed in every part of the County: in towns, villages and open country alike. Apart from the coastal areas, Maidstone, Tonbridge, Tunbridge Wells, Sevenoaks, Tenterden, Cranbrook, Ashford and the Medway towns suffered most severely, with many dead and injured. During that period, 152 people lost their lives and over 1,700 were injured. Nor were these the final figures. The *Messenger* article stated that they referred only to "that part of Kent which is known, for war purposes, as S.E. Region and that the areas of Erith, Crayford, Bexley, Chislehurst, Sidcup, Orpington, Bromley, Beckenham and Penge, while attached to London for operational purposes, were still part of the administrative county of Kent".

At the beginning of September 1944, the assault by flying bombs tailed off, but they were partly replaced by a new weapon, the rocket (V2). Although carrying about the same amount of explosives as the flying bomb (2,000 lbs), it could not be seen or heard, and they could not be destroyed by gun fire or fighter planes. A total of 1,054 rockets fell on English soil, with about half in the London Region. Many fell also in Kent, especially in the Bromley, Penge and Orpington areas. It is interesting to note that both the last flying bomb and the last rocket of the war fell on Kent. The final rocket struck Orpington during the afternoon of March 27th 1945, causing one death, probably the last civilian killed in the country as the result of enemy air action. A few hours later, in the early morning of March 28th, the last flying bomb of the war exploded in Scadbury Park, Chislehurst, injuring a number of people. Kent's ordeal by fire and high explosives was over.

It is now necessary to go back a little in time to the autumn of 1944. With the Allied advances in Europe, the dangers for the south-east had lessened considerably, and plans were put into operation to 'repatriate' the Colour Scheme men and women to their home stations. In Kent large Departure Centres were established to receive and prepare N.F.S. units for their long journey home. One of the largest of these centres was established at the Star and Garter Homes at Sandgate, a former hospital. On October 18th 1944, the King and Queen visited the bombed and shell-torn ports of Folkestone and Dover. In a sports ground in Folkestone, large detachments of civil defence workers and members of the N.F.S. were inspected by their Majesties, who also met fire-fighters from reinforcing units who had come to Kent during the period of greatest danger. Then, on October 25th, the first detachments left on their long trek home.

They took with them a letter from Mr G. H. Robinson, Fire Force Commander, 30 Fire Force which read: "The time has now arrived for you to return to your Home Fire Force after a stay in No. 30 Fire Force, in most cases, for a period of some eight months. Credit is due to all personnel that the blend of North, Midlands and South has been a happy one, and I am certain that had we been called upon to perform the duties which most of us anticipated when the move southwards was made, the team spirit which had been built up and existed would have been more than enough to combat the worst that the enemy could send against us. We in this part of England have been privileged to act as the shield for London against the enemy's fly-bomb attacks on the Metropolis, and the work of you all has earned the National Fire Service nothing but praise. All of you will, I am sure, take back with you memories of many varied experiences, and of friendships made. Those of us who remain in Kent will, I know, forever remember 'Colour Scheme' with the most pleasant of our thoughts, and I know I speak for all those remaining when I say to you 'bon voyage', good luck, and thanks for your good comradeship".

Part IV

Kent County Fire Brigade 1948 to the

present

During the war the medley of professional, volunteer, A.F.S. and war-time only firefighters had been welded, literally, in the fire of experience, into probably the finest fire service in the world. They were used to huge conflagrations never experienced in peace time; they had to accept conditions of exceptional severity, go without sleep and food, overcome shortages of water and equipment and be ready to be sent to any part of the country without notice.

Although the N.F.S. was not finally de-nationalised until 1948, a slow contraction began as early as May 1945. The Government was uncertain what to do about the future of the N.F.S.; some thought that a continuation of a national service would be better for the country than a return to local authority control – promised in 1941 – and division into 1600 fire authorities. Local authorities protested against this breach of faith, but a bill was prepared and passed in 1947 handing over the Service to county boroughs and counties in England and Wales and to fire areas in Scotland – approximately 147 in total.

Nationalisation had brought about many improvements in equipment and appliances; and the gradual standardisation of uniforms, hydrants, statistics and conditions of service during the war period, unified the Service and divorced it, in many areas, from a parish pump mentality. But when, on April 1st 1948, the new brigades started, they were faced with huge problems. Fire stations and appliances were often old and dilapidated, new stations in the right locations had to be found or built, standardisation, especially of hydrants, had not been completed, and the country was short of manpower, materials, and above all money. Kent, which was fortunate in being able to continue to use the former 30 Fire Force H.Q. at Tovil as the H.Q. of the new Kent Fire Brigade, appointed as its first Chief Officer Mr J. H. Fordham, affectionately known to all as 'Bim', a war-time Regional Fire Officer and Chief Adviser on Fire Defence at the War Office.

On April 1st 1948, the New Kent Fire Brigade took over 79 fire stations, many of which were classified as retained, i.e. manned by part-time personnel, and many dating back to the pre-war local and volunteer brigades. During the war years many hut-type fire stations had been erected in places, and of a type unsuitable to the requirements of a modern fire service. The County faced the same problems with appliances. Those taken over were mostly old, in poor repair and unsuitable for modern fire-fighting. The K.C.C. as Fire Authority was therefore immediately faced with the necessity to work out a far-reaching and very costly programme for building and re-siting fire stations and for replacement of appliances and vehicles.

With its headquarters at The Godlands, Tovil – itself an interesting old country house, much of which was built from stone quarried in its own grounds – the County Brigade was divided into four divisions: 'A' with H.Q. at Bromley, 'B'–Chatham, 'C'–Maidstone and

'D'–Canterbury. At the time of take-over the Brigade covered an area of 975,960 acres, with a population of over 1½m and a rateable value of over £11½m.

It must have been a daunting task for Chief Officer Fordham and his senior officers. A new administrative machine had to be created, a Brigade Training School established, and there was talk of integration with the County Ambulance Service; a workshop was needed and a huge building and replacement programme had to be implemented. The Brigade now had a total of 1,653 officers and men of which 780 worked in a part-time capacity. While all this re-organisation was going on, the Brigade had to deal with 5,724 calls in its first year of existence. Although figures for calls attended by the many local brigades in the last year before the war are not available, it is believed that the 1948/49 figures are treble those of the 1938/39 ones. To this must be added the new duties of a County Brigade: training, fire prevention, communications and call-out systems.

Nor did it take long before the efficiency and indeed the courage of the new brigade were put to the test. On April 28th 1948, only four weeks after the establishment of the Brigade, fire-fighters from a wide area had to face their first major fire at the plant of British Cellulose Lacquers Ltd at Sydenham. Fire first broke out in a large garage and rapidly involved out-buildings and a large open-air store of highly flammable solvent. The mutual assistance arrangements with the London Fire Brigade had to be put into operation and the fire was eventually put out with the help of 12 jets. Not long after, on May 11th, another fire involving oil, paints and varnish, at Sargeant and Parks in Maidstone, severely damaged a large warehouse and spread to four adjoining buildings. The premises were situated in a highly congested part of Maidstone and it took the combined efforts of the firemen using again 12 jets to bring the fire under control and stop it from spreading further.

A most unusual incident occurred on May 24th when Kent Control received a call from Boulogne reporting a serious ship fire and the local brigade unable to cope with it. The fire was in the M.V. *Clan McLaren*, a practically new vessel, loaded with jute. Kent immediately agreed that the ship should be brought to Dover. During the passage the flames were kept under control by injecting CO_2 into the burning hold, which later severely hindered fire-fighting. On arrival in Dover, Kent fire-fighters began the long and arduous task of controlling the fire in the burning jute. Men from all parts of Kent had to work in shifts aboard the vessel and it took five days of strenuous efforts in the smoke-filled hold to extinguish the fire. Most of that time the firemen had to work for long periods in breathing apparatus because of the presence of smoke and carbon dioxide. This was by no means the only time that Kent helped its French colleagues. A year later they sent appliances and men to the South of France to assist in one of their worst forest fires on record.

160

Disaster struck the Open Day at Manston Aerodrome on September 18th. Once again, Kent firemen together with crews of the R.A.F. fire service were heavily involved when a Mosquito aircraft crashed into a stream of vehicles approaching the display. When firemen arrived at the scene they were confronted by a major disaster. The crashed aircraft and many vehicles were blazing fiercely; bodies, some burnt beyond recognition, were everywhere, and many injured were crying for help. Together with the big crash tenders of the R.A.F., the men extinguished the flames, removed the bodies and assisted the injured. The final total of the disaster was 12 dead and 10 injured, 4 very seriously.

Not all fires attended by Kent fire-fighters were so spectacular or tragic. The County, with its hop gardens, oast houses, hay barns, paper mills and wide agricultural areas, kept men and machines busy, day in and day out. Many of these fires, while hardly mentioned in the Press, involved long hours of hard and tiring work, work of great importance to the sufferers, but unspectacular and unglamorous. Add to this the many special service calls, the cats in trees, the little children with parts of their bodies stuck in unmentionable objects, the flooding, the storms, and the cattle in ditches, and one begins to appreciate that a fireman's work is almost never done, and refutes the snide remarks sometimes heard that firemen spend most of their time playing snooker or darts in their stations.

No two incidents are exactly alike. A most unusual one occurred at Coal Washer Wharf, Queenborough on November 23rd. This wharf can only be approached by sea or along a railway track which is built on a causeway, one mile long and unusable by vehicles. Firemen approaching the wharf could see a very large single-storey building well alight out to sea, but how were they to get their pumps to the fire? Not only must a fireman be well trained, brave and dedicated, he must also be resourceful. No wonder their motto is "the difficult we do at once, the impossible takes a little longer". This seemed indeed an impossible situation but a solution was quickly found. A flat bogey and a railway engine to draw it were organised, and a trailer pump and fire fighting equipment were loaded on it. When they had 'chuffed' their way to the fire they found not only a large building blazing from end to end but a large number of railway trucks loaded with coal, had become involved. The pump was set in, water was obtained, but their troubles were not yet over. Suddenly the water became a trickle and then stopped altogether. There was a shout of "the tide is going out" and a new way had to be found quickly to stop the fire spreading even further. It was a classic case of "all hands to the pumps", the crew lifted and manhandled the heavy pump over one ship and then onto the deck of another moored at the jetty. The pump was set into new deep water and the fire was finally extinguished.

Ninteen forty-eight drew to a close with more fires and special service calls. In December it was realised that a vehicle was needed that could co-ordinate operation and information at large-scale incidents. A double-decker bus was purchased for adaptation as a mobile fire station, wireless station and control unit. This vehicle played a major and useful part for several years to come.

Nineteen forty-nine brought to the Kent Fire Brigade, barely nine months old, an incident which strained all the resources of men and machines, but also proved that the Brigade after such a short time was alive and well and ready for whatever the elements had in store for them. Shortly after midnight on March 1st 1949 messages were received that a very high tide was causing flooding at various points between Margate and Gravesend. By 2.15 a.m. appliances were engaged in pumping operations at Chatham, Rochester, Strood, Upnor, Gravesend, Sheerness, Sittingbourne, Faversham, Herne Bay, Whitstable, Dover and Margate. So bad was the flooding in certain areas that Herne Bay, Whitstable and Chatham districts were declared one incident. Hundreds of calls for assistance were received and these had to be dealt with according to their immediate necessity. Throughout that night and day the tired and wet firemen battled on, trying to stem the flood waters which engulfed more and more areas.

The following day, March 2nd, the Brigade was asked by the Kent Rivers Board to assist in the clearing of very extensive agricultural land and orchards which were deeply under water in the Gillingham area. Normal pumping operations would have been costly and ineffective so it was decided to operate a system of syphons, using armoured suction hose, to reduce the water level. These syphons operated continuously for four days and three nights by which time the water level had been sufficiently reduced for the work to be stopped. Throughout the emergency, the Brigade worked 1,876 man hours, used 88 pumps and 765 gallons of petrol.

The presence of many paper mills in Kent has already been mentioned. A high fire risk, two of them kept firemen busy within one week of March 1949. The first broke out on March 9th at the Dartford Paper Mills in a 250 ton stack of wood pulp. Despite gallant efforts by the works brigade they quickly asked for the assistance of the County fire-fighters, who, on arrival, found about 80% of the stack burning furiously. Eighteen jets were put to work and a fire break had to be cut through the stack by removing bales with the help of an overhead crane. So fierce was the fire in the hard-packed bales that active fire fighting continued for two days and a watch had to be kept for several weeks because of the danger of re-ignition as the stack dried out.

Four days later, on March 15th, a call was received to Lloyd's Paper Mill at Sittingbourne, where an extensive range of buildings covering about three acres was well alight. It took ten jets to extinguish the fire and although the buildings were damaged the Brigade managed to save most of the contents.

Since the Brigade had been formed communications had become a problem with only one wireless in use at Bromley and it was decided to establish a joint Police/Fire Brigade scheme with 44 mobile two-way units, 15 fixed receivers and one two-way fixed sub-control. It was also decided to dispense with Street Fire Alarm systems as they became obsolete. These street alarms had always been the source of many malicious false alarms to the Brigade, especially at weekends and at closing time of public houses.

Nineteen forty-nine which had started off with a major operation dealing with wide-spread floods, gave the Brigade a lot more trouble weather-wise, when suddenly too much water was converted into far too little. A long hot and dry summer again strained the resources of the Brigade which brought the total calls for the year to a new record of 8,636, of which 3,066 alone were due to the hot summer. The worst day was July 31st, when no fewer than 141 incidents had to be dealt with. First attendances had to be restricted to one appliance and during this period property damaged included nearly 3,000 acres of grass and woodland, 1,400 acres of standing crops and stooked corn, 2,277 tons of unthreshed corn and over eight miles of hedgerow. Urgent requests were made to British Railways, unfortunately without result, asking for controlled burning of grass on railway embankments to create fire breaks, and to fitting spark-arresters to locomotives which by themselves caused no fewer than 927 fires.

In June and July the Brigade was represented at rallies of the French Fire Brigades and the West Flanders Fire Brigades Federation, Belgium, thus further strengthening the already existing bonds between Kent and its continental neighbours.

But difficulties still abounded. In his annual report for 1949/50, Chief Officer Fordham states that no new major appliances had been obtained and no new fire stations built or acquired. Again he refers to "the deplorable inheritance received from the National Fire Service" but is able to compliment his men on a very high level of morale, despite bad conditions at many stations. Some rural areas, having not yet got used to a County Brigade and longing for their old volunteers, complained about fire cover provided for them. Goudhurst, for example, which in the old days had a Brigade glorying in an imposing name of "Weald of Kent Fire Brigade", having had their request for a pump to be stationed at Goudhurst refused by the County Council, complained to the Home Office. At an R.D.C. meeting angry councillors stated that farmers were disturbed, especially during the hop-picking season because high rates had to be paid for fire services yet without proper protection, money was being obtained 'under false pretences'. A Goudhurst councillor said that he was so disgusted with the position that he had bought his own fire-trailer.

Carelessness and stupidity, two of the major causes of fire, claimed a life and two serious injuries to men in Canterbury at the beginning of

August. Tractor vaporising oil was being unloaded from a tank lorry at the garage of the Invicta Motor Engineering Works, when an explosion occurred which was heard all over the city and which set the whole of the premises ablaze. It appeared that the driver claimed that there was no danger in smoking near the tanker and to prove his point he flicked a lighted match towards the back of the lorry; in the explosion that followed he escaped, but his mate was killed and two others badly injured.

Dreamland Amusement Park at Margate has an unfortunate post-war history of being attacked by fire. Again and again its large amusement arcade, its scenic railway and its zoo were damaged in a succession of blazes. On August 21st 1949 a large part of the scenic railway and many timber show booths were severely damaged. When the Brigade arrived, parts of the park were well alight and seven jets had to be used to bring the flames under control. A year later, on August Bank Holiday, an even bigger blaze nearly destroyed the park.

An incident now occurred which will go down in the history of the British Fire Service as a shining example of the close co-operation between fire-fighters the world over. Throughout July and August of 1949, the worst forest fires France had known were raging throughout the Bordeaux region. Already the uncontrollable fires had claimed a hundred dead, including twenty-eight soldiers who were trapped while fighting the fires; over a hundred people were missing and several hundred had been badly injured, while the damage to property amounted to many millions of francs. On August 20th, when the French fires were at their height, and the pompiers and soldiers who had been sent to the region from all over France had been nearly overwhelmed, the then chairman of the Kent Fire Brigade Committee, Mr G. J. Gully, and Chief Officer Fordham, decided to send help to their hard-pressed French colleagues. On Sunday August 21st the Chief Officer called for volunteers, bureaucratic obstacles were overcome, Home Office agreement was obtained within hours, and the Foreign Office gave permission for the party to travel without passports.

The French authorities were contacted and the French Consul at Folkestone issued, on a single sheet of headed notepaper, a collective visa for the eleven men and one woman to travel – passportless – to France. By Monday morning, August 22nd, the party had been assembled. It consisted of Chief Fire Officer Fordham, Assistant Divisional Officer V. G. Love, Station Officer W. Adamson, Firewoman Dorothy Hood, Sub-Officers A. Loosely and G. E. Ranner, Leading Firemen R. C. Green and G. G. Nye and Firemen A. E. Martin, G. D. Foster, H. H. Howell and J. M. McHugh. They were to take with them a large staff car and a two-ton tender with trailer-pump. The detachment also had walkie-talkie sets, shovels, picks, axes, electric hand-lamps, petrol supplies and emergency rations for several days including drinking water.

164

Fig. 19. *a* Above: the burning French forests near Bordeaux. *b* Below: Kent fire-fighters at the funeral of some of the many victims of the disaster.

But this was to be no sight-seeing party. "We are going to France to do a job", said Chief Officer Fordham, "and we are going to give what help we can, few though we are, to our French colleagues who are so terribly hard pressed." So, in the early hours of Monday morning, the party set off for Dover. Firewoman Hood had produced a couple of Union Jacks which fluttered proudly on the fenders of the vehicles, and with a set of maps, travellers' cheques for a hundred pounds, and ten pounds in francs, everything was ready for their five hundred mile no-sleep journey to Bordeaux. After a minor delay at Dover, they finally got the green light at 4.45 p.m. when a message came from the Ministry of the Interior in Paris welcoming the British firemen to France "in our hour of need". As the ship sailed for Dunkirk, Brigade Headquarters stated "If every Kent fireman who volunteered for this job had been allowed to go, the County would have had no Brigade today."

They arrived at Dunkirk at 11 p.m. where they were met by the town's fire chief, had their tanks filled with petrol and, to the cheers of English holiday-makers on the dockside, left on their five hundred mile journey. Driving throughout the night, they reached Rouen at dawn on Tuesday 23rd where the local Brigade gave them breakfast. By midday they had reached Le Mans where the local firemen, their wives and children, had gathered to welcome them and entertain them to a three-hour lunch. With a short rest that night at Poitiers, the party left early on Wednesday 24th, on the last stage of their journey. At 11.15 a.m. on that day, the staff car led the way into Bordeaux and drew up in front of Police headquarters. While they were eating lunch as the guests of the city of Bordeaux, large crowds gathered in the street, waving flags, cheering and blowing car-horns.

But there was to be no more rest for the Kent fire-fighters after their forty-eight hour journey. With the fires roaring in the distance, they drove straight to the front-line Saucats sector, eighteen miles from Bordeaux. On arrival they were told that they were urgently needed to work throughout that night. And so they set to work fighting the advancing flames; on their right flank units of the Paris Fire Regiment, and on their left thirty young R.A.F. fire-fighters who had been flown out from England. Late that evening they were ordered on patrol duty in an area several miles away and finished the night on standby, bedded down in the open on salvage sheets. Thursday August 25th brought the Kent contingent to a group of new fires, forty miles south of Bordeaux. With the fires beginning to be brought under control, the Kent fire fighters returned to Bordeaux in the evening where they were presented with badges and made honorary members of Bordeaux Fire Brigade.

On the following morning, Friday August 26th, after an air reconnaissance of the area, the Kent contingent received orders to return home. At noon they left Bordeaux with the thanks of the Prefecture and the French colonel in charge of operations and started on their two-day journey back to England. They arrived in Paris on the afternoon of Saturday 27th and after a thorough clean-up, they attended a reception for them at the British Embassy, followed by a dinner at the Paris Fire Brigade Headquarters and a visit to the Casino de Paris. The final stage of their journey started at 2.30 p.m. on Sunday 28th when they left Dunkirk.

When they arrived at Dover, having driven a total distance of one thousand and thirty-six miles, they were received by the Chairman of the Kent Fire Brigade Committee, the then H.M. Chief Inspector of Fire Services, Sir Henry Smith, and the French Consul from Folkestone. There followed an enthusiastic reception at Dover Fire Station after which the contingent was stood down.

Although only a token force from Kent went to the French disaster area, the effect of their gesture reverberated throughout France and indeed the whole of the continental fire services. Not only could they give practical help, however small, but their immediate response to the catastrophic situation in which their colleagues found themselves raised the morale of the French fire-fighters which after weeks of struggle and with hundreds of casualties, was at a low ebb. The tiny Kent contingent was received in France with flags waving and people cheering as if it were a liberating army. Kent had proved once again the bond that exists between fire-fighters throughout the world, and the dedication and courage of a body of men who consider their work a vocation, not an occupation.

On September 5th 1949, Fireman A. C. Young of St Margaret's was killed by falling from an appliance while en-route to a fire and during the year 1949/50 as many as 68 men were injured in the course of their duties. Towards the end of 1949, arrangements were made with the military authorities in the County for soldiers to be put at the disposal of the Kent Brigade in case of need. Three days before Christmas, four people in a crashed car owed their lives to a most unusual coincidence. Their car had skidded in Westwell, Ashford, over-turned and caught fire. The occupants were trapped facing certain death, when a fire appliance, driven by a single fireman came along the road. He immediately stopped, rescued the trapped people and then, single-handed, put out the fire. In March 1950 began the delivery of 1,700 plastic fire helmets, to replace the heavy war-time steel helmets and others.

Shortly before midnight on August 8th 1950, the fire-prone Dreamland at Margate was once again blazing from end to end. Flames could be seen over a wide area and reinforcements had to be drafted in from many parts of Kent. When the Brigade arrived, the whole of the Arcade was well alight, with the steelwork beginning to collapse. Neighbouring boarding houses and the zoo were threatened and attendants stood by with rifles (to shoot the lions if necessary). Huge crowds had gathered to watch the fire and U.S. Military Police were drafted in to support local police in crowd control. The fire spread rapidly owing to the flimsy construction of the stalls and it needed 12 jets to bring the flames under control. Over half the structure and contents of the Arcade were destroyed in the fire.

Exactly two weeks later on September 22nd, the portion of Dreamland which had been saved on August 8th, was again found to be on fire and after the use of seven jets to stop the fire from spreading, 95% of the original Arcade had now been destroyed.

In the late evening of October 24th 1950, all that remained of the ill-starred Crystal Palace following the great conflagration of 1936, was wrecked in another major outbreak. Many calls were received by Control to the Palace, which was situated at Penge, and when the Brigade arrived they found much of the structure well alight, with a strong wind fanning the flames. A total of 25 appliances and over 100 fire-fighters were in action and assistance was received from brigades in London, Croydon and Surrey. The glow, which could be seen for miles, attracted thousands of spectators, among them the most famous, Winston Churchill, who had spotted the fire on his way to Westerham. He left his car and, smoking his usual cigar, advanced within yards of the burning buildings where he was asked by a Kent Officer to move back out of the danger zone. His reply has not been recorded!

Cheers went up in parts of Kent when it became known that the offices of the Inland Revenue were damaged by fire at The Rookery in St Mary Cray at the beginning of November; although records and registers were destroyed, onlookers had cat-calls for the efficient fire-fighters.

At the end of November, Canterbury firemen were called out for the tenth time in 1950 to save the city's bacon ration. But already on the way, they were certain that they would find no fire. The reason? – on the previous nine occasions, all they found was smoke from the bacon-curing plant.

In March 1951, in the Chief Officer's report for 1950/51, improvements in appliance replacements, communications and buildings were reported. More street fire alarms were discontinued; The Godlands, Fire Brigade Headquarters, was finally purchased; walkie-talkie sets were supplied to all four divisions; 15 new water tenders were received as well as 15 vans and 5 cars. Non-emergency work continued and increased during the year. The War Office requested the Brigade to undertake the entire training of Army Officers in fire-fighting to be carried out at the Kent Training School. During the summer the Mobile Unit made a tour of the County and was visited by 27,000 people.

At the beginning of June 1951, firemen were called to a job which must have been unique, certainly in Kent, if not in the country. When the Margate unit was turned out to a fire in an underground burial vault at Emmanuel Church cemetery, they thought that April Fools' day had come late that year. But, on arrival, they found smoke pouring from the vault which belonged to the well-known Margate brewers' family, the Cobbs. They entered the vault, having had to don breathing apparatus because of heavy acrid smoke and found a lead-lined coffin, buried for over a century, alight. When the flames, which had spread to other coffins in the vault, had been extinguished, they discovered that one coffin, belonging to Mrs Harriet Cobb, who died in 1845, had been completely destroyed as had that of her son who had died in 1836. Nine other coffins in the vault were damaged by fire and water. No positive cause for the fire could be established but bricks had been removed from the vault coping and it was believed that children had dropped lighted matches through the hole into the vault. For some time afterwards the Margate Unit was known as the Coffin Brigade.

Not so amusing was the call received on June 18th to Biggin Hill Aerodrome. Following a display, attended by Mr Winston Churchill, seven R.A.F. Meteor jets took off for a display flight. One failed to gain height, tore across a main road and crashed, blazing, into a bungalow. Two of the other jets circled low over the crash scene but collided and also crashed. All threee pilots were killed. The incident covered a wide area and fire-fighters from the R.A.F., Surrey and Croydon assisted the Kent Brigade. Apart from the three dead pilots, a number of firemen and civilians sustained injuries.

Another major outbreak hit Canterbury on August 11th 1951 when fire, followed by a flash-over nearly destroyed Barton Flour Mills. In November, Tonbridge firemen took part in a 'rodeo'. Called to Tonbridge Electricity Works where a steer had become impaled on top of a pointed iron fence which it had tried to jump, they freed the animal by cutting away part of the fence and lifting it away with poles. Although injured, the steer bolted round the field as soon as it felt firm ground beneath its feet. To prevent further escape, the firemen chased it, hung on to its tail and gripped it round the neck. Finally, the Tonbridge cowboys lassooed the steer and returned it to its owner. A painful decision faced Dartford firemen at the beginning of December 1951 after they had attended a fire at Longreach Smallpox Hospital – whether to be vaccinated or not. The Hospital Medical Superintendent advised it. The Station Officer in charge called Senior Brigade Officers for advice. They referred the matter to the County Medical Officer who said that the men should choose for themselves. Finally all volunteered for the jab.

On December 22nd, when the London Fire Brigade was dealing with one of its biggest peacetime fires, an urgent request went to Kent for assistance. Immediately a Station Officer with five pumps and crews was sent to Broad Street, London, where a vast goods depot was ablaze.

Shortly after noon on March 4th 1952, Margate and indeed East Kent faced its biggest fire since the end of the war. Fire broke out in the Cliftonville Hotel, Margate, which, a year previously, had been converted into private flats. So severe was the blaze that appliances from as far away as Folkestone, Canterbury and Maidstone had to be called and altogether 13 units of the County Brigade were in attendance. Fifteen appliances including turntable ladders were in use and the County Chief Officer personally took charge. As 70 firemen fought the blaze, 63 men, women and children were evacuated to a quickly set up relief centre at the nearby Greylands Hotel. It took eight jets to bring the fire under control and the hotel was badly damaged.

After the fire, the Chief Officer commented about the smooth working of "closing in moves" to give cover to stations emptied of appliances attending the fire. These moves affected stations as far away as Gillingham.

At the end of March 1951 the annual report for 1951/52 reported further progress. All part-time fire stations had been provided with calling-out systems, and Kent scored a 'first' by the introduction of aluminium alloy extension ladders to replace the wheeled fire escapes which, with only slight alterations, had been in use all over Europe for over 100 years. Kent was also the first to use 'water fog' as a standard method of attack for small fires in premises, thus minimising water damage. New appliances put into commission were nine water-tenders, two pumping appliances, 18 utility vans and six motorcycle combinations.

Kent, particularly the coast and Medway regions, has always been subject to heavy floods and inundations. Severe gales with an abnormally high tide breached and destroyed sea walls and river defences all along the coast between Folkestone and Erith, shortly before midnight on January 31st 1953. The operation, which severely strained Brigade resources, went on throughout the month of February and was not finally finished until March 2nd. Hundreds of calls for assistance were received and officers and men on duty had to be augmented by personnel recalled from leave, and volunteers. All available and reserve appliances were called out to assist in the rescue of persons trapped by the floods, to protect and maintain public services, and to render whatever humanitarian services were possible.

Pumping had to be carried out in 33 different parts of the County with the biggest problems at Whitstable where 51 pumps were needed, Erith 24 pumps, Dartford 18 pumps and Sheerness 12 pumps. Ten pumps were sent by the Surrey and East Sussex Fire Brigades to help in the disaster. During the emergency, 47 miles of hose were in use and 21,000 gallons of petrol consumed.

The summer and autumn of 1953 kept the Brigade busy. Although there were few major outbreaks, a number of serious fires gave the men little rest. In the early hours of May 14th a fire in a very old multi-occupancy building in Canterbury caused severe damage to the structure; Snodland Paper Mills was again involved on July 17th; and on

170

August 13th Beachborough Park House, at Newington near Folkestone, was severely damaged by fire. In this instance, the occupiers tried to fight the fire themselves which resulted in a delay of 40 minutes before the Brigade was called. Do-it-yourself fire-fighting by untrained persons can result in loss of life and usually in far greater damage than necessary. Fire Chiefs have always insisted that however small the fire and even if there is only a suspicion of fire, the Brigade should be called. In the event it needed five pumps, a turntable ladder, and a hose-laying lorry to put out this fire.

On September 13th a large toy factory in Chatham went up in flames; most of the Christmas stock was destroyed and the large building was severely damaged. On September 26th two firemen were injured by chemical fumes in a fire at a paper mill at St Mary Cray.

In the early hours of the morning of November 18th, Kent firemen were called to a fire which turned out to be one of the biggest and most disastrous of 1953. The call to Russell's Garage, Chatham, was given by a night watchman at the adjoining Gammon's Wharf, who saw a sudden flash inside the garage and heard an explosion. When the Brigade arrived minutes later, the whole garage was ablaze and the fire was threatening to spread to an adjoining timber warehouse containing large stocks, and also to houses across the street, a public house, and merchandise on the river wharf at the rear of the burning building. Inside the garage were quantities of wood and 33 motor vehicles. At an early stage the roof collapsed, threatening the men advancing into the fire, and exploding oxy-acetylene cylinders created a warlike scene. The fire, which had now reached the timber store and had caused paint work on nearby premises to burst into flames, had to be contained. This was achieved by strategic siting of jets and the constant cooling by water-jets of the underground petrol tank which was in danger of imminent explosion. When the fire was finally put out the whole of the garage, its contents, including the 33 motor vehicles, had been destroyed.

Nineteen fifty-four started with the virtual destruction of the Ritz Cinema in Pudding Lane, Maidstone. In the early hours of January 11th, a police constable called the Brigade to the cinema but on arrival of the first attendance, the whole building was well alight. Reinforcements were immediately requested but with the whole of the auditorium burning, the risk to adjoining premises in the heavily built-up area was considerable. The asbestos cement roof was exploding violently in the fire, showering red-hot material over a wide area, on roofs and on parked vehicles. The roof of a garage, occupied by Fremlin's Brewers caught fire and part of the fire-fighting force had to be diverted to attack the fire-spread in the area, remove vehicles and cooling-down. It took many hours, eight pumps, a turntable ladder and a hose-laying lorry finally to subdue the main fire with nine jets.

Fire-fighters narrowly escaped when a severe fire at the Baltic Saw

Mills, Tonbridge on March 31st melted the lift wires of a crane, causing the jib to fall across a timber store. In the annual report for 1953/54 further progress in the re-building of the Brigade after the war was reported. Although the number of calls was on the increase again, having reached a total of 7,578, the first new fire stations had been completed and put into operation – a whole-time station at Medway and a part-time station at Headcorn. Thirteen new appliances had been commissioned during the year; and 13 water tenders, six pumping appliances and two hose-laying lorries had been received.

An innovation which caused much comment from the public was the introduction of unpainted aluminium bodies on fire appliances. The departure from the traditional red fire engine – there was only a minimal amount of red remaining on mudguards and fenders – met some sadness and opposition, but it quickly became obvious that money could be saved on paint and maintenance, especially as the new livery eliminated the many scratches caused when machines had to go through the many narrow lanes with overhanging hedges.

During the summer and autumn of 1954 the Brigade dealt with the usual crop of fires and special service calls, some major, some unusual. Occasionally there is light relief in the serious business of a fire brigade. A nurse from Linton Hospital, having attended a dance at Linton Training School, met a nice fireman there. A few days later, knowing his name but not his telephone number, she decided to make contact again and phoned Directory Enquiries. Asked whom she wanted, she replied 'the Fire Brigade'. Immediately, she was connected to Maidstone Fire Station on the 999 emergency line, and when greeted by the words 'Fire Brigade', she hung up in terror.

Now things really began to happen. The Exchange operator thought the call had come from the Isolation Hospital in Barming, so down went the bells and a pump; wireless van and Station Officer raced away to Barming to be followed by the Maidstone retained appliance. A couple of minutes later, the Exchange, realising that they had made an error, advised that the call had actually come from Linton Hospital. The retained unit, just about to leave, were given the new address; Loose was alerted and the appliances on the way to Barming turned back by radio. Even the Deputy Chief Officer, who happened to be in Maidstone at the time, became involved in the saga. Having seen the first attendance proceed over Maidstone Bridge at a cracking pace with bells ringing and lights flashing, he saw them return in the opposite direction, with bells still ringing, a few minutes later. Naturally he followed them. Finally they all met in front of Linton Hospital, (three senior officers, three appliances, two wireless vans), only to be assured that there was no fire and that no call had come from their official switchboard. Investigations followed; the origin of the call was traced to a phone in the Nurses Hostel and the 'culprit' was 'apprehended'. Nothing is known about the fate of the amorous nurse but it is believed that the senior Brigade Officer present pleaded for mercy.

An extraordinary accident at Chatham Dry Dock on December 15th 1954 involved H.M. Submarine *Talent*. The accident, which cost four dock workers their lives, caused the submarine to shoot across the Medway and embed herself, half full of water, on the mud flats. The accident happened at 3.30 p.m. and shortly after 7 p.m. the Naval Authorities requested assistance from the Kent Brigade. Two feather-weight pumps were immediately despatched to the dock-yard and loaded on to a launch. There followed a hazardous journey, fog having reduced visibility to zero, and with a strong tide running, the only means of locating the stranded vessel was to steer for the sound made by men on board hammering the hull. So effective were these two pumps that four more were loaded onto two launches which inched their way through fog across the river. But now more difficulties faced the firemen. The falling tide had left a ten-yard strip of deep mud between the submarine and deep water. Planks had to be laid on the mud and the pumps manhandled over them.

Then came the hazardous task of hoisting the pumps on board, as the sides and deck of the vessel were covered with slime and oil, and festooned with wires, cables and shoring timbers. Once aboard, the pumps were set in different compartments and as these were pumped dry, shipwrights sealed all openings to prevent reflooding when the tide rose. By 3.15 a.m. in the morning of December 16th the submarine had been pumped dry, and shortly afterwards she was afloat and riding on an even keel. As the tide fell, she again grounded and Brigade personnel and equipment remained on board in case she shipped water, but fortunately she remained dry and refloated easily on the afternoon tide. But this was not the end for the tired fire-fighters. Crews which had worked all night were relieved, but the launch in which they were returning to the dockyard lost its way in the thick fog and stuck on a mud bank. Cold and wet, the men waded ashore and groping their way through the fog, found themselves alongside the submarine once more. They remained on board until the fog cleared partially hours later and they returned to dry land by launch. Appreciation of the Kent Brigade's work which helped save the vessel and avoid the complete blockage of the River Medway for at least a week was received from many sources. The Captain of the Dockyard sent a signal thanking the Brigade without whose assistance the Royal Navy would not have been able to refloat the submarine. Similar messages of thanks and congratulations were received from the Commander-in-Chief, The Nore, and from the Home Office.

By the beginning of March all street fire alarms in Kent had been scrapped, resulting in a sharp decrease of malicious false alarms. The Brigade was further strengthened by the addition of 28 pumps, two hose-laying lorries and two-foam tenders. An exceptionally hot and dry summer kept firemen throughout the County busy. Several major fires, of which the one at Queen's Highcliffe Hotel in Margate was the biggest, added to the work.

As soon as Margate firemen turned out of their station at 6.35 a.m. on Monday May 12th 1955, they knew they were in for a long and dangerous battle. A pall of black smoke hung over the town and the first call for assistance was already made over radio before the crews arrived at Margate's biggest hotel, the 220-bedroom Queens Highcliffe. Situated at the edge of the cliffs at Cliftonville, it had recently been bought by Butlins as a holiday hotel. Recently completely redecorated, it was fortunately unoccupied at the time of the fire, although it was due to be opened for the holiday season in three days' time. Fire-fighters were faced with a fierce blaze which involved large parts of the six-storey building and further assistance was requested from stations in East Kent. At the height of the blaze over 100 firemen from 11 stations with 20 appliances were in attendance. Several firemen were injured when the roof collapsed over the central section, and although this part of the hotel was severely damaged, and the dining-room and ballroom destroyed, the men managed to save the rest of the building.

In the early hours of June 20th, Maidstone lost its second cinema, through fire, in 18 months. Despite heroic efforts by firemen who came from six stations, the entire roof of the Central Cinema collapsed onto the balcony and stalls, leaving the interior of the building a twisted, burnt mass of metal and rubble. A member of the staff who had discovered the fire gave the first call but returned to the cinema to try and fight the blaze. Overcome by smoke, he collapsed and was found unconscious by the first crew to arrive. He was rushed to hospital and later recovered. Only 18 months earlier the Ritz cinema was destroyed by fire.

The hot, dry summer and autumn of 1955 was followed by a winter of extreme cold and snowy weather. Calls rose sharply, with over 9,500 recorded by the end of March 1956. Paradoxically, many of these fires were caused by the cold weather, especially in February, through the careless use of blowlamps for thawing out frozen pipes and through oil stoves and candles left unattended in attics and roof voids. More fires were caused in hearths through overstocking of grates. Because of ice and snow, fire-fighters had great difficulties in reaching incidents; machines were damaged and some delays in attendance occurred. Having finally defeated the fires caused by frost and snow, April 1956 brought them back to the old routine of woodland and grass fires. During that month, over 400 fires were attended by the Brigade. So extensive were some of these outbreaks that at Ashford Warren, over 100 troops from a nearby R.E.M.E. depot had to be called in to assist the firemen. At the beginning of June an extensive outbreak near

Cranbrook, covering many acres of trees, grass and peat, required more help from the Army. To prevent the fire from spreading even further, 50 soldiers from Hythe Garrison were sent to the area with trenching tools. A mile-long trench had to be dug around the perimeter of the fire area and it took 24 hours of difficult fire-fighting to contain the blaze.

Two serious fires devastated Dartford Paper Mills in April and June of the year. In the first, the machine house was found to be alight on arrival of the Brigade and within minutes, a huge extractor fan from the burning roof collapsed onto the paper-making machinery below. In the second fire, another machine house, adjacent to the one severely burnt in April, was badly damaged, with the roof collapsed and machinery rendered useless. During that operation a fireman was badly injured when he fell through the burning roof. In July, a fire near Brigade H.Q. at Straw Mill Hill, Tovil, involved 2,500 tons of waste paper. During fire-fighting, which lasted for five days, the Brigade laid six-inch plastic piping for water relays and to bridge the public highway.

Many people in the past believed, and some still believe, that the work of firemen is almost entirely concerned with fires. Usually they see the Brigade at work at spectacular fires, see engines with blaring sirens and flashing lights rush through the streets, and have it in their minds that between these comparatively rare occasions the men sit cosily in their stations, playing games or sleeping. Nothing could be further from the truth. Apart from fire prevention work, which takes up hundreds of man-hours each week, apart from cleaning their appliances, hydrant inspection, training and lectures, perhaps the majority of their work consists of special service calls, anything from a child's head stuck in railings to pumping out flooded premises and rescuing Farmer Giles' cow from a ditch. The Fire Service is a 'maid of all work' and success depends largely on its ingenuity, its equipment and its untiring dedication.

Perhaps 1956 is a good year to look at these Special Services. In May the Brigade received a request from the police to pump out a stretch of the River Eden below a weir at Penshurst where the body of a drowned boy was believed to be. After four pumps had been at work for several hours, the body had still not been found. When it was decided that the weir could only hold back the increased weight of water for another ten minutes, two firemen, with lines attached, jumped into the icy water and eventually found the body in a cavity under the weir. An unusual call, typical of the wide variety the Brigade has to perform, came at the end of May. Called by a frenzied householder to Park Lane, Sevenoaks, firemen found a swarm of bees had settled on a chimney stack and inside a flue of a private house. No protective clothing against bee stings was available, but ingenuity won through again and the bees were dislodged by simultaneously smoking them out from the flue and playing a jet of water onto the chimney stack. No accurate record exists of bee sting

Fig. 20. Another plane crash – another Special Service call.

injuries to firemen, but it was rumoured at the time that local chemists completely ran out of anti-sting creams and lotions. Next, in June, the pilot of a glider whose machine had crashed onto the roofs of a pair of houses at Hawkinge after hitting overhead electricity cables, had to be extricated by a turntable ladder.

July and August 1956 saw once again the return of wide-spread floods throughout the County. In July severe gales caused much damage and crews from 29 fire stations worked for many hours at a variety of incidents: from freeing passengers from cars hit by falling trees, to removing dangerous television aerials from chimney stacks. At the beginning of August, large-scale flooding hit the Tunbridge Wells, Tonbridge and Faversham areas. In Tunbridge Wells alone 53 calls were received in a short space of time and pumping-out work was made even more difficult by packed ice from a freak hail storm.

In the darkness of a November evening, cries for help were heard from the direction of the Seasalter Mud flats. Two men, out shooting, had lost their bearings in a sudden mist and were trapped by the rising tide. The Brigade was called out and with the searchlight of one of the appliances directed vertically as a beacon, firemen, spacing themselves out along a 100-foot line, waded into the murky dark. They followed the cries and eventually found the men exhausted and waist-high in icy water, and led them to safety.

In the year 1956/57 there was a total of 384 special service calls and it is interesting to see a breakdown of these non-fire events. About this time a new issue of raincoats with loose fleece lining was given to all whole-time personnel below the rank of station officer; jerseys to all whole-time and retained personnel and coat hangers to all whole-timers excluding firewomen who, one presumes, were not supposed to strip off even their jackets.

In April 1957 the Kent Fire Brigade entered its tenth year. It was to be a year of new developments and of tragedy. Three members of the Brigade lost their lives at a hospital fire. Calls soared, reaching for the first time over 1,100. At the end of May, the 56-hour week duty system was introduced which made it possible to have a three-watch system of duty at stations. Although better than the previous system, appliances were still undermanned and an application was made to the Home Office to have the Brigade establishment increased. There was a sharp decline in the number of retained firemen, which led to some stations being operational only at night, while others operated with undermanned appliances. The new turntable ladders were delivered as was the first consignment of plastic hose. An unusual, new, retained station was opened in a prison at Eastchurch, where premises were made available by the Prison Commissioners who also agreed to members of the prison staff volunteering to become retained firemen. No mention was made whether prison inmates would also be allowed to ride machines at times of emergency.

The 'haunting' of the Dreamland Amusement Park at Margate by fire continued and on June 3rd 1957, the Brigade was once again called to a serious fire there. But on this occasion it was the 'Haunted House' itself that was on fire. Although men and appliances from five stations fought for ten hours to save the building, the 'Haunted House' was destroyed, and would haunt children and adults no more. During the weekend June 29th/30th the Brigade was stretched to its utmost when 250 calls were received to fires in growing crops, woodlands, grasslands and undergrowth, caused by sparks from passing trains, children playing with matches and discarded lighted cigarettes. Periods of torrential rain during the weekend did not lighten the work of the firemen who received many calls to flooded buildings and areas. At the end of July, a fire at Bowater Lloyds Paper Mill at Sittingbourne, kept busy for 24 hours ten units of the brigade, assisted by the Bowater Works Brigade, fighting a blaze in paper and straw stacks. It took 23 jets to bring the outbreak under control.

November 29th 1957 will long be remembered by the Brigade. In a fire and collapse at Oakwood Hospital, Maidstone, six people were killed, three of them fire-fighters, and many were severely injured. At half past six in the morning, the Night-Superintendent at the mental hospital saw flames in the upstairs part of the printers' block and what should have been a fairly routine incident turned, less than four hours later, into a major catastrophe for the Brigade. Five minutes after the first call, Maidstone fire-fighters were on the scene, and because of the severity of the fire, four extra pumps were sent on. The blaze was in a wing adjoining the main block of the Hospital used for workshops, library and offices, and started in a tailors' shop on the first floor. It rapidly spread down in a television lounge and upwards into the roof.

The main building contained four wards, in which 350 mental patients were being cared for at the time of the fire. Six jets got the fire under control in less than an hour, and at 7.30 a.m. the 'Stop' message had been sent back, and firemen stood by to clear up and tackle small outbreaks of fire in the debris. At 9.00 a.m., relief crews arrived at the hospital to continue clearing up, and the job seemed nearly finished, when at 9.55 a.m., without any warning whatever, a 120-foot ventilation tower collapsed onto the wing building, demolishing it, and burying many fire-fighters and hospital workers under tons of bricks and debris. At that time, 24 Brigade personnel were on the scene, and for some time it was unclear how many were missing, trapped under the rubble. Brigade Control immediately set disaster procedures into operation, and more firemen with special equipment were sent to the Hospital. Meanwhile, Civil Defence Rescue Squads from six Kent towns had been alerted and rushed to the scene. Twelve ambulances stood by, and took the injured in relays to hospitals. At West Kent Hospital, the Casualty Department was cleared of patients to receive the injured, but soon the doctors could not cope, and ambulances were diverted to St Bartholomew's Hospital, Rochester. While rescue workers were digging away to reach the trapped, several of whom were already assumed to be dead, doctors stood by with morphine injections for the badly injured.

Despite the efforts of nearly 100 men, working in highly dangerous conditions, and under the threat of further collapses, it took a long time for the first casualties to be brought out. Of the first six men to be carried out, two were found to be dead. One of them was the Officer-in-charge, Assistant Divisional Officer Leslie Pearce, aged 49, and a member of the Fire Service for nearly 30 years. Two Retained Firemen were also killed – Albert Farrow, 44, of Linton, and John Hawkes, 33, of Boughton Monchelsea. In addition, six Firemen and two Senior Officers were severely injured, some during rescue operations. Three of the hospital staff were also killed, and seven badly injured, including the hospital's Chief Fireman. It was not until the afternoon two days later, that the last body was recovered from the debris.

A cruel coincidence in an already tragic situation happened when Station Officer Pearce, from Maidstone, was tunnelling through blocks of fallen masonry, searching for casualties. In the basement, under heaps of rubble, he discovered a partly visible body; tearing away at the rubble with his bare hands, he uncovered the man's face, to discover to his horror that it was his own brother, Assistant Divisional Officer Leslie Pearce. He collapsed with shock, and had to be removed to hospital. On December 6th, the three fire-fighters who had lost their lives at the Hospital, were laid to rest. Before the Service at All Saints Church, large crowds lined the street to watch the procession, headed by Senior Officers, and 100 Firemen from all Kent Divisions. The flag-draped coffins were carried on a turntable ladder, and were followed by a Fire Service lorry carrying some of the thousands of floral tributes, which had been sent by other Fire Brigades, Local Government and the townspeople.

The beginning of December saw another most unusual special service call, to add to the variety already mentioned. When the Brigade was called to Whitehall Road, Canterbury, they found a boy firmly wedged inside an 18-inch gas pipe lying at the side of the road. The boy, intending to crawl through the pipe, finally became trapped about three feet from the end and, terrified, screamed for help. Liberal application of heavy grease all over his body, and combined pulling by several firemen on ropes attached to the boy, finally released him from his prison.

It is interesting to record that while the cost of the Brigade during its first year 1948/49 was just under £400,000, this had risen at the end of the tenth year, 1957/58, to just under £1 million. During the year 1958/59 further progress with new buildings and new appliances was made. In September, the new Maidstone fire station was opened by Sir Alfred Bossom and the ceremony was attended by Officers from France, Belgium, Holland and Luxembourg, together with representatives from their embassies. A Standard for ceremonial use was also presented to the Brigade. In January 1959, the Eastchurch Retained Fire Station – the one inside a prison and staffed by prison officers – was brought into operational use, as was the new Ashford Station in March of that year. Charing, too, had a new retained station. A new development, at first regretted by firemen and public alike, was the installation of the first Continental two-tone horn on one Maidstone appliance, to replace the traditional bells. Although drivers and police reported the definite superiority of the horn, it seemed a sad day when the calming and reassuring sound of the bells would no longer be heard approaching an emergency. But with the changing times, heavier traffic and bigger lorries, it became inevitable that the two-tone horn and the blue flashing light should in the end be adopted nationally. Four more turntable ladders and eight pumps were added to the Brigade strength during the year.

April 1958 saw the sudden death of 3,000 chicks, when a poultry house at Marden caught fire following a gas leak. Despite the attendance of men and appliances from three stations, and the use of four jets, neither the building nor any of the chicks could be saved. On the evening of August 1st 1958, tragedy struck in Bromley. Lighted candles left burning by children in a private house caused a disastrous blaze which cost two lives and severely damaged the building. Malicious false alarms, one of the Brigade's biggest worries, most likely contributed to the fatalities. Minutes before the call to the fire was received, men and machines from Bromley had answered a call which turned out to be malicious. The next nearest appliance had to be despatched, and when they arrived, they found the house well alight. Two occupants, a man and a child were trapped in the inferno. Ladders were pitched to windows and in spite of the flames and intense heat, firemen managed to recover the bodies of the child and man. Later it was discovered that the man was a passer-by who, hearing the screams for help, rushed into the blazing building in a rescue attempt and was killed himself.

On September 5th 1958, an electrical storm of unprecedented intensity struck the northern and north-western areas of Kent; so severe was the tropical-like storm, that in less than five hours, a total of 1,345 calls were received by the Brigade for assistance. Buildings had been struck by lightning, premises flooded, people trapped in upstairs rooms of their houses, while torrents of water rushed through the streets, over fields and wastelands, marooning trains, buses and cars. All available personnel, men recalled from leave, extra appliances and A.F.S. units with their 'Green Goddesses' were mobilised, and worked for long, wet and exhausting hours, trying to stem the floods. Out of thousands of incidents, a few particularly stood out. On the railway line at Bickley, power cables short-circuited due to the flooding, causing a severe fire. At Gravesend, 45-foot ladders had to be used to build a bridge across flood waters to the upper floors of a building, to rescue three trapped persons. At Hever Castle, flood water overflowed the moat and entered the historic building; the electrical installations were threatened and extensive damage was done to the Castle and its valuable contents; pumping had to be continued for five days.

At the height of the storm, an incident happened which is the nightmare of any fire-fighter – a call to a refinery, one of the most difficult and dangerous fires a brigade has to tackle. The call came from the B.P. Refinery at the Isle of Grain. Two tanks, each 140 feet in diameter and containing crude oil, had been struck by lightning, starting rim fires on both tanks. The large refinery brigade immediately set to work and, with the addition of 12 appliances from the Kent Brigade and the use of eight water and four foam jets, managed to contain the outbreak. Nor was this the only incident involving the Refinery. A few weeks earlier, the Cracker Unit was damaged when waxy feed-stock ignited a control valve; four foam jets had to be used. Then, in February 1959, the Reformer Unit containing a 1,000 gallon tank of naphthalene went up in flames. This time it took eight foam-branches to bring the outbreak under control, and involved men and appliances from eight Kent Fire Stations in addition to the refinery's own brigade.

In October 1958, Alderman T. Prior, a former Chief Officer of the pre-war Lydd Fire Brigade, was made a Freeman of the Borough. He joined Mr H. J. Blacklock, another Freeman, who had also been in charge of the Lydd Brigade many years before. The exceptionally dry summer of 1959 caused the biggest increase in calls the Brigade had received since its inception 11 years previously. During that time the average number of calls was about 8,000 per year, but they now increased dramatically to more than 14,500. From June to mid-October, grassland and woodland fires raged relentlessly throughout the County. Troops had to be drafted in to assist the hard-pressed fire-fighters, and in many incidents, volunteers from the public rendered valuable service. So many calls were received each day that crews had to be re-directed by radio from one area to another, and often attended several incidents before they returned, completely exhausted, to their stations for a short rest. Meals were often delayed, and at times, impossible to arrange, and many firemen received burn and eye injuries.

It took over a week of fire-fighting, when a blaze damaged Gibraltar Farm, Sharstead, on November 18th 1959. A barn, an oast house, and a range of buildings used as a piggery and for farm machinery, were involved with a large Dutch barn 15 feet away also ablaze. The only water available was a small 8,000-gallon reservoir. With extra water tenders and a hose-laying lorry requested, two jets were got to work; but the water in the tank lasted less than five minutes. When the extra appliances arrived, a three-pump relay from a hydrant one mile away was started, and more jets brought into play. Water supply was still insufficient, and once again, the firemen's ingenuity was tested. Quickly some of the men dug a ditch round the affected area, and channelled the hot water flowing from the burning building into a dry well from which two further jets could be used. Nor was the firemen's inventiveness over yet: the Dutch barn was in danger of collapsing onto a nearby thatched-roof barn, but by using two aluminium ladders to prop up the gable end of the former, they saved the other building.

In December, a serious fire wrecked the offices and plant of the *Kentish Times* in Sidcup; 12 firemen had to receive treatment for burns, cuts and eye irritation. The day before Christmas 1959, fire-fighters found themselves in the unusual role of temporary delivery drivers, when they had to help quickly to evacuate 120 vans threatened by a major fire at the Tip-Top Bakeries, Orpington. The vans were endangered when the huge building and its contents, including large quantities of fats and sugar, became completely enveloped in fire. Although the building was badly damaged, most of the main bakery was saved, and only one of the 120 vans was slightly damaged, whether by fire or bad driving is unknown.

A macabre scene faced firemen when they were called to a toy factory at the County Works in Ramsgate, on March 31st 1960. Entering the building in breathing apparatus, they suddenly saw through the thick smoke and flames, the newly-made bodies of dolls and, hanging from hundreds of smouldering wooden pegs, their as yet eyeless heads.

In contrast to the exceptionally dry and hot summer of 1959, the summer of 1960 was one of the wettest on record in the County. Slight flooding was already being experienced during August and September, but towards the end of October a week of monsoon type rains, whipped up by 80 m.p.h. gales, confronted the Brigade with its biggest Special Service since it was formed in 1948. The first calls to the emergency came on October 31st and rapidly built up. At the height of the emergency, November 4th, hundreds of firemen, units of the A.F.S., and volunteers, battled against rising floods, and the B.B.C. announced that 10,000 acres of land in the Medway Valley were under water; roads and railways were cut, vehicles had to be abandoned; and houses had been hit by fallen trees. The areas most affected were along the River Medway, including Maidstone, Yalding and Tonbridge, but practically every part of the County was in a state of emergency. At any one time 40 pumps and the 'Green Goddesses' of the A.F.S. were employed, and one of the biggest tasks of the Brigade was to protect and restore essential services, fresh water supplies and communications. Close liaison was maintained with the police and the W.V.S. supplied much-needed refreshments to the wet and tired firemen. It was not until November 7th that the emergency was over, although some pumping continued, especially in the Canterbury area. But every cloud has a silver lining, even for an embattled fire service. November 5th, usually a hectic day for the firemen, fell right in the middle of the emergency, and senior officers could report that hardly any calls were received to bonfires out of control.

New Year's Eve 1960 was spoiled for some fire-fighters when their celebrations took the form of ten hours work at a serious blaze at the British Road Services Depot at Sittingbourne. February 1961 saw the virtual destruction of the 300-year old Syndale House at Ospringe. The building, known since the war as the Mumford Arms Hotel, was closed for the winter, and the only person in residence was the owner's 87-year-old father. On arrival of the Brigade, with men and machines from five stations, they found the whole building in flames and the old man asleep and unaware of the danger; men with breathing apparatus rescued him. Priceless panelling, paintings, antique furniture and silver were lost in the blaze.

In March, Kent and Essex County Councils chartered a badly needed fireboat, the *Fireflair*, from the War Office, to give improved cover for shipping and the oil ports between Barking Creek and the Estuary. A 66-foot vessel, it had a speed of ten knots and could throw 1,500 gallons of water a minute. It was situated off Gravesend, with a permanent crew of four firemen, and additional crew members were available from the Gravesend station. Chief Officer Fordham commented at the time:

182

"Before this fireboat, we were the only major oil port in the country, or in the world, which did not have this kind of protection".

During the next 12 months, Kent firemen were heavily involved in a series of difficult ship fires and in at least one, the new fireboat *Fireflair* proved its worth. In August 1961 the Brigade was informed that the 5,500-ton motor vessel *Kindat* was approaching Gravesend with a serious fire in No. 2 hold. The fireboat was mobilised and sailed out to the stricken vessel and escorted her to Gravesend Reach, where she dropped anchor. A large cargo of plywood, timber and palm kernels was involved, and fire fighters with their pumps and other equipment, had to be ferried out to the ship by police launches. The men experienced great difficulties in gaining access to the seat of the fire and holes had to be cut into the metal deck. While this fire was being dealt with, nine appliances had to be sent to an oil refinery at Hoo, where two high fractionating columns were involved in a major fire. Foam and cooling jets had to be used to bring the blaze under control and avert what could have been a major catastrophe.

Three weeks later, in September 1961, fire was discovered in the cargo of the S.S. *Kayseri* which had broken down in the Channel. After a delay of 11 hours, she was finally towed into Dover Harbour, where eight jets were used to quell the flames in the cargo consisting of sunflower, cotton seeds and oil cake. Firemen narrowly escaped death when two explosions suddenly ripped through the ship, causing extensive damage and badly affecting its trim. It was found necessary to tow the vessel away from the harbour and beach it. It took eight appliances and their crews nearly three days before the vessel could be safety left.

In the early hours of December 16th, another ship, the S.S. *Tauri*, was burning in midstream off the ship pier at Rochester where she was anchored. Local residents were awakened by the continuous sounding of the S.O.S. signal from the ship's siren, but it took over 30 minutes before the third mate could make his way to the shore to call the Brigade. Thirty firemen on six appliances rushed to the pier, but once again found no boats to take them across. Eventually the landlord of the nearby Ship Inn found a boat and rowed eight of the men across in two journeys. On the second trip he saw a dinghy with two firemen and an armless man who had volunteered to help, capsize, throwing the three men into the freezing water. He managed to rescue two men, while the second fireman fought his way through the heavy swell to the shore. When the blaze was under control, firemen wearing breathing apparatus searched through the smoke-blackened ship and found the vessel's Second Officer, a Swede, badly burned, and dead.

A huge explosion, followed by a fire, ripped the Motor Vessel *Alignity* apart, while loading 300 tons of motor spirit at No. 1 jetty, B.P. Refinery, Isle of Grain, on March 19th 1962. So fierce was the fire, and so much of the refinery was threatened, that 12 Kent appliances and five from the refinery brigade, as well as two fire tugs, had to be mobilised. Foam was used to blanket the tanks and 14 water jets fought the fire and cooled down the surrounding risks.

Once again, special service calls took up much of the Brigade's time. There were literally hundreds of them, ranging from a child's head trapped in a metal dish, to a person stuck in a turnstile. Trapped animals, cats, dogs, cows, horses and swans had to be rescued and fun was had with the recovery of a large weather balloon. Two incidents, one amusing, one tragic, typify these services. A child, playing with a bayonet at his home in Tunbridge Wells, jammed the securing ring on one of his fingers. His father managed to saw the bayonet away but could not remove the ring. At the Kent and Sussex Hospital it was decided to amputate the finger, but as a last resort, that 'Maid of all works', the Fire Brigade was called. They applied plenty of lanolin, and slipping a thin key between the ring and the finger used a hacksaw blade to cut open the ring. The operation was completed without injury to the finger or the boy. One of two boys who had gone to 'lay a ghost' at Oxney Court, a ruined 11th century mansion at St Margarets, was not so lucky. While attempting to lift a heavy door off the ground, one of the boys slipped and fell into a 180-foot well. The Brigade was called and a fireman was lowered by line to rescue the boy who, on arrival at hospital, was found to be dead.

During the year, the first major re-organisation at Fire Brigade Headquarters since the formation in 1948 took place. Central mobilisation from Brigade H.Q. Control became fully operational on January 1st 1962 and was staffed entirely by firewomen. In September, Kent Fire Brigade became the first in the country to start a major training scheme for junior firemen. The first 18 boys, all 16-year old school leavers, were taken on for a two-year training course.

The year from April 1962 to the end of March 1963 kept firemen in Kent busy with the kind of jobs which had become routine over the years: fires, big and small; special service calls; and a considerable amount of fire prevention work. However, calls increased to a 'high' of 12,000, mainly owing to the twin curses of any fire service – chimney fires and malicious false alarms. While the first is usually due to neglect and bad housekeeping, the second can endanger life and limb, not only of those in real need of the Brigade, but also of the firemen themselves, rushing, often in hazardous weather conditions, to non-existing emergencies. During the winter of that year, abnormal weather conditions threw a heavy strain on the Brigade. Fire-fighting had to be carried out under intensely arduous conditions; driving the appliances, especially at speed, was difficult, and even travelling to report for duty required great devotion to the job. To give just one example: on January 13th 1963, farm buildings at Wrotham became involved in a serious fire which destroyed cattle feed and fertilisers, and killed 53 cattle and ten sheep. Working in sub-zero conditions, firemen found their wet tunics frozen at the back while they were roasting in the front. Hoses used had to be abandoned at the scene, hard-frozen and could not be recovered for three weeks.

Once again a serious and dangerous ship fire kept the Brigade busy in December 1962. The Dutch Motor Vessel *Temar*, in passage from Silvertown to Rotterdam with a cargo of sugar, found itself in a desperate situation when fire swept through the crew's quarters, trapping a sailor. Nearby tugs, answering the vessel's S.O.S., made a dramatic rescue of the trapped man by cutting away deck plating and releasing the man. A lifeboat stood by and took the injured man to hospital. Meanwhile, the fireboat *Fireflair* battled its way through very bad weather conditions to the scene and began fire-fighting operations. Suddenly, the ship developed a severe list and the fire crews had to be withdrawn because it was feared the ship would capsize. The 'trim' had to be adjusted; firemen went back on board and managed to bring the blaze under control. Eventually the vessel had to be towed into Sheerness Dock.

Two special service calls deserve special mention. In August 1962 gale force winds were sweeping over Margate and were threatening to tear the 'Big Top' of Sanger's Circus to shreds. Alarmed at losing the huge marquee and disappointing the children, the owner called the Brigade and asked for whatever help it could give. Ready with the answer as usual, the Brigade sprayed jets of water on the dried-out canvas, tightening it and increasing its weight, and saved the day. In January 1963, the Power Station at Northfleet was in imminent danger of a complete shutdown, due to the failure of the cooling water-main. Hoping to avert a wide-spread electricity black-out, the Brigade was called. A temporary pipeline to the river was laid, and with two heavy pumps, cooling water was supplied to the power station. This it continued to do for five and a half days, while workmen laid a completely new pipeline to the station. Meanwhile the power station continued working and the area had its usual supply of electricity.

The next 12 months brought a large increase in major fires but the year 1963/64 could be called the year of farm fires and the Arsonist. Despite the increase in work, important developments in the Brigade took place. Four new fire stations were opened, a whole-time one at Tunbridge Wells and retained stations at Cliffe, Borough Green and Hawkhurst. The joint Police/Brigade radio network which had existed for several years was terminated and an independent Brigade scheme became operational, covering, with the help of police booster stations, the whole of the County. Kent took a lead once again when it introduced safety belts on all vehicles; these belts quickly proved their worth when they saved the lives of firemen whose machines were involved in accidents shortly after their introduction.

Farm fires were so numerous that it is impossible to go into details. In July 1963, 13 pigs were prematurely roasted when fire severely damaged a farm at Petham. In October, six pumps were needed to bring a blaze under control at Penshurst, when blazing fuel oil from a ruptured tank caused the flames to spread to a two-storey barn and three oast houses which were destroyed. In February 1964 a range of farm buildings and their contents were severely damaged at Weavering Street, Maidstone. In the same month, three Dutch barns were destroyed at three separate farms at Deal within minutes of each other. All three were of suspicious origin and were believed to have been started by arsonists.

Major fires included one of particular difficulty and hazard. On May 10th 1963, the Brigade was called to Dungeness Nuclear Power Station where a reactor vessel under construction was on fire. Having been told that it was highly dangerous to use water on the reactor, firemen had to begin the difficult job of removing the burning materials manually and extinguishing these at a distance from the incident. After two days work, the vessel was finally sealed off and flooded with carbon dioxide.

In September, firemen from Margate, Westgate and Broadstairs were once again called to their old battleground – the Dreamland Amusement Park at Margate. When the men arrived, they were met by a fusillade of exploding ·22 bullets spraying in all directions, and a fire which illuminated the sky over the town. Trying to get to work, the men were further showered by fragments of bursting asbestos tiles which were disintegrating in the heat. A large section of Dreamland, wrecked by fire on several occasions, both before and after the war, was again severely damaged, but fortunately, none of the 30 firemen was shot, hit or otherwise injured. October saw St Paul's Church, Maidstone, nearly destroyed by fire, an outbreak for which three small boys were found to be responsible, and on the next day a multiple store of three floors in the High Street, Deal, was alight from top to bottom when the Brigade arrived. It took eight pumps and a turntable ladder to bring the blaze under control, but despite all efforts by the fire-fighters, adjoining premises had been damaged by radiated heat. During five hours on the day before Christmas Eve 1963, appliances from Strood to Dartford were busy attending five fires in the High Street area of Gravesend. Going from job to job, firemen found all of them to be of doubtful origin. In the middle of it all, an irresponsible joker found it amusing to put through two malicious false alarms.

The New Year 1964 started badly, with a tragic fire at Samaritan Grove, Northfleet. When the Brigade arrived at a small terraced house in the early hours of January 7th, they found the building smoke-logged and on fire. A couple and their two children had already made their escape through thick smoke and intense heat. Being warned by neighbours that more children were in the house, the firemen braved the smoke and flames to try and rescue them. Eventually three more children were found and brought out, but all were dead.

January 24th saw the lighter side of Fire Brigade work. Early in the afternoon, two gorillas from John Aspinall's private zoo at Howletts, Littlebourne, decided on an unauthorised outing, and escaped while their cage was being cleaned. For a time, Kula, the husband, weighing 16 stone, and wife Shamba, roamed around the estate and resisted all attempts to lure them back to their cages with oranges and bananas. Meanwhile a small army of nine policemen, led by a superintendent from Canterbury, were trying their unsuccessful best to corral the animals. The police were ignored, and the gorillas helped themselves to milk bottles from the doorsteps of nearby cottages. Zoo workers remembered that gorillas don't like water, and the cry went up "Send for the Fire Brigade!" They arrived with blaring horns and flashing lights, and having assessed the situation, connected hoses to the swimming pool. Then a merry chase began. The gorillas tried to climb a wire fence but were dissuaded by streams of water. Kula climbed high up into a tree from where he was dislodged by a spray of ice-cold water, proving right the theory that gorillas don't like water. Kula shambled back into his cage. Meanwhile, Shamba had disappeared but was suddenly seen looking out from the upstairs window of a cottage and waving to the firemen below. When the first stream of water hit the window, she quickly clambered down, jumped to the top of the wall and was finally cornered in a walled garden, where after watery persuasion, she was finally reunited with her husband.

It took 10 pumps using 12 jets, to bring the fire under control in a timber-yard at Sandwich on February 15th 1964. On March 17th, Fairmeadow Mill at Maidstone, a range of buildings used as an agricultural merchant's granary and mill was severely damaged in a fire which brought 15 appliances and crews from a wide area of Kent to the scene. Eight hundred tons of corn involved in the fire began to swell under the mass of water from 20 jets, and fire-fighting became very difficult when walls started to collapse inwards, covering the burning materials. Brigade personnel had to remain at the scene for over a month to deal with occasional new outbreaks.

The year April 1964 to March 1965 saw once again a considerable fluctuation in the number of calls received. Once again the trend was upwards – over 13,000 calls received, and in his Annual Report for the year, Chief Officer Fordham stated that in his opinion, "increasing human carelessness" was a main factor, combined with "the disturbing increase in malicious calls which is a further indictment of the age in which we live". Fire Prevention work increased too, as did the number of major fires. The cost of the Brigade during that year was nearly £1,700,000.

In the early hours of April 7th 1964, flames could be seen shooting into the night sky miles out to sea off Deal. The Brigade and Walmer Lifeboat were alerted and reports were received that the M.V. *Perseus*, carrying a mixed cargo including drums of petrol, was involved in an explosion, followed by a severe fire. The crew had to abandon ship and were picked up by the lifeboat, while the burning vessel was taken in tow by a German tug and anchored a mile off shore at Deal. Fire crews were ferried out by tug to meet the ship and, wearing breathing apparatus, confined the damage to the upper structure, saving the cargo. A month later another ship, the *Chalcrest*, caught fire while berthed at a wharf at Dartford. Severe damage was caused to the upper structure and the crew's quarters, and firemen had to work under very dangerous conditions when five gas cylinders became involved in the flames. Fortunately none exploded. Shipping in the Eastern Dock, Dover, was threatened when a large supply pipe fractured and poured large quantities of petrol into the harbour. Firemen laid a blanket of foam over the petrol, which had spread over a wide area of the harbour, to prevent what could have developed into a serious fire situation.

At the end of May 1964, Oakwood Hospital, Maidstone, was once again in the news. Less than seven years before, six people, including three Brigade members, were killed there when a tower collapsed on them during clearing-up work. This time, two men were buried under tons of earth when a 20-foot deep trench on which they were working collapsed on them. Firemen had to work in a very confined space and succeeded in uncovering the head of one of the men; but it was nearly two hours before he could be released and taken to hospital suffering severe injuries. Eventually the second man was dug out, but on arrival at the hospital was found to be dead.

Kent fire-fighters are used to dealing with animals, whether they be escaped steers, trapped cows, sheep or dogs, or even playful gorillas that do not like water. But a new situation faced them when they were called, shortly after midnight on June 19th, to a farm at Speldhurst. When the men from Tunbridge Wells Station arrived at the farm, they found that following a heavy cloudburst, dozens of pigs and hundreds of assorted poultry were in immediate danger of drowning in the flooded area of the farm. But how were they to reach the squeaking and squawking animals? Off went one crew to a park with a lake five miles away, 'borrowed' four rowing boats from the boathouse, and returned now fully prepared to the rescue. Assisted by the police and members of the public, they rowed out to the fast-sinking animals, and after a considerable struggle, especially with the terrified pigs, ferried most of them to safety.

At half past four in the afternoon of July 13th 1964, the Kent Brigade was called to its largest fire since the war, when two factories, covering an area of 19 acres, processing oils, waxes, paints and resins were involved in fire. Flames were shooting over 100 feet into the air, and with 12 buildings and their highly inflammable contents burning fiercely, the scene was reminiscent of the Blitz. General mobilisation was put into operation, and appliances from a wide area of Kent converged on Thames Road, Crayford. Working in clouds of choking, black smoke and amidst exploding oil drums catapulted high into the air, the men were further threatened when they nearly became surrounded by a blazing river of molten wax. Two Dartford firemen received burns when they fell into the burning wax, as did two of the factory employees who were trying to help. The fire, which could be seen 30 miles away, attracted thousands of spectators, and created huge traffic jams severely hindering fire appliances from London Fire Brigade called to assist. Altogether 26 appliances including foam lorries, turntable ladders and A.F.S. pumps from Kent and London were on the scene, and it took 13 jets and over three hours of hard and dangerous work to bring the blaze under control. Even then, work had to continue for another 24 hours before the incident could be safely left.

On August 25th, Hoo Oil Refinery was seriously threatened by a deep-seated fire in nearby peat and grassland covering about a square mile. With flames steadily advancing towards the refinery, ten appliances were rushed to the scene, and worked for over 50 hours, using 12 jets, before the danger was averted. An arsonist was responsible for a series of fires over two days, which severely damaged 35 acres of young conifers at Mereworth Woods in September. At the height of the fire, a bulldozer had to be used to cut a fire-break to prevent further spreading. It needed nine appliances to bring the blaze under control, but two further outbreaks, again maliciously started, had to be dealt with the following day. On October 27th, the Oil Refinery at the Isle of Grain was once again threatened by a major fire in an oil reformer. This was brought under control by the use of foam jets, but just as the appliances were leaving for their home stations, a new fire was reported in a nearby vacuum unit, which was in imminent danger of exploding. This too, was extinguished with foam jets after two hours of dangerous work.

Margate, always prone to spectacular fires, was the setting again on November 7th 1964, when the pavilion at the end of Margate pier, and much of the pier building and structure were severely damaged by fire late at night. Flames, which could be seen by shipping at sea 15 miles away, brought a flood of radio calls from them to the local coastguard station, many of them believing that another large ship was ablaze. The flames, fanned by a strong east wind, spread rapidly, and fire-fighters were hampered by a shortage of water because all supplies to the pier had been cut off the previous day because of fear of frost damage. It took 30 minutes to reconnect the supply, and in the meantime, floating pumps had to be used which were not very effective in the heavy swell. When the mains supply was restored, hose had to be hand-laid along the 400-yard jetty before jets of water could be brought to bear on the blaze. Lifeboatmen removed rockets and explosives from the Margate lifeboat which was lying in the harbour nearby. A party of 40 Royal Engineers from Dover, who had been on a visit to Margate, were about to board their return coach when the fire started. The Officer-in-charge immediately offered their services, and the soldiers assisted the Brigade in carrying hoses, and with crowd control.

A serious situation arose at the Shell Mex and B.P. depot at Northfleet at the beginning of March 1965, when a tank containing 2,000 tonnes of petrol exploded, killing a 40-year-old man. Fire following the explosion threatened 14 nearby petrol storage tanks, and it took ten pumps, four foam-tenders, a hose-layer and a fire-boat over four hours before the fire could be brought under control with nine foam jets. A further 12 water jets had to be used to cool down the surrounding tanks. Crews and appliances had to remain on the scene for five days before the depot was judged to be safe. When Maidstone firemen were called to an outbreak in the boilerhouse of 13th century Leeds Castle, near Maidstone, the leading appliance, after negotiating the narrow drawbridge, got caught in a low stone archway leading into the castle. Not to be defeated, they laid extension hoses over a long distance and successfully fought the fire in the boilerhouse.

On April 1st 1965, the whole of the Kent Fire Brigade 'A' Division was transferred to the newly-created GLC Fire Authority. The transfer included eight whole-time stations at Bromley, Beckenham, West Wickham, Biggin Hill, Orpington, Sidcup, Bexley and Erith. The transfer of a whole division and the consequent reduction of the area covered by the Kent Brigade meant a fall in the number of the calls during the year 1965/66. The year also saw major changes in other areas of brigade work. All fire calls were now centrally received and handled from a new Control at Brigade Headquarters. This new system proved entirely satisfactory and fire stations no longer needed manned watchrooms and were, at times when all appliances were out, unattended. A new arrangement with the Port of London Authority had placed four powerful modern fire-fighting tugs at the disposal of the Kent and Essex fire authorities, and the fire boat called *Fireflair* which for several years had done sterling service was honourably retired.

Two new retained stations at Dymchurch and Marden became operational and work on two others, Swanscombe and Teynham, and on two whole-time stations, Canterbury and Larkfield, were well advanced. In July 1965, the Kent Brigade had a stand at the International Fire Exhibition and Conference at Olympia which attracted a large number of visitors from home and abroad.

After 18 years service as the first Chief Fire Officer of the Kent Fire Brigade, Lt-Cmdr J. H. Fordham C.B.E. retired in August 1966. Following the war and denationalisation Cmdr Fordham, under extremely difficult circumstances, quickly created one of the biggest and most successful county fire brigades. International in his outlook, he quickly realised the value of association and exchange of views between British and foreign fire services. Under his command, the Kent Brigade carried out much pioneering work such as the adoption of the 45-foot alloy ladder; the development of the Bikini boat; the use of aluminium bodies for fire appliances; the introduction of the two-tone horn and central brigade mobilising and the start of one of the first junior fireman schemes in the country.

Kent's new Chief Fire Officer was Mr W. Babbington C.B.E., Q.F.S.M. He came from Lancashire where he had been deputy C.F.O. since 1963. Before that he held appointments in Warwickshire, Hampshire, and Suffolk and Ipswich fire services. During the war he was one of a team of officers who went to India to organise the fire services to meet the threat of Japanese air attacks.

The last year of Chief Officer Fordham's command was one of the busiest the Brigade had to cope with since its inception in 1948. Major fire followed major fire and one, in Dover, was the biggest this century. Special Service calls too, were many and unusual. On May 8th 1965, the Pakistani freighter *Yousof Baksh*, seriously involved in fire in the Channel, was in imminent danger of sinking and had to be beached in Sandwich Bay, about 300 yards off Deal. Before the operation was over nearly four days later, a leading fireman had died aboard ship; a helicopter and a lifeboat had to be called in; and crews from many Kent stations had to be ferried to the scene in relays, for relief duties.

When the first crews arrived at the shore, they saw the vessel, carrying a highly inflammable cargo of jute, cotton and oil cake, well alight from bow to stern. Most of the crew, and women and children, had already been taken off by lifeboat. An urgent call went to R.A.F. Manston and within minutes, a helicopter had been scrambled and arrived at Deal. Firemen and their equipment were ferried out to the burning ship while motor boats were requisitioned to take reinforcements to help those already on board. In the meantime, two fire-fighting tugs, one from Germany 300 miles away, had arrived at the scene and had begun pouring thousands of gallons of water into the stricken vessel. With the flames still spreading, firemen added 20 jets of water to the deluge, but eventually it had to be decided to cut two large holes in the ship's side, below the water line, to flood the deep-seated fire in the holds. Thousands of people stood on the sea-front to watch the burning ship, flames from which could be seen as far as Ramsgate and the French coast.

On the third day of fire-fighting, Retained Leading Firemen Reginald Deveson, who had been at work for many hours, suddenly collapsed. Walmer lifeboat was launched with a doctor on board, but Mr Deveson was found to be dead. When, after nearly four days of hard and dangerous fire-fighting, involving crews from a wide area of Kent, the flames were finally brought under control, the vessel was refloated and towed, badly damaged, to Germany.

Two weeks later, on May 23rd, Dover experienced its biggest conflagration this century. Once again, scenes were reminiscent of the wartime Blitz, as a wide area of the night sky over the town was lit up by flames shooting hundreds of feet into the air. The fire, in a vast factory complex, housing ten separate firms, was discovered by a night-watchman who was patrolling the buildings with his Alsatian dog. Seeing smoke pouring from underneath a door, he pushed it open and was met by a wall of flames. He managed to get to a phone to call the Brigade, but found his retreat cut off and shouting into the phone that he was trapped, he climbed out of a window. As soon as firemen turned out of Dover station, they could see the extent of the blaze and immediately radioed for reinforcements. Eventually, 15 appliances and a turntable ladder were on the scene as well as over 100 firemen from a wide area of Kent.

The most urgent task of the first men to arrive on the scene was the rescue of the night-watchman who was precariously perched on a window sill still shouting for help. They were at first hampered by the Alsatian watchdog who, although scorched, had escaped into the open and was fiercely trying to prevent the firemen from cutting their way through the main gate. The dog was eventually removed. With only seconds to spare before the window with the night-watchman was engulfed in flames, he was brought down a ladder by firemen. More reinforcements had to be called and as fire-fighters drove towards Dover, they could see the huge pall of smoke from as far away as Deal, Folkestone and Canterbury. Even in Calais, across the Channel, crowds gathered at the water front to see the glow in the sky. So fierce were the flames that the top of the cliffs backing onto the burning building were scorched. Burning debris, forced up by the intense heat, showered all over the town, and crews of ships in the docks nearby had to turn out to stamp out burning embers as they landed on decks and cargoes.

As the fire spread, fresh dangers arose. Cars had to be driven to safety; a massive wall overlooking the Dover-Folkestone railway line was found to be unsafe so that all trains had to be stopped, and passengers had to travel between the two towns by bus. It took nearly five hours and 16 jets to bring the blaze under control, but firemen had to remain on the scene for several days.

On July 3rd, the 800-year-old Norton Court, near Sittingbourne, which was once a monastery, was badly damaged by fire. Nine appliances and 50 firemen fought the blaze for several hours, while villagers helped to carry out valuable antique furniture from the building. In August 1965, another potentially dangerous fire occurred on a Swedish ship, the M.V. *Portia* on the River Thames, carrying a cargo of cotton, paper and explosives. The first task of the fire crews was to isolate the explosives to avoid the vessel being blown to pieces. This they succeeded in doing and the fire was brought under control with eight jets.

Another serious ship fire happened in September when the crew had to take to their lifeboats six miles off Margate. A Kent fire officer was lowered aboard by helicopter and, with the help of three fire-fighting tugs, managed to confine the damage to the crew's quarters and the upper structure. The vessel was eventually towed into Gravesend. Shortly before midnight on October 16th, over 100 blind and partially-blind children had to be evacuated from their beds when fire badly damaged their school at Dorton House, Seal. While firemen fought the blaze, the children had to spend the rest of the night in a nearby gymnasium.

October brought once again National Fire Prevention Week and what was described in the Press as "probably the most imaginative contribution to Fire Prevention Week in the country" happened in Tunbridge Wells. I must declare a personal interest in the matter, because it all happened in my own offices when I was the Editor-in-Chief and Proprietor of the Fire Group of Journals. We 'conspired' together with senior officers of the Kent Fire Brigade and Kent Police to show, in a realistic way, what would happen if a building were involved in fire while many people were present. So we invited the Mayor, council officials, members of the business community, cinema and dance hall managers, to a talk on fire prevention and emergency evacuation. Careful preparation had been laid and two of my co-workers concealed themselves, one in the attic and the other in the basement. Both had harmless smoke bombs which they were to release at the appropriate moment.

Half way through the talk by a divisional officer, our internal fire alarm was operated and the startled dignitaries and businessmen were ushered out of the now smoke-filled building. Cries for help were heard from the basement and our man in the attic hung, shouting out, from the top storey. Our telephone operator dialled 999 and then left the building herself. Within two minutes the first pump arrived in Dudley Road, quickly followed by a second one, and a turntable ladder. Police in the meantime had sealed off both ends of Dudley Road and groups of people began to gather, pointing out the 'poor chaps' trapped in there. The man in the basement staggered out through the smoke and was revived by firemen, while the turntable ladder was brought into position, extended, and the man at the attic window was lowered by sling to the ground.

After a roll call had been taken in the street and everyone found to be present, the evacuees, now realising that the whole affair had been 'laid on' to hammer home the dangers of fire, trooped back into the building, and after refreshments to help them over the shock, departed more ready, we hoped, to prevent fire from happening on their premises.

In his first report for the year April 1966 to March 1967, the new Chief Officer, Mr Babbington, had to report once again a considerable increase in large fires in the County. Some of these occurred during the

Spring and early Summer, but the first disastrous one, both from a damage and historical point of view, happened on July 12th, 1966 at H.M. Dockyard, Chatham. When the Brigade was called at 10.15 a.m. the whole of the dockyard was already blanketed by a heavy pall of smoke. On arrival, they found the historic No. 2 Slipway with its 200 year-old timber building well alight. The slipway, with its close association with Lord Nelson, and the place where Nelson's Flagship H.M.S. *Victory* was built, had been designated an ancient monument; and despite all efforts of firemen from ten Kent stations and supported by dockyard workers, the building, blazing from end to end, finally collapsed in a shower of sparks. Employees from nearby offices and workshops had to be evacuated; many parked cars were destroyed; Medway House – home of the Flag Officer, Medway – was damaged by radiated heat; and 41 persons including some fire-fighters were injured during the blaze. At the height of the fire 20 appliances, ambulances and control cars were in attendance but nothing could be done when it was recognised that the figurehead of Lord Nelson, taken from the 7th *Vanguard* (launched at Pembroke in 1835), was also ablaze. However, the badly-charred mask of the figurehead was rescued and, after renovation by the Royal Navy, presented to the fire station at Chatham in recognition of their efforts. A further fire on November 8th at the R.N. Barracks, Chatham, caused severe damage to the NAAFI cinema, ballroom and mess, and it required nine pumps to bring the outbreak under control.

Two very serious fires in August 1966 strained the resources of the Brigade over a wide area of Kent and caused severe damage to property and injuries to firemen. The first was on August 2nd at Marley Tiles Limited, Riverhead where a large building, containing eight drying ovens and 50 tons of magnesium, was on fire. During very dangerous operations because of the chemical involved, four firemen were injured and despite the use of 16 pumps, the building collapsed and adjoining properties were damaged by fire and radiated heat. The second fire, on August 25th, badly damaged the large Woolworths store in the centre of Gravesend. The fire occurred during the busy lunch-time period and on arrival, firemen were told that people were trapped on the first floor. Crews, wearing breathing apparatus, fought their way upstairs through the heavy smoke and heat, and managed to rescue eight female employees. But during the rescue two firemen and two civilians were injured. Twenty-two pumps including two turntable ladders were in use, and the incident could not be left for several days.

In November, a private nursing home at Ramsgate, housing female patients aged between 74 and 93, was involved in a serious fire which cost the life of a 93-year-old patient. Four others had to be removed to hospital. Later in November, the furniture store of Court Bros. at Ramsgate, was ablaze on all floors when the Brigade arrived. Because of

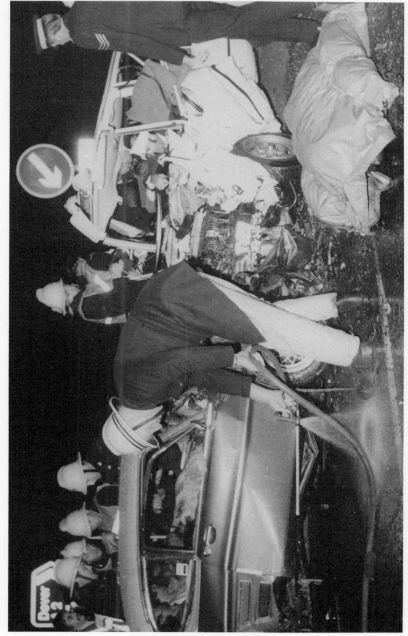

Fig. 21. Firemen at work at a serious night-time road accident, involving several dead and seriously injured.

195

the large stocks of furniture, the flames spread rapidly throughout the building and it became necessary to evacuate occupants of adjoining premises. Finally, the fire was extinguished with the help of 12 pumps and two turntable ladders.

In February 1967, two small children lost their lives when a large aluminium caravan at Stockbury was destroyed by fire; and in March, a Tenterden tanker driver who was trapped in the blazing cab of his overturned vehicle carrying white spirit, was burnt to death before crews from four pumps could rescue him.

Special Service calls once again provided the usual variety of people and especially children trapped in the most unlikely situations, but during the year some assumed a more tragic aspect, with persons killed or injured. In May, a double-decker bus overturned in Broadstairs, trapping and killing an elderly passer-by and injuring 47 passengers. In June, it took several hours of Brigade work at Canterbury to extricate an injured workman trapped in a 25-foot deep, collapsed trench. In August in Swanley, a man, buried in the collapse of a deep trench, died despite the attempts by firemen to administer oxygen while he was still buried up to his neck. But on two occasions, the Brigade was instrumental in providing assistance when new lives came into the world. On a dark night in December, just as a young woman was starting labour in her house at Strood, a power cut plunged her, her husband and a midwife into darkness. The alarm was raised by the husband and minutes later, an appliance from Strood Fire Station was on the scene with two powerful hurricane lamps which provided essential light during four hours of darkness. The operation, logged by the Brigade as 'Emergency Service – Maternity' was a success and the woman bore a healthy 8 lb boy. History repeated itself in January when emergency lighting was again provided at a maternity case in Stirling Close, Borstal, during a power failure.

A fire at Fawkham in April 1967, showed again the foolishness of laymen trying to tackle a blaze on their own, without calling the professionals. A large country house dating from the 16th century, was almost destroyed in the fire when the occupier tried to fight the flames for 20 minutes before calling the Brigade. By the time they arrived it was too late. An explosion and fire in the nitration plant of a chemical factory in Willesborough, later that month, killed one operator and seriously injured two others. The difficult fire required four pumps and a foam-tender before it could be brought under control.

A tribute was paid to Kent firemen by the Archbishop of Canterbury, Dr. Michael Ramsey, when he opened the new Canterbury Fire Station in May 1967. Speaking on behalf of all the ordinary citizens of Kent, the Archbishop said that the Fire Service had won the gratitude of the people in protecting our villages, towns, cities and persons. But, the Archbishop added, because of the great competence and reliability of the

Brigade, people did not think about its work as much as they should.

A difficult and hazardous job faced fire-fighters from five Kent Stations when they were called to the disued R.A.F. Radar Station at Cliftonville, on the morning of August 4th. Wearing breathing apparatus, the men had to fight their way through smoke-logged underground passages to try to locate the seat of the fire. It took 14 hours of hard work by relays of men before the fire, found eventually in the central control section, was brought under control. November 1967 was a heavy month for the Brigade with five major incidents: Timothy Whites at Folkestone; a shirt factory was badly damaged at Sittingbourne, where one fireman was injured during the operations; Turkey Mill, covering a site of half an acre at Maidstone, was badly damaged when high voltage electrical switch-gear became involved in fire; and 11 pumps had to be mobilised when a storage shed containing many tons of paper reels was on fire at Snodland – there the Brigade was in attendance for seven days. Finally, an explosion at the rear of Dover Town Hall caused a fierce fire which damaged large parts of the building and seriously injured three persons.

December was once again the month of ship fires. On the 5th, a large motor tanker, the *Thomas B. Kimball*, was berthed alongside the oil jetty at Cliffe when, during the discharge of gas oil, fire broke out in the pump room. Firemen found it very difficult to gain access to the seat of the fire and it took 12 pumps, a fire tug and two-foam tenders to bring the blaze under control. On the 14th, two ships were involved in fire: the M.V. *Hilda* in the River Medway and the M.V. *Seriality* in the Thames at Greenhithe. At the end of January 1968, fire broke out in the engine-room of the M.V. *Hawick* when five miles off shore, and while the vessel was escorted into harbour by a tug, five pumps and a foam-tender were waiting at Dover to put out the fire. On St Valentine's Day 1968, the 13th century 'Star and Eagle' hotel at Goudhurst was on fire, with the flames rapidly spreading throughout all floors and into the roof. Seven pumps and their crews from several fire stations fought for several hours to save this historic building from destruction.

March 31st 1968 saw the disbandment of the Auxiliary Fire Service under a Government decision to place Home Defence on a 'care and maintenance' basis. The men and women of this service who, since the beginning of the war and indeed during the post-war period, had contributed so much to the fire defence of the country, were suddenly, together with their appliances the 'Green Goddesses', put into moth-balls as an economy measure. Recruitment to the A.F.S. after the war was always disappointing nationally, but Kent had one of the strongest units in the country. They took part in many weekend exercises and, on occasions joined forces with other brigades to carry out mobile column exercises and 'war games'. On the same day, the Admiralty Constabulary Fire Service was also disbanded, and the Kent Fire Brigade became responsible for all fire-fighting measures in H.M. Dockyard and H.M.S. Pembroke at Chatham.

The Spring and early Summer of 1968 was comparatively free from serious fires or extraordinary Special Service calls. In April, the offices and printing works of the Kent Messenger in Maidstone, a paper which so often reported the activities of the Fire Brigade, itself became involved in a serious outbreak which severely damaged large parts of the building. Firemen wearing breathing apparatus and crews from the London Salvage Corps fought the flames for several hours, using ten pumps. Another major outbreak, at the premises of Plant Protection in Yalding in May, when a range of buildings, used as garages and store for packing materials, was badly damaged. Firemen from a wide area fought the blaze with 12 pumps and a foam-tender and after it was brought under control, damping-down had to continue for another 18 hours.

Kent firemen had their first taste of dealing with a nuclear hazard when fire broke out on August 14th 1968 in a reactor compartment of the Nuclear Submarine *Valiant*, in dry dock at H.M. Dockyard, Chatham. On receipt of the call, a full alert was set in motion and appliances from as far away as Canterbury raced to the scene. Pumps, foam-tenders and control units were in attendance, and firemen wearing breathing apparatus had to fight the fire in extremely cramped and dangerous conditions. The men worked in short shifts and on re-emergence from the submarine were immediately checked by doctors with Geiger counters. Although the fire was not serious, it took several hours to put out because of difficult conditions. Constant checks for radiation leakages had to be made, and after the fire was out, all firemen who had been on board were examined by health physicists.

Kent, which has always been plagued by widespread floods and inundations, suffered again during four days in September 1968. Following tropical-storm type rainfall – described as the worst in living memory – the Brigade for the next four days had to mobilise every available pumping appliance (including reserve and workshop pumps), every officer and man (on or off duty), to stem what seemed an unstemmable tide. Hundreds of people had to be rescued from upstairs floors of their houses, others had to be saved from being swept away by raging flood-water, houses were damaged and communications interrupted. Calls for assistance began to flood into Brigade Control at 6 a.m. on Sunday 15th and it quickly became evident that a serious situation was developing. In the first hour 700 calls were received, and all off-duty officers were immediately recalled and sent to the worst affected areas to assess priorities and estimate requirements.

The areas worst affected were Dartford, Gravesend, Strood, Isle of Grain, Isle of Sheppey, Maidstone, Tonbridge, Tunbridge Wells, Larkfield, Sevenoaks, Edenbridge, Yalding and Whitstable. By 2 p.m.

the situation at Whitstable had reached crisis point when the storm-water reservoir overflowed inundating much of the town with several feet of water. Thirty extra pumping units were immediately sent to the town but the problem recurred at each high tide during the next 48 hours. By evening of that day every available appliance was at work, although a few had to be retained at strategic stations to deal with possible fire calls. Much of the success of the operation depended on communications, and although many telephone lines were damaged and the landline radio link from Central Control was out of action during the whole of the emergency, the reserve radio proved satisfactory.

Movement of the Brigade was badly hindered because of impassable roads, dangerous bridges, fallen trees and deep flood-water. Some appliances were put out of action through being driven through deep water, and had to be manhandled by men, waist-high in water, to safer ground. By Monday 16th, the situation showed some slight signs of improvement and allowed for relief to some of the crews who had been working non-stop for nearly 24 hours. But a whirlwind at Hoo which badly damaged the roofs of over 50 houses brought new problems. A temporary H.Q. was set up at Hoo Fire Station and extra crews had to be drafted in to sheet up roofs, fill sandbags, divert flood water and pump out premises.

The emergency showed, once again, the value of the Fire Service at times of natural disasters, with its specialised equipment and highly-trained personnel. There were some incidents of special interest. At Chiddingstone Causeway, two men and a woman were trapped and in immediate danger of their lives on a river bank; they were rescued under great difficulty by firemen. At Tonbridge, two men, a woman and several youths were rescued seconds before being swept into a raging river. At Edenbridge, 25 people had to be rescued from flooded houses by firemen, shoulder high in raging water, and themselves in danger of being swept away. At Hildenborough, two elderly women had to be rescued and 20 others evacuated to a village hall. Continuous pumping for 48 hours was necessary to prevent the Dartford Tunnel from flooding completely, and to maintain traffic flow and essential services. Many more pumps had to be used for long hours at the Nuclear Submarine Base, Chatham, to keep this essential naval establishment operative.

On Tuesday 17th, much of the water had cleared from roadways but left behind many hundreds of basements and cellars, together with areas of low ground, in need of pumping-out. New priorities had to be established to help public utility premises, post offices, chemists and food shops; and large-scale pumping operations continued until the evening of Wednesday 18th. At the end of the emergency, the whole of the Brigade was commended by their Chief Officer for the difficult and dangerous work they had carried out so well.

From floods to a tragic fire at Dover on November 5th, when shortly after midnight, a fierce fire claimed the lives of two small children and a man. When the Brigade arrived with five pumps at the three-storey private house, three persons had already jumped from the first floor and another had climbed down a drainpipe. Firemen immediately pitched a ladder to the burning building and brought down two more persons, but on searching the premises, found the three dead.

When, in the late evening of January 4th 1969, the main line London-Ramsgate passenger train ploughed into the back of a parcels train near Marden, all rescue services in the County were put on major disaster procedure. The crash, in thick fog, occurred in open country and fire appliances and ambulances could not drive over the roughly one mile of wet and muddy fields to the crash scene. Nine appliances, a control unit and 14 ambulances were mobilised, and tractors were requisitioned to carry the injured to the waiting ambulances, and then to three hospitals in Pembury, Tunbridge Wells and Maidstone. It took two hours before the first dead were found in the twisted wreckage and nearly 12 hours before the last, the driver, could be extricated. Altogether four people lost their lives and 20 were badly injured. Throughout the night, firemen used hydraulic lifting-gear and gas-cutting equipment to free the trapped people, often under difficult and dangerous conditions.

In February, Divisional Officer Eric May was awarded one of the first Churchill Travelling Fellowships to study fire services in many parts of the world, including Germany and the Soviet Union. Mr May, who began his fire service career in Margate in 1941, travelled for three months gathering valuable information on foreign fire-fighting and fire protection methods. He later became Deputy Chief of the Brigade and is now an Inspector of Fire Services at the Home Office Fire Department.

The year April 1969 to March 1970 presented the Kent Brigade with a number of new challenges, new progress in administration, buildings and appliances, and a series of major fires. New fire stations at Whitstable and Thames-side were opened, work started on a new Training Centre and Stores adjoining Maidstone Fire Station, and work on a new retained fire station at St Margaret's was underway. Retained firemen at eight fire stations were equipped with personal call-out wireless equipment, much to the delight of the general public who had, for many years, suffered from the noise of the wartime sirens that called out the retained men in an emergency. Twenty-two new pumps, two emergency tenders and 23 other vehicles were added to the strength of the Brigade. Also put into commission was a hydraulic platform, a new type of extendable ladder which, while not replacing the turntable ladder, could be used for easier rescues and for fire-fighting in inaccessible places. The number of calls during the year was over 10,800 and the cost of the Brigade reached nearly the £2 million mark. With the development of modern and high-technical fire-fighting methods and equipment, the

Fig. 22. 1970: Herne Bay Pier badly damaged by fire.

recording of many fires, even major ones, can easily become routine. While it is the historian's duty to research and record as much as possible, he could easily fall into the trap of becoming tedious. However, a compromise has to be found, and giving the basic facts of the more important incidents only, in the year, might provide the answer.

When firemen had to battle for 16 hours with a fierce fire at the Kemsley Mill at Sittingbourne on April 19th 1969, high expansion foam was used to good effect. This foam, mixed with air and water and expelled under pressure, resembles that of a vast over-filled bubble bath, and is especially useful in cellars, holds and confined spaces where it creeps along, filling every inch of the room, and by excluding oxygen, kills the fire. Large quantities of waste paper in the mill were destroyed, despite the attendance of eight pumps and two hose-layers. High expansion foam was again used in a fierce fire at Folkestone Harbour Railway Station on April 22nd; the fire, fanned by a strong wind, badly damaged platforms, store rooms, offices and the station buffet. Two fire-fighters were badly injured when a fire severely damaged a garage and workshops at Ashford on May 22nd. Another fireman was seriously injured when he was struck by falling roof timbers during an incident which nearly destroyed a large country house at Borough Green. Firemen wearing breathing apparatus had great difficulties in locating a fire in a series of underground workings 90 feet below, at St Margaret's on July 13th. Six pumps were needed and high expansion foam was again used to great advantage, but it took 20 hours before the Brigade could leave. Three fire-fighters were injured during a blaze at the Pricerite Stores at Swanley on July 16th. Ten pumps, a hose-layer, a foam unit and crews from the London Salvage Corps were mobilised but the warehouse was badly damaged.

Strood's most disastrous fire occurred in the evening of October 9th 1969, when large sections of Luxrams Electrics were destroyed by a fire which proved more dangerous to fire-fighters than usual. When the first appliances reached the factory, which manufactured a wide range of light bulbs and electrical fittings, flames were already leaping high into the sky and the blaze could be seen for many miles around. Reinforcements were ordered on by radio and eventually 100 men from fire stations all over north-west Kent were joining the battle with 15 pumps, emergency tenders, foam units and control cars. Suddenly, fire-fighters, who had managed to fight their way into the blazing sheds, came staggering out and some collapsed on the ground. Chlorine gas escaping from the burning materials inside had badly affected their lungs, eyes, noses and throats. The most severely affected were taken to a nearby hospital where they were treated for severe headaches, soreness of eyes and throats, and gas sickness. With thousands of gallons of water per minute being poured into the blazing building, firemen quickly ran out of a sufficient water supply, and a mile of hose had to be laid to the river at the Strood Yacht Club. The cause was never definitely established, but children had been in the vicinity of the factory just before the fire, playing with fireworks. A disaster was narrowly averted on October 30th, when fire broke out on a 67,000-ton oil tanker laden with crude oil, at the B.P. Refinery, Isle of Grain. Quick intervention by firemen with six pumps, two emergency tenders, two-form tenders and two hose-layers confined the damage to the pump room of the vessel, and saved the ship and refinery from a major catastrophe. One fireman was badly injured on December 6th when parts of the large supermarket of Tesco in Folkestone were damaged by fire. Another fireman received injuries and burns to his arm, back and hands when a fierce fire severely damaged a service station and tyre store at Chatham on December 27th 1969.

Once again the Chief Officer's Annual Report for the year April 1970 to March 1971 reported an increase of calls of 15% to 11,600 which included a record number of malicious false alarms (1,188 in all). As throughout the nation, Kent also suffered from this stupid and dangerous practice. Arrangements were being made to install voice-recording apparatus at Brigade Control to assist in tracing the callers. Fires, too, not only increased but were both of a bigger and more destructive type. Research into the reasons for this showed that the general increase in the cost of buildings, machinery and materials contributed to the heavier fire losses, but the main reasons were the use of new techniques and processes in factories and the greater storage of high risk chemicals and materials.

On May 9th 1970, Ramsgate's biggest fire since the war devastated part of the town centre. The call was received in the early hours of the morning and as soon as the first pumps left Ramsgate Fire Station, the men could see flames leaping high into the air over the burning shopping centre. Reinforcements were immediately ordered on and firemen with their appliances closed in from a wide area of Kent. Eventually, there were 20 appliances including pumps, turntable ladders, emergency tenders and a control unit from Maidstone on the scene. For hours they fought the flames, cooling down premises not yet affected by the radiated heat which scorched the uniforms of fire-fighters and spread the blaze through a range of shops and flats. When the blaze was eventually brought under control, a public house, two shoe shops, a big store, a wool shop, an outfitters and an ice cream parlour, as well as a block of flats, had been extensively damaged.

Heavy rain and high tides caused havoc at the end of July 1971 in the Folkestone area. Hundreds of homes and buildings were flooded, beer supplies in the cellars of public houses spoiled, road surfaces cracked and power supplies disrupted. Firemen from Folkestone, Hythe, Dymchurch, Dover, Deal and Whitstable worked non-stop for 16 hours, pumping out, rescuing trapped persons and manhandling some of their own appliances which had become stuck in the floods.

When shortly after six o'clock in the evening of September 2nd 1970, the Red and Blue watches at Maidstone fire station were about to change shifts, none could foresee the horror that was in store for eight of their colleagues. The alarm went for a pump to go to the assistance of hard-pressed crews at a fire in Bentlif Close, Maidstone, but minutes after they set out, their appliance skidded, hit a tree and exploded into flames. The blazing vehicle was left perched 12 feet in the air against the broken tree and almost immediately three firemen tumbled to the ground, their uniforms ablaze. Rolling themselves in rainwater puddles, they tried to smother the flames. With the whole of the appliance now a mass of flames, the other trapped men desperately tried to escape through windows and jammed doors.

This is the story of one of the injured firemen, Retained Leading Fireman Don Bates, after he was released from hospital. "After the crash, flames were leaping up everywhere. The heat and smoke was intense. The off-side door was a mass of flames and it was clear we could only get out on my side. But this door was partially jammed, but I managed to squeeze through a gap of about eight inches. Only then did I realise we were 12 feet up in the air and I crashed down onto a fence. I got to my feet and saw two of the lads following me. Then another fireman who was trapped in the front shouted for help. I grabbed a ladder, raced to the front and propped it up against the door. I pulled him through the shattered window and onto the ladder. It collapsed and we both fell to the ground. I knew the driver had not got out, so I put the ladder up again to try to rescue him. I grabbed his arm, but he was badly burned and I lost my grip and fell again. I shouted to the people standing around 'there is a man burning alive in there'. I don't think I went up the ladder again, I don't remember very much after that". The driver, critically injured, was in fact rescued by another fire-fighter, Mr George Stone, a member of the Aylesford Paper Mills Fire Brigade, who was passing by at the time. Meanwhile, other Kent appliances had arrived on the crash scene and four ambulances took the badly burned and injured men to the accident centre at Medway, 15 miles away, since the accident department at West Kent Hospital, Maidstone, had been closed for the night.

Of the eight men taken to hospital, two were critically ill in the intensive care unit, one had to be transferred to Roehampton Special Burns Unit, and the other five were in fair condition. One of the critically ill firemen, Malcolm Farrow, died four days later in hospital. By a cruel twist of fate he was the second member of the Farrow family who had died in the fight against fire. Thirteen years previously, his father, Albert Farrow, was killed in the disastrous fire and collapse at Oakwood Hospital, Maidstone. The driver Mr Roger Lynn, who was trapped in the blazing cab of the machine and was the last to be rescued, had to have his right leg amputated below the knee; and the other members of the crew, Firemen John Page, Albert Foreman, Albert Bray, Alan Bush and Leading Firemen Peter Whent and Donald Bates were suffering from various degrees of serious burns. When Fireman Farrow was laid to rest at Vintners Park, Maidstone, flags on fire stations throughout Kent were flying at half-mast and officers and men from many Kent stations attended the funeral.

Millions of greetings cards were destroyed in a fire at Photo Productions, Gillingham on October 19th 1970. Arson was the cause and it kept 16 appliances and their crews from a wide area of Kent busy for over 12 hours before the outbreak could be brought under control. A security patrolman discovered the fire around midnight, and after calling the Brigade, he went back into the now blazing factory to try to fight the fire single-handed. Badly injured, with burns to the hands and face, he had to be taken to hospital on arrival of the firemen. The whole of the large building was severely damaged and 100 women were put out of work. With the usual number of fires keeping the Brigade busy, some special service calls deserve mention. On August 17th, a workman whose hand had been torn off at the wrist in a machinery accident was delivered to hospital. Doctors who believed the hand could be sewn back, called the Fire Brigade for assistance and a crew rushed to

Bearsted, found the hand and got it back in time to the hospital. On December 8th, an operation was carried out at the Ophthalmic Hospital, Maidstone, when a power cut left doctors and patients in complete darkness. The Brigade provided emergency lighting to the operating theatre and the situation was saved.

Taxis were damaged and the ticket office was wrecked when a train failed to stop at Sheerness Railway Station on February 26th 1971. The leading carriages overshot the buffers, and came to rest outside the station on the taxi rank. Several passengers were injured and a woman in the ticket office was killed. Firemen assisted in the rescue of the injured and recovery of the body. One man was killed and 15 injured under tons of rubble and twisted metal when part of a new motorway bridge at Leybourne collapsed without warning on March 22nd 1971. The Brigade sent six pumps, two emergency tenders and a control unit to the scene to help with the rescue work. April 1971 was a particularly busy time for the Brigade. On April 10th, fire involved the Pilkington Sheet Glass Works at Queenborough. When, because of the heat, a retort containing 1,000 tons of molten glass fractured, a stream of the white-hot substance flowed through the factory processing area. Firemen, their faces and hands blistered by the intense heat, used cooling jets which solidified the

Fig. 23. A hydraulic platform in action.

205

glass and stopped its progress. Three days later, fire swept through Rochester Airport, destroying most of the terminal buildings and flight control systems. Firemen from Medway, Strood, Maidstone and Thames-side, fought the blaze for four hours, using eight pumps and five special vehicles. Cricketers throughout the south-east were alarmed when they heard that a blaze had severely damaged a factory manufacturing cricket balls and bats at Tonbridge on April 24th. Firemen, many of them cricketers themselves, fought to contain the outbreak, but so fierce were the flames that most of the contents were destroyed and adjoining property damaged.

The dangerous job of a fireman was once again emphasised when fire broke out at a range of buildings used as laboratories and chemical stores at Novadels, Gillingham, on June 2nd 1971. Soon after the arrival of the first appliances, thick, acrid, white smoke began to pour from the buildings, blanketing the whole area. Police sealed off surrounding streets and with loudhailers warned householders to stay indoors and shut all windows and doors. Fire-fighters who had started to tackle the fire became affected by the choking toxic smoke, and a fleet of ambulances were called to take them to hospital. Eventually 18 firemen were detained for observation in hospital but later released. Despite a prolonged and difficult fight, using 12 appliances, the range of buildings and their contents were very severely damaged.

Malicious false alarms were still one of the biggest unnecessary problems the Brigade had to face. Despite an intensive publicity campaign, a new record was reached in the year 1971/72 with 1,361 false alarms, an increase of 40% over the average for the previous six years. In his annual report, Chief Officer Babington pleaded for fines to be related to the maximum penalty allowed under the Criminal Justice Act 1967 and not, as often happened, only to the misuse of electricity. During 1971 three new retained fire stations were opened, at Sandwich, Tenterden and Edenbridge. When the R.A.F. Helicopter Squadron withdrew from Manston, the long-standing arrangements with the Brigade for use of the helicopters for fire-fighting at sea had to be terminated, but a new arrangement was made with H.M. Coastguards to use their machines. In order to improve further operations at sea, transportable radio sets for ship-to-shore communications were provided at Dover, Margate, Sheppey, Strood and Thames-side fire stations, with a fixed radio at Medway Ports Authority Control, at Sheerness.

Nor was the year April 1972 to March 1973 any easier for the Brigade. Calls went up to a new record of 13,125 and malicious calls increased still further. Fire prevention inspections, under the various Fire Precaution and Factories Acts, also reached a new record and kept fire prevention staff busy on over 18,000 occasions. New fire stations were opened at Thanet, Sevenoaks and Lydd and many new appliances and special vehicles were added to the Brigade fleet. The year also saw the death of two firemen in action and the biggest fire Kent had to deal with since the establishment of the Brigade nearly a quarter of a century before. On the morning of April 28th 1972, the Post Office buildings at Bearsted, including a general store, a butcher's and a newsagent's, were well alight when firemen from three stations arrived. Because of the heavy smoke, breathing apparatus had to be worn and firemen had great difficulty in getting into the building because of intense heat. During these operations a retained sub-officer C. S. Homewood, collapsed and had to be removed to hospital, where he later died. Heavy damage was caused at the Post Office and shops.

Shortly after midday on June 8th 1972, Brigade Control received the first of many calls to what turned out to be the biggest fire in the Brigade's history. By the time fire-fighters could be withdrawn, nearly 48 hours later, 330 officers and men had been involved at the scene, 60 appliances and 40,000 feet of hose employed for fire-fighting and relay purposes. The fire, at the Bowater Kemsley Mills, Sittingbourne, involved 42,000 tons of wood and pulp, and damage caused was £500,000, then a huge amount. As soon as the first pumps roared out from nearby stations, firemen could see what they had to face. The sky over a wide area was an angry red and flames shooting high into the air could be seen as far away as Canterbury. As the men started to fight the inferno with jets of water and monitors fixed into the ground, station after station throughout Kent was alerted, and men and machines raced to the aid of their hard-pressed colleagues at Sittingbourne. With hundreds of thousands of gallons of water being poured on the flames every minute, water became in short supply and long relay lines of hose had to be laid. The intense, radiated heat threatened nearby large stocks of wood pulp logs, and more fixed ground monitors had to be used to flood these with water to stop the advancing flames. With so many men and machines fighting the fire at Kemsley Mills, large movements of appliances and crews had to be made to provide fire cover in the depleted stations. Men and machines from all over the County were re-located in a complicated closing-up movement which involved a further 180 officers and men and their appliances. During the period that the Brigade was fighting the major fire, another 52 incidents had to be attended.

In September, cricketers received another blow when a large joinery works at Chiddingstone Causeway was badly damaged by fire. A large stock of cricket equipment was destroyed. Twelve appliances were in attendance. Two firemen were injured when a blaze wrecked shops and offices in the centre of Maidstone on November 3rd 1972. Nearby shops had to be evacuated and roads leading into the town centre closed. The fire spread rapidly because of photographic and pharmaceutical materials stored in the premises and it took 13 appliances to bring it under control.

Two officers received serious burns to face and hands and a fireman was injured when a road tanker carrying 4,000 gallons of petrol overturned and exploded at Greenhithe on November 22nd. On December 19th, one of Chatham's best known landmarks was badly damaged in a fire which swept through the Sun Pier buildings. At the height of the blaze, the roof of the 100-year-old pier caved in and sent the cast-iron clock tower crashing to the deck below.

Tragedy struck again in January 1973 and once more Kent firemen had to record that one of their men "was killed in the execution of duty". During the morning of January 9th, 1,600 pupils at the Upbury Manor School, Gillingham, had just finished their first lessons after the Christmas holidays, when the fire alarm sounded. They were quickly evacuated into the playground when it was found that the science laboratory on the first floor of the three-storey building was involved in fire. Brigade received the first call at 10.57 a.m. and because of the many children at risk, appliances and crews were turned out from all over North Kent. Two teams of nurses were also sent from Medway Hospital in case children were hurt. When the first crews arrived, they were faced with dense black smoke issuing from the burning laboratory and two of the men, Fireman Neil McCulloch and Fireman Raymond Plumley, were ordered to enter the school wearing breathing apparatus. They entered through a storeroom and moving on hands and knees tried to find the seat of the fire. Having done so, they started to make their way back to get a jet when that most feared danger to firemen, a flash-over, occurred. With the force of an explosion, a sheet of flame raced through the laboratory, knocking over Fireman Plumley and badly injuring him. Despite his injuries he managed to crawl to safety and was taken to hospital. There was, however, no sign of Fireman McCulloch, and a second team of men with breathing apparatus, Firemen Fred Jackson and Ben Murray, were sent into the now fiercely blazing laboratory to search for him. Eventually he was found slumped against a wall with his face mask off and with extensive burns to his head and face. The position had now become totally untenable, but despite burns to his own hands, face and neck, Fireman Jackson dragged McCulloch out of the laboratory to safety. Both were taken by ambulance to hospital where Fireman McCulloch was found to be dead. The fire, which severely damaged the laboratory and part of a new wing of the School, was brought under control in just under two hours with the help of ten appliances.

A most unusual rescue, which brought firemen from the scene of a road accident to assisting in the operating theatre of a hospital, happened at Green Street Green on December 30th 1972. The driver of a van which had collided with a barrier of metal piping on concrete posts was impaled on his seat by a length of piping that had passed through the front of the vehicle, through the leg of the driver, pinning him firmly to the seat. With the man still conscious and in considerable pain, firemen cut away the piping where it entered his leg and he was taken by ambulance, still attached to the seat to hospital. In the operating theatre, under the watchful eyes of surgeons, firemen then gently cut away more of the piping, finally releasing the man from the seat. Surgeons then managed to remove the remaining piping from his leg. This was eventually handed to the crew as a souvenir and can still be seen as an exhibit in the Brigade's Museum at Headquarters, Tovil. Firemen were shocked when they were called out to one of their own fire stations at Sheerness in the early hours of January 18th. Following a collision between a milk-float and a tanker (in which the float driver was killed), the tanker crashed into the fire station demolishing a pumping appliance stationed inside.

When the Local Government Reorganisation Act 1973 came into force at the end of March 1974, the fire service was affected in many ways. Through creating larger brigade areas by incorporating county borough brigades into counties and metropolitan areas, the number of brigades in the country was reduced from 166 to 63. However, there was little change in Kent where the only county borough, Canterbury, was already receiving fire cover from the Kent County Fire Brigade under a special arrangement in force since 1948. The reorganisation might, however, be a convenient point to look back over the past 26 years since the formation of the Kent Brigade in 1948. In that year, Kent had to take over the stations and appliances from the disestablished National Fire Service and all the problems that go with old and dilapidated fire stations; many temporary erections in the wrong locations, and appliances (mostly old and in poor repair), were unsuitable for modern fire-fighting requirements. Communications were poor; standardisation of equipment and hydrants, although greatly improved during the war, was still incomplete; and there was a shortage of manpower, materials, and above all, money.

It took many years of dedicated work by the officers and men of the brigade, and the officials of the K.C.C. to change this situation, so that by 1974, 14 new whole-time fire stations had been built, as well as 30 retained stations, a training centre and a brigade store. With new technology, communications had been improved with a central control, radio on all appliances, pocket alerts for the retained men, walkie-talkie sets, and special ship-to-shore links. A big appliance replacement scheme had been completed and Kent now had some of the most modern fire-fighting machines in the country. It is interesting to note the increase of fire and special service calls during that period. In the first year of the Kent Brigade, 1948/49, there was a total of 5,724 calls to which the brigade responded. This number increased year by year, so that in 1973/74, calls recorded reached a record figure of 13,125.

Not only did the number of calls increase, but where in past years the attendance of more than two or three appliances at an incident was rare and fully reported in the Press, the situation had changed through new technology and the increased use of dangerous materials, where the presence of several machines and perhaps 50 firemen was a frequent occurrence. It is not possible, even for the historian, to give details of the majority of these calls and so he has to confine himself to recording only the biggest events.

One such event cost the lives of two Medway firemen and badly injured four others. In the early morning of November 8th 1974, a naval patrol discovered a fire at H.M.S. Pembroke, R.N. Barracks, Chatham.

Upon arrival of the brigade, the ground floor bedding store of a three- and four-storey building used as stores, offices and sleeping accommodation was found to be smoke logged. Firemen Holley and Bell, both wearing compressed air breathing apparatus, entered the store with a charged line. Shortly after their entry, a violent explosion, followed by a severe fire, occurred inside the store, which trapped both breathing apparatus wearers. Other members of the Brigade who were immediately outside the building suffered burns to exposed parts of their bodies and some were knocked off balance.

Emergency measures were immediately implemented and two pairs of breathing apparatus wearers entered the building for search and rescue purposes. Ambulances were ordered and the attendance increased to six pumps, and later increased to ten.

The two breathing apparatus wearers who first entered were located and upon their removal from the storeroom were immediately conveyed to Medway Hospital by ambulance where, upon arrival, they were found to be dead. Four other members of the Brigade were also conveyed to hospital by ambulance suffering from shock and burns received at the time of the explosion.

The store contained approximately 180 latex foamed rubber mattresses, some of which had a loose cotton outer covering and, from evidence given at the inquest, the explosive condition was brought about by the mattresses smouldering for an appreciable time during which an explosive vapour was produced. The intense fire which followed the explosion caused heavy damage to the entire store and spread by convection to a first floor dormitory.

Calls continued to rise during the first few months of 1975, and although few fires achieved really major proportion, the brigade was kept busy with special service calls; with the increasing number of visits for fire prevention inspections under the various Acts; and with responding in one month alone, January, to no fewer than 850 alarms, many of which required the attendance of men and machines from several stations. In the late evening of January 22nd, the brigade received an unusual call to a 30-ton cabin cruiser in distress at Allington Lock on the River Medway. On arrival, the brigade found that the vessel was hanging precariously across the arresting wire on top of a weir, after going out of control due to engine failure. On board, 18 people, including children, were trapped, and firemen laid a 45-foot ladder from the bank to the deck of the listing vessel to rescue them. This was achieved by leading them to safety over the ladder with the aid of life-lines. Two appliances and an emergency tender were in attendance and two ambulances were called to take three people, including one small child, to hospital. The river, which was in flood, make the rescue operation and the consequent mooring of the boat by the brigade, particularly hazardous.

February saw several serious farm fires at Farningham, Leigh and Lyminge, and in April, a serious fire at Redmans Garage, Lamberhurst, injured two civilians, and brought men and appliances from six fire stations, including an emergency tender and the Control Unit from Brigade Headquarters to the scene. Breathing apparatus had to be used and the garage and an adjoining house were severely damaged in the blaze. In June, the Westminster Mill at Horton Kirby, a former paper mill but then in multiple occupancy, was severely involved in fire and it took men and appliances from ten fire stations with 15 machines to bring the blaze under control. The building of three floors was severely damaged when, at the height of the fire, the roof crashed in. Nurses had to flee in their night clothes when fire swept through a wing of the Nurses' Home at Oakwood Hospital, Barming in September 1975. The fire was discovered at 11 p.m. and spread so rapidly that some of the nurses were trapped in their rooms by smoke and flames. When firemen from stations over a wide area arrived, several rescues had to be carried out, and one ancillary worker, just about to jump from her bedroom window, was only saved from certain injury by a charge nurse climbing up a drain pipe to calm her and to await the arrival of the brigade ladder.

Meanwhile, appliances from Maidstone, Larkfield, Halling, Borough Green, Marden and Medway were arriving, including turn-table ladders and an emergency tender. Firemen, wearing breathing apparatus, fought their way into the blazing building and when the roof collapsed into the first floor, two firemen had to be taken to hospital with severe eye injuries. Three of the nurses also had to be taken to hospital but were not detained. Many of the 106 rooms in the Home were badly damaged and many of the nurses, mostly from overseas, lost all their clothes and belongings. The fire was finally brought under control after four hours, but crews were in attendance for another 24 hours. Oakwood Hospital was once again involved in a serious fire in November, when a range of single-storey buildings, used as a laundry, was destroyed. The new outbreak again required men and appliances from six Kent stations with 12 machines, before it could be brought under control with eight jets. In December 1975, 11 firemen were overcome by chemical fumes at an incident at Denton Wharf, Gravesend, and had to be taken to hospital by ambulance. The alarm was caused by the accidental spillage of 350 kilos of titanium tetrachloride and the brigade had to neutralise this dangerous chemical by the application of 1,500 kilos of light sodium carbonate.

The summer of 1976 kept Kent fire-fighters again very busy with wood and grassland fires, and several major incidents, particularly in June and July, kept the brigade fully stretched. On June 16th, fire severely damaged the Amusement Arcade at Herne Bay. The blaze, which could be seen over a wide area, brought firemen from five stations, and appliances were gradually built up to ten. Despite the efforts of the men, the whole structure collapsed in a shower of sparks, ruining the contents of the many booths and other equipment. Many jets, high expansion foam and breathing apparatus had to be used, and two firemen were injured in the incident.

The very next day, June 17th, saw one of the biggest store fires in Medway for many years when Giles furniture store in Chatham High Street suddenly burst into flames. Fully stocked for a forthcoming sale, the fire was discovered about 8 p.m., and before the brigade arrived, a "flash-over" caused by the sudden influx of oxygen into a fume-filled, over-heated area, blew out the windows and spread the flames rapidly over most of the building. When firemen from five fire stations arrived, large parts of the High Street were threatened, and shops and buildings on the other side of the road were already affected by the heat and smoke. Windows cracked, and customers in the "Royal George" public house opposite the blazing store had to flee through the back when the heat melted paint on the bar and charred the carpets in the lounge. At the height of the blaze, fire-fighters had to put a curtain of water between the store and properties nearby, while others, wearing breathing apparatus, fought their way inside and tackled the flames which were threatening to spread to the shops on either side. Police closed off large parts of the High Street and kept back thousands of sightseers who streamed to the scene, attracted by the flames and smoke.

One shop and its occupants in the direct line of fire-spread was a pet shop and the owner organised a team of animal lovers to form a rescue squad. Dozens of animals in their cages were evacuated and found temporary refuge in a dry-cleaners', an optician's, and a camera shop. In the middle of the evacuation, a pet rat gave birth but it is not recorded whether firemen assisted during labour.

July was the brigade's worst month for 1976. An extensive period of hot and dry weather resulted in many fires in woods and grassland, especially in the northern part of Kent where the brigade received an average of over 100 calls a day to these incidents. On July 7th, the Brigade Control had to deal with 161 calls for assistance, and appliances had to be moved over long distances to cover the denuded station

212

grounds of the busier areas, but quickly became involved in incidents themselves. Appliances from Canterbury fought fires in the Maidstone area, and crews from Herne Bay and Whitstable dealt with grass fires in the Medway Towns. During the month, large quantities of trees, corn, and heathland were destroyed.

With all sections of the Kent Fire Brigade stretched to the limit, three major incidents further depleted remaining appliances, and it was only due to the dedicated work of the firemen, already tired and over-stretched from the continuing battles in the countryside, that these major fires were dealt with efficiently. All happened within the space of a few days in July 1976 and during the time when the wood and grassland fires were at their very worst.

The first, at Reed International Paper Mills, Aylesford, needed 15 pumps and firemen from ten stations from a wide area of Kent to bring it under control. At the height of the blaze, which involved contractors' buildings and 13,000 tons of baled waste-paper and pulp, over 100 Kent firemen were joined by the mill's own fire-fighting crews. While some of the men fought the main fire, where flames were leaping hundreds of feet into the air, others desperately tried to prevent the fire spreading to the nearby machine shops, and to cool down an oil pipe running along the burning bales from bursting in the heat. In the thick smoke, some of the men had to wear breathing apparatus, and despite the use of 22 jets, the buildings, bales, and six trailers were badly damaged by the fire; assessed at over £½m.

Continuous grassland fires probably caused the near-destruction of a Napoleonic fort at Chatham in which many thousands of new and old tyres were stored. Discovered by an employee of the tyre firm, the flames spread rapidly among the highly flammable tyres and very soon the whole of the town and the surrounding area were blanketed in black, acrid smoke. Appliances, with headlights blazing in the murky atmosphere, raced to the scene from eight fire stations, which included Medway, Chatham, Strood, Thames-side, Gillingham, Larkfield and Maidstone. The smoke could be seen as far away as Maidstone, and police had to close off a wide area round the fort and divert traffic to allow easy access to fire appliances and to water hydrants. When the first crews arrived on the scene, they were warned that fuel tanks, holding 20,000 gallons of heating oil at the neighbouring College of Technology, were threatened by the flames. While some fire-fighters were diverted to cool down these tanks, others faced the difficult task of fighting the flames in the stacked tyres, most of which were stored in the underground rooms of the fort.

Time and time again, firemen trying to fight their way into the underground passages, were beaten back by heat and smoke issuing from the narrow entrances, and vast quantities of water had to be poured into the building before access could be achieved. Meanwhile, further men and appliances had to be diverted from fighting the grassland fires and had to go to the assistance of their hard-pressed colleagues. Staff were evacuated from the Maidstone and Medway Technical College and joined the thousands of spectators who watched the firemen at work. At one stage, fire officers were worried about the possible collapse of the fort itself. As one commented: "The Fort was built to last, but it was never designed to withstand this sort of heat". Eventually, the blaze was brought under control with 12 jets, but some crews had to remain at the fort for another 48 hours to dampen down and prevent new outbreaks in the still smouldering debris.

Firemen from five Kent stations had to fight a shrub and woodland fire amidst a hail of exploding ammunition at the Lydd Army range in July 1976. At the height of the blaze, help had to be called in from the East Sussex Fire Brigade as soldiers and firemen tried to quell the flames in the bone-dry gorse and scrub of the 40-acre site. Eight appliances and other special vehicles were on the scene; and when two soldiers were seriously injured and there was a threat of more casualties from the continuing explosions, two ambulances were ordered on. Senior officers were particularly worried about the nearby Dungeness Atomic Power Station; electricity supplies were disconnected, and both nuclear reactors were switched off. At the height of the blaze, a pall of smoke 500 feet high spread for miles downwind and could be seen as far away as Ashford and Folkestone. A coastguard at Lade, several miles away, said that he could see fir trees exploding into balls of fire. Exploding ammunition was not the only hazard fire-fighters had to face; there was also the danger of hitting high tension electricity cables with their water jets which could conduct fatal shocks to the men on the branch. The fire was not brought under control for six hours but, apart from the two injured soldiers, only minor burns were sustained by the firemen.

A flaming July passed into a flaming August. With the drought now into its 12th week, the whole countryside was ready to explode, and tired and exhausted Kent fire-fighters stood by their worn-out machines for a last-stand battle against the flames which roared across woods and grassland, beauty spots, and caravan sites. Every available man and appliance was brought into action; retained men hardly ever saw their regular employment; training and workshop pumps became front-line appliances; and soldiers and sea cadets were equipped with beaters to assist the firemen. Fire Brigade Control became swamped with calls, and during June and the first two weeks of July, four times the usual number of alarms (3,000) were recorded.

Not only did the fires do untold damage to Forestry Commission plantations, crops, farms, and woodland, but the cost to the County and ratepayers was also high. An extra £20,000 a month had to be found to pay the retained and full-time men. Men and machines had to be drafted from one corner of Kent to the other, returning exhausted to their own

214

stations, only to be ordered to stand by somewhere else. Hardly had they established themselves in a new station, when the alarm went and they had to turn out again to fight the flames, maybe for several more hours. The drought also brought water shortages, and with water rationed to ordinary consumers, the firemen had to use as many ponds and streams as possible.

At the famous Warren at Folkestone, three miles of grass were blazing, and it took firemen from six stations ten hours to bring that blaze under control, using ten jets, two ground monitors and numerous hose-reels. A forest fire at West Blean Woods, Herne, blazed for four days and destroyed thousands of young fir trees, killed wild life, and threatened a caravan camp. Firemen from Herne Bay were soon joined by crews from Faversham and Ramsgate, and as resources became stretched, more assistance was ordered on from Sturry, Sittingbourne and Sandwich. They fought desperately to keep the flames away from the Westlands Caravan Camp (from which holiday-makers had been evacuated) and succeeded when the wind direction changed. At one point, a group of firemen was cut off by flames and by blowing whistles to keep in touch, they escaped just before the wall of fire closed behind them.

More holiday-makers had to be evacuated from the Blue Channel caravan site at Capel, near Dover, when a huge forest fire threatened to engulf it. Firemen from several stations, with the help of volunteers and soldiers, managed to keep the flames away from the mobile homes, but several acres of trees were destroyed. It was only at the beginning of September that the long nightmare for the Kent firemen drew to an end. Small amounts of rain began to fall, and although insignificant as far as the water shortage was concerned, it gave the fire-fighters their first respite for nearly four months.

The first signs of unrest and discontent in the British Fire Service began to appear during the latter part of 1975, and increased considerably during 1976. Government economies, inadequate wage increases for a vital and dedicated service, and the threat of job losses, made Britain's fire-fighters realise that the old parish pump attitudes had not been forgotten completely. Feeling that their efforts were not appreciated, they protested through their organisation, the Fire Brigades Union; and many stations throughout the country worked "to rule" for long periods, which meant responding only to emergency calls. Morale slumped, bitterness and frustration held the once-proud service in its grip, and the intransigence of those in power led eventually to the first ever national firemen's strike at the end of 1977. This lasted ten weeks and did great damage to the service, the public and the country alike.

Like the rest of the country, Kent was affected during 1976/77, and the "work to rule" lasted longer in the County than in most other areas. When in October 1976 the *Kent Messenger* reported, under the heading "Fire Service to Cut its Strength", that "fire brigade economies

215

will leave the Brigade 55 below strength", it caused great concern throughout the Brigade and forced the then Chief Fire Officer to point out that there would be no redundancies but that no new recruits would be taken on to bring the Brigade up to its authorised strength of 751 – a difference of 55. This statement does not seem to have satisfied most members of the Brigade and a further notice was posted asking the men to "refer for clarification of doubts to their officers".

It was in this atmosphere of misgivings and low morale, that Chief Officer Babington retired at the end of December 1976; and Mr Reginald Doyle, Chief Officer of Hereford and Worcester Fire Brigade, took over the command of Kent on January 1st 1977. Born in Birmingham in 1929, the new chief, after seven years in the Royal Navy where he saw action in the Korean war, joined the Service in Birmingham in 1954. He quickly made his mark at the Central Fire Station and gained rapid promotion to Leading Fireman, Sub-Officer, and Station Officer, before transferring with the rank of Assistant Divisional Officer of the Devon Fire Brigade where he was in charge of Tavistock Station. Further promotions followed, and in 1967 he moved to Gloucestershire with the rank of Divisional Officer, Grade 1. Two years later, he was appointed Assistant Chief Fire Officer of the important Lancashire Fire Brigade, and in 1973, became Chief Fire Officer of the Worcester City and County Fire Brigade which, under the local government re-organisation of 1974, became the Hereford and Worcester Brigade. But it was on January 1st 1977, on the retirement of Chief Officer Babington, that Mr Doyle took over the command of Kent and started a process of developments and rehabilitation which made it one of the premier brigades in the country.

Nor had the new chief long to wait before he saw his men in action. Only a week after starting his duties, the newly-modernised printing plant of Kent Art Printers at Rochester went up in flames, causing a major alarm and mobilising men and machines from eight fire stations over a wide area of Kent. Eventually, 12 appliances (including a hydraulic platform) were in attendance. The 100-years-old main building, formerly a church, was badly damaged, as was valuable machinery and stock, but firemen succeeded in saving the rest of the large works.

Shortly after 0245 hours on Sunday March 27th 1977, firemen at Dover Station received a call to the Crypt Tavern restaurant in Bench Street. When they arrived, they found the large building heavily smoke-logged and several people shouting for help from upstairs windows. In front of the building stood the distressed manager, shouting to the men that more people were trapped inside, including members of his family. This was the situation that faced the Acting Leading Fireman who was in charge of the first water-tender to arrive on the scene. With his limited number of crew members, he ordered ladders to be pitched to the upper floors and sent other men wearing breathing apparatus to enter the building and search for the missing persons. Three children were successfully carried down a ladder and two other persons rescued from the third floor windows.

Meanwhile, a major alert had been called in the Division. At 0256 hours, pumps were made up to three, the Divisional Officer and the Deputy Chief Officer had been informed, and at 0302 hours, pumps were made up to four, and the Chief Officer informed. From then on, officers of rising seniority arrived on the scene to take charge of operations, and by 0310 hours, 15 appliances, including pumps, turntable ladders, a control unit, and emergency tenders were in attendance. With the arrival of more men and appliances, a turntable ladder was pitched to the roof of an adjacent building and another person was rescued.

The first breathing apparatus crew to enter the building fought their way through dense smoke and extreme heat to climb the stairs to the first floor, and being forced to crawl to gain further access up the stairs, located the trapped persons. Both men re-entered the building on three successive occasions to locate and carry out the casualties. The fire by now had gained a firm hold of the building and the heat and smoke intensified to an almost explosive level. By the time the breathing apparatus crew had carried out the third casualty from the building, both men were suffering from extreme fatigue and were in a state of near collapse.

Station Officer Peters arrived at the scene soon after 0300 hours and saw thick black smoke issuing from all levels at the front of the building and drifting over the roof; the last of the persons being rescued by ladder was being brought down and the officer-in-charge, Acting Leading Fireman Dadd, was in the process of giving mouth to mouth resuscitation in the street to a small child whom the breathing apparatus crew had just brought out. The search continued until a flash-over occurred on the ground floor which engulfed the front entrance, blowing out the doors, and seriously threatening the main staircase used by the breathing apparatus crews. The evacuation whistle was sounded and the crews withdrew from the building. The additional appliances had now arrived and crews from Folkestone were attempting to control the fire at the front of the building. The fire vented itself through the roof of the two-storey section in the centre of the complex which caused an inrush of air and intensified the fire. The turntable ladder was directed to be put into operation as a water tower to assist in the control of the fire, whilst crews with branches worked hard in punishing heat and smoke to drive the fire back. As soon as the staircase was accessible again, crews were directed to re-enter the building on the second and third floors to continue the search for the remaining three missing persons.

At about 0330 hours Divisional Officer Evans arrived to take over control of the incident, and after a reconnaissance of the site and a brief appraisal of the situation from Station Officer Peters, he entered the building via the main staircase. He climbed the stairs to the half landing between the first and second floors, and there discovered the bodies of Miss Anita Lee, aged 19 years, and Janusia Ashton, aged 5 years, huddled together with their heads resting against a door. Assisted by ambulance crews, the bodies were removed from the building to the waiting ambulances. The crew searching on the second floor, having completed the search of the flat, were in the rear bedrooms when they found the body of Shane Clay, aged 7 years, lying between two single beds. The crew carried the child to the front of the building where they handed him to a fireman waiting on the ladder.

Conditions on the upper floors were slowly improving due to the sustained efforts of the fire-fighting crews on the ground floor. At about 0400 hours, part of the two-storey section of the building collapsed on top of the fire-fighting crews, completely burying some of them under tons of rubble, timber flooring and roof sections. The devastated area was soon filled with rescuers; the two men who were trapped by the lower half of their bodies were quickly released and carried to safety. The search continued for others known to have been involved in the fire-fighting operations. A faint voice was heard coming from beneath a large section of timber flooring and all hands were called to assist in its removal. Due to the large amounts of rubble and debris pinning the section down on top of the men, systematic cutting away of small sections had to be undertaken.

Rescue operations were hampered by fire which was beginning to regain a hold, and men were detailed with branches to try to control it. Meanwhile, one of the two men trapped beneath the debris had become unconscious and it was feared that both might suffocate under the heavy load. Air line equipment was brought in from the emergency tender and fed down to the trapped men. After a period of determined efforts by all concerned, one by one the men were freed and placed on stretchers and removed to waiting ambulances. The search continued for another member of the crew who had led the fire-fighting teams and who had done so much in the initial stages of controlling the fire. After a considerable amount of systematic searching and digging had been done, the tunic of the missing man, Leading Fireman John Sharp, was uncovered. His lifeless body was lying partly on its side with his face downwards, his helmet was still in position on his head. Following the removal of his body from the scene, the area was deemed to be unsafe and instructions were given that no further fire-fighting operations were to be carried out within this area.

This was one of the worst fire tragedies in Kent for many years. With six civilians and one fireman dead, and seven other fire-fighters seriously injured in hospital, investigations into the cause of the blaze were started. The Mayor of Dover started an appeal fund for the dependants of Leading Fireman Sharp, and for days the shock of the tragedy affected the whole town. The investigations revealed that during the night of the fire, the restaurant manager, Mr Colin Clay (who lost his wife and two of his five children in the blaze), had made a routine check of the premises when the restaurant closed at about midnight and had found everything in order. The fire was believed to have started in an electric fryer in the steak bar about one hour before it was discovered. The verdict of the inquest on those who died was that they were killed by acute carbon monoxide poisoning and asphyxia. None were killed by the fire itself.

Leading Fireman John Sharp met his death while he was leading a crew of men in the ground floor bar when the roof collapsed on them. All five men were trapped under the debris and all available personnel were ordered to move the debris by hand and to use power saws to cut through the timber. All were eventually brought out with serious injuries and taken to hospital where Leading Fireman Sharp was found to be dead. The two most seriously injured fire-fighters were Fireman James Wraight who sustained broken ribs, a punctured lung and burns to both legs, and Leading Fireman David Waters with severe compression to the chest and burns to the legs. Sub-Officer John Davison and Fireman Albert James, Ian Radford, Malcolm Carolan and Michael Page, all suffered from various degrees of burns, cuts, bruising and shock.

When Leading Fireman Sharp was laid to rest, more than 600 firemen from 40 brigades throughout the country, including a contingent of French fire-fighters from Boulogne, attended his funeral. His coffin was carried on a fire engine along the main street of Canterbury which was lined by firemen and thousands of townspeople, to Canterbury Fire Station where a contingent of firemen from other Kent stations saluted the cortege. From there, the procession continued round the city to St Stephen's Church. While the procession was in progress, all traffic and trains were stopped, and on arrival at the church, six of Leading Fireman Sharp's colleagues carried the coffin inside.

Chief Officer Doyle told the large congregation that firemen came face to face with tragedy and disasters almost every day of their lives. Leading Fireman Sharp had been a fireman for 12 years and left a wife and two young children. The last act in the drama came when four firemen were awarded the Chief Fire Officers' Certificate for courage and bravery during the Crypt fire. They were awarded to Fireman David Dadd (28), Fireman James Hogben (29) and Fireman Kenneth Fairchild (28). A posthumous award to Leading Fireman John Sharp of Canterbury was made to his widow, Mrs Gloria Sharp, who also received her husband's axe, rank marks and cap badge, mounted on a plaque.

The Citation for Fireman Dadd, who was acting leading fireman in charge of the first crew to arrive at the scene of the Crypt fire, told how he set his men to work rescuing children and adults from upper storey windows and from the roof. He also ordered two men to enter the building in breathing apparatus to search for casualties. He restrained the restaurant manager – who lost his wife and two children in the fire – from re-entering the building.

During this early stage of the fire, when manpower and resources were so limited and the situation demanded so much, Fireman Dadd acted far beyond the highest expectations for a man in his position.

The joint citation for Firemen Hogben and Fairchild recalled how they entered the blazing building, wearing breathing apparatus, and went up the main staircase. Both men were forced to crawl because of the extreme heat. Three times they went back into the building to recover the bodies of the casualties.

Leading Fireman Sharp led his crew from Folkestone Fire Station into the ground floor of the building to attack the seat of the blaze. Crouching low to avoid dense smoke and hot gases, the crew inched their way forward into the building. Slowly the fire was driven back and Leading Fireman Sharp with his crew eventually penetrated to the centre of the building, where their sustained efforts under extremely hazardous conditions were having a marked effect on the control of the fire.

Suddenly, without warning, the roof collapsed, killing Leading Fireman Sharp and completely burying other members of his crew. The courage, determination and leadership displayed by Leading Fireman Sharp was in the highest traditions of the Fire Service.

But there are lighter sides to a fireman's job, and indeed situations where they can admire the bravery of others. Such an occasion happened in July 1977, when lightning struck a house in Salisbury Close, Sittingbourne, setting a bedroom on fire. Alone in the house, with her one-year-old baby brother, was four-year-old Jeanne Baillie, while her blind mother was out at a meeting. Despite the smoke and heat, the little girl did not panic but lifted him out of his cot and guided him downstairs to safety. She refused to hand him over until firemen arrived; they had to fight the fire wearing breathing apparatus. So impressed were the firemen by her courage and calmness, that she was made the guest of honour at a ceremony at Sittingbourne Fire Station, given a bracelet subscribed to by the men, and received a letter from Chief Officer Doyle, together with a Kent Fire Brigade badge, mounted on a wooden shield. The letter stated that "the firemen of the Kent Fire Brigade would like to say how proud we are of the way you acted when your house was on fire and you helped your little brother".

Now, however, we are entering one of the saddest periods in the history of the British fire service. The discontent of pay and conditions which had been smouldering in the brigades since 1975, suddenly erupted on November 14th 1977, in the first national firemen's strike in history. Men, who for years had risked and sometimes given their lives in the service of their fellow men, who had sustained terrible and maiming injuries, who had worked long and exhausting hours under the most terrible and dangerous conditions, suddenly felt that their own living conditions were becoming unbearable. When the call for a total strike came from their Union, men were torn between their devotion to the service and their own needs; between the realisation that their action may lead to the death of people and the apparent indifference the authorities showed to their problems. Most Fire Brigade Union members joined the strike, while officers and senior officers belonging to different organisations remained on duty. The government quickly brought the war-time Green Goddesses out of mothballs, mobilised units of the armed forces who, after a few hours of fire training, assumed the responsibility of the nation's fire cover.

In Kent, the Royal Engineers were stationed in various parts of the County. The Royal Navy, stationed at the Invicta Barracks, Maidstone, manned a large mobile column to go to major incidents, and another Royal Navy "quick response breathing apparatus and rescue" unit operated out of Chatham Dockyard. Some of the Kent retained fire stations were also on strike, while others responded to emergency calls only in their own area, or their own village. Practically all fire stations were closed, with picket lines manned day and night in the bitterly cold winter weather. Nor did the public forget the firemen who had helped and assisted them so selflessly and so often. Gifts of money, food and drink were showered on the men as they stood before their closed stations, and motorists and lorry drivers hooted their support.

Nor did the firemen forget the public. Knowing the lack of experience and training the soldiers and sailors had in fire-fighting, they were ready to assist where lives were in immediate danger. Thus, when they were informed of a fire in which people were trapped, several of the strikers with their breathing apparatus sets, would jump into their own private cars, race to the incident, carry out the rescue, and immediately afterwards, return to their picket lines. Senior officers would respond to calls to act as advisers to the soldiers and sailors who often had great difficulties in containing even comparatively small fires.

Week after week, the strike which had started over government policy on pay awards, dragged on. Fire calls, which in the first weeks of the strike had fallen dramatically (because people, feeling unprotected, took greater care), began to rise again. Negotiations dragged on between the union and the authorities. Eventually, on January 15th 1978, after ten weeks, the strike ended and the brigades, nationally and in Kent, went back to work. The dispute was resolved by the men's acceptance of a 10% increase in wages, a 42-hour working week, and a promise of more money in the future; the so-called 'formula' which would put firemen on a par with the salaries of the upper quartile of skilled workers.

With the end of the industrial troubles, morale and good relationships

221

had to be built up again, Kent was fortunate in their Chief Fire Officer who, less than a year after he took command, had become trusted and respected by officers and men alike, as a man who understood the firemen's problems; and whose stated ambitions were to reconstruct good relationships, and to release the latent abilities of the Kent Fire Brigade to their full potential. In this, Chief Officer Doyle succeeded, and his brigade suffered less and for a shorter time than many other brigades, from the aftermath of the strike.

Since the days of the volunteer fire brigades, fire-fighters have not only cared for and assisted the victims of fire and disasters, but have also looked after their own injured, maimed, and dead. Perhaps it is not surprising that, in a service that relies so heavily on team work and true comradeship, a great organisation was built up to give real and unqualified assistance to the men and their dependants who had suffered, sometimes terribly, in the service of their fellow men. It was during the last war, when less than generous provisions by the government for injured fire-fighters created great hardships, that many brigades started their own benevolent funds. At first, these consisted mainly of a voluntary "whip-round" of all members of the brigade to assist the widows and families of firemen who had been killed in the 'blitzes'.

These funds were often supplemented by contributions from a grateful public, and in 1942, they were amalgamated in the National Fire Service Benevolent Fund, with special responsibilities to the orphans of firemen. After the war, this was changed to the Fire Services National Benevolent Fund, an organisation which over the years paid out millions of pounds to distressed members of the service, provided invalid chairs to maimed fire-fighters, supported widows, and greatly assisted in the education of orphans. Huge sums are raised by the brigades themselves, through highly original and inventive happenings, which outshine both in concept and income, the usual fund-raising methods of dances, raffles and jumble sales.

And, once again, the men and women of the Kent Fire Brigade were in the forefront of raising moneys for the Fund through extraordinary efforts and events which put them year after year right at the top of the first division. So impressive were their achievements that at the beginning of 1984, the Fund's Honorary Secretary, Mr George Pollock, wrote to Chief Officer Doyle telling him that from 1968 to 1983, Kent had raised £306,313. The amount for 1983 alone was £54,362, a magnificent sum, states Mr Pollock in his letter, "which exceeds by a staggering £18,570 any contribution made by a single brigade in the past".

While not ignoring the more conventional fund-raising activities such as collecting-boxes, draws, dances, waste-paper collections, bingo and jumble sales, the Kent firemen dreamt up such a variety of original schemes that earned them, from the public, the nickname of the "Crazy Gang with the golden hearts". They went on 1,000-mile rides through Britain on a bicycle made for two, pushed a crazy-looking four-man scooter from Dover to Edinburgh; rowed a boat from Deal to France; took part in the London and other marathons; participated in the Royal Tournament; staged their own pantomime; pushed prams with uniformed firemen in them for many miles; pulled old fire engines half-way round the County; made parachute jumps; swam in relays across the Channel; went carol-singing; and organised fashion shows, auctions, firework displays, pram and raft races; and played Santas in Christmas grottos.

During 1979 a new national duty system for wholetime firemen, the "42 hour week", was introduced into the British Fire Service and a new establishment scheme had to be prepared for the Kent Fire Brigade. This provided for a 4th shift on each whole-time station with a consequent increase in the number of personnel. At the same time, the County Fire Officer commissioned a comprehensive analysis of the standards of fire cover in the County in order to determine the future needs of the Brigade. This highlighted one of Kent's unique features in the very extensive seaboard, which prevented reinforcements being brought in quickly from adjoining brigades outside Kent in the event of large fires. Because of this disadvantage, Kent required to support itself and therefore needed more fire stations than would be the case in most other county brigades.

Meanwhile, fires and special services continued to rise, with nearly 14,000 in the year 1979/80. A completely airborne operation in November 1978 tested the co-operation between the Kent Fire Brigade, the R.A.F. and the Coastguards, when a Swedish vessel was on fire in the Channel, about 19 miles south of Dungeness.

The call came from the Straits of Dover Coastguard Control at 0606 hours on November 7th, the predetermined action was initiated – plans which have been used operationally and practised over many years in close co-operation with the R.A.F. Search and Rescue Flight, R.A.F. Manston, H.M. Coastguard and sea-going boat operators all round the Kent coast.

Because of the distances involved, it was decided to use airborne transport only. An officer and two men were flown to the ship by helicopter with predetermined fire-fighting equipment – e.g. breathing apparatus, light pump, etc. – to carry out a reconnaissance.

On arrival, it was found that the vessel involved was the 5,000 ton *Birkaland* en route from Israel to Hälsingborg, Sweden, laden with general cargo, citrus fruit, timber and containers. It was found that a severe fire had occurred in the engine room and, by conducted heat, had spread to the captain's quarters and the cargo in No. 4 hold.

The engine room had been flooded with CO_2, completely using up the supply carried on the ship. Since the fire had affected both the ship's main engines and its auxiliary engines, the ship's fire-fighting pumps were inoperative.

Following the officer's initial reconnaissance, a message was received

Fig. 24. A fireman being lowered onto the deck of the MV *Birkaland*.

at Brigade Control requesting 12 Proto breathing apparatus wearers, high expansion foam unit and ancillary equipment – all sent on by helicopter.

The breathing apparatus crews entered the captain's quarters and dealt with incipient fires in this area and, despite intense heat and very smoky conditions, breathing apparatus crews entered No. 4 hold via two entry points.

The main fire in No. 4 hold involved a cargo of timber boards. The freeboard of the vessel necessitated the use of the companionway which had to be manhandled by crew and firemen over the side to be used as a pumping platform for the light pump. Due to determined efforts by personnel, a 'stop' message was sent at 1402. Crews and equipment were transported back by helicopter and the last appliances returned to home station at 1817 hours. The vessel was towed by its sister ship, *Batticland*, to Dunkirk for repairs.

In the early hours of June 14th 1979, firemen from Folkestone and Hythe had to deal with an unusual case of arson, when they were called to Peacock's Garage in Folkestone. When the first attendance arrived, they found the ground floor car showroom well alight, and immediately radioed for assistance which resulted in crews from Hythe attending. Jets were positioned at the front and sides of the building and firemen wearing breathing apparatus fought their way into the blazing showroom. There, they discovered that a petrol-soaked string had been passed from one car to another, and so on, forming a continuous fuse. Meanwhile, a stand-by crew from Dover, which had arrived to cover for the depleted Folkestone and Hythe stations, received a call to a car on fire in the centre of the town. This car, earlier stolen from opposite the Peacock Garage, had also been set on fire deliberately. Investigations revealed that both fires were started by a gang who had hoped to divert police attention, while they carried out a robbery at a local antique shop. Later, three men and a woman were convicted of arson and theft.

Rapid fire-spread and two flash-overs severely damaged the Domestic Science block of the Sheppey Comprehensive School, Minster, on April 20th 1980. Brigade Control received 50 calls to the incident, which had been started deliberately. When the first firemen arrived, they were confronted by a severe fire situation and pumps were rapidly increased to four, then six, and finally eight. Officers found that a window on the ground floor had been broken and was fully open. This and a separate fire in an office, led them to suspect arson. Flames, fed by highly combustible materials, spread rapidly through the block, and within minutes of the arrival of the first fire-fighters, the blaze had grown to such an extent that two flash-overs at either end of the building, spread the flames to the whole of the first floor. Shortly afterwards, the roof collapsed, injuring two firemen who had to be taken to hospital by ambulance. It took over five hours before the fire had been brought under control and the last appliances withdrawn.

Two of the major mistakes one can make with fire is to smoke in bed, and then spread the flames by trying to fight the flames oneself, instead of calling the brigade at once. Such mistakes were made by a Margate flat tenant which resulted in him having to be rescued, unconscious and badly burnt, and five other people (including a police officer), being trapped in the four-storey building, also having to be brought down by fire brigade ladders to safety. At 0328 hours on July 17th 1980, a patrolling police officer saw smoke coming from the first floor flat of 17, Hawley Street, Margate. He immediately called the brigade and six appliances (including a turntable ladder) attended from Margate and Thanet. On arrival, they were told that several persons (including a police officer) were still in the smoke-logged building, and two firemen, wearing breathing apparatus, immediately went in to search for them. In the kitchen of the first floor flat, they found the occupier, a Mr Bishop, lying unconscious near the sink. It appeared that some time before, he had been awakened by the smell of smoke and saw some flames in the corner of his bedroom. He crawled along the floor to a sink, wetted some towels, and put them on the fire. This was unsuccessful, so he went back to the sink to fill a bucket with water, but at this point, he was overcome by smoke and collapsed.

Meanwhile, the occupants of the second floor flat, a Mr and Mrs Sayer, smelt the burning and rushed downstairs, and into the street. Mrs Sayer and a policeman went back into the building to waken Mr Bishop and the occupier of the third floor flat, a Mrs Wood. Unable to rouse Mr Bishop or Mrs Wood, Mrs Sayer returned to her own flat to dress. By this time, the policeman had arrived on the third floor where he was cut off by thick smoke. He and Mrs Wood took refuge in her flat while Mrs Sayer was trapped on the second floor. She was rescued by ladder and Mrs Wood and the policeman were brought down from the third floor by turntable ladder. The fire originated in a bed in the kitchen of Mr Bishop's flat and the 71-year-old man later agreed that he had smoked in bed.

A fault in an electrical circuit caused a fire that severely damaged the three-storey building of the National Westminster Bank in Swan Street, West Malling, in October 1980. Fire-fighters from three Kent stations with six appliances, including an emergency tender, fought the blaze for over four hours, and succeeded in preventing serious fire-spread to nearby properties, although houses on either side of the burning bank were damaged.

In the years 1980/81, the equipment, training and fire cover of the Kent Fire Brigade were reviewed, and as a result, 58 new fire appliances were purchased. These appliances, designed to replace the ageing Brigade fleet, were of the most modern design, and included a skid check; a crew safety cab; power steering and automatic transmission. The Brigade was also re-equipped with compressed air breathing apparatus, airline equipment and protective clothing against chemicals. At this time, Kent also re-introduced the Junior Fire-Fighter Course with 16 young men recruited at the age of 16.

The year 1981 began with a series of major fires and the trend for four, five and six pump alarms continued throughout the year. Thus, in January, the Brigade attended fires with six pumps at a dutch barn in Fawkham Green; five pumps in the Dartford Tunnel; five pumps at a warehouse in Sittingbourne; five pumps at a school in Sevenoaks and at a large house in Longfields; four pumps at Lydd army camp; four pumps at a hotel in Barham and at a private house in Norton where a woman died and a small girl suffered severe burns; four pumps at the Nurses' Home of the Kent and Sussex Hospital, Tunbridge Wells; and in 44 incidents during the month, breathing apparatus had to be worn.

Firemen from seven stations narrowly averted a disaster when fire broke out in a chemical storage tank at the ICI Plant Protection Unit in Yalding on August 2nd 1981. On arrival, the brigade found one tank, containing highly flammable solvent, well alight. With the immediate danger of the flames spreading to surrounding tanks and nearby

Fig. 26. Elephants watch with interest – and with trepidation – as fire engulfs their foodstore at Howlett's Zoo, Canterbury, in June 1981.

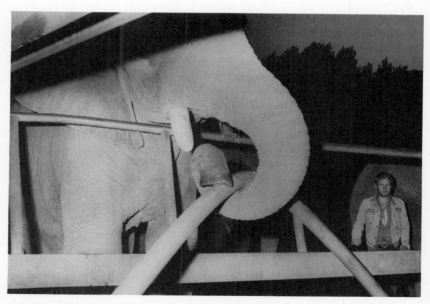

Fig. 27. "Make trunks 1" – an elephant assists the firemen by holding a hose in position.

buildings, a major alert was declared, and men and machines from Maidstone, Paddock Wood, Marden, Tonbridge, Matfield, Larkfield, Canterbury and Strood raced to the scene. Even the London Fire Brigade became involved, sending a foam-tender to stand by at a Kent station. Because solvents were ablaze, water could only be used for cooling surrounding tanks, and the main blaze had to be tackled with foam and light water. Special equipment, too, had to be used, with three heavy-duty ground monitors and five cooling jets preventing the heat and flames igniting the other tanks. Off-duty senior officers were informed and rushed to the fire while more special appliances arrived at Yalding. Eventually, Assistant Chief Officer Edmonds took charge of the fire. It took over two hours to bring the blaze under control, but although there was heat damage to surrounding tanks and pipework, the efforts of the fire-fighters had prevented a major disaster at the high-risk ICI plant.

Later in August, the Claremont School in Tunbridge Wells was wrecked in a night-time fire which was believed to have been caused by arson. Men and equipment were sent from Tunbridge Wells, Rusthall, Southborough, Tonbridge and Maidstone, and the London Salvage Corps was also on the scene. The large two-storey school was severely damaged by fire and collapse.

Once again an electrical fault caused a fire which badly damaged the Nayland Rock Hotel and private flats above it, in the Royal Crescent, Margate. During the morning of February 2nd 1982, the Brigade received a call to the hotel, and when the first appliances arrived, the officer in charge was told that a number of persons were still in the smoke-filled building. Concerned about the possibility of a heavy loss of life, a major alert was put into operation, and men and machines from Margate, Thanet, Ramsgate, Westgate, Herne Bay, Deal, Whitstable, Canterbury, Folkestone, Dover and Sittingbourne converged on Margate. Eventually, there were 20 appliances at the scene, including two turntable ladders, a hydraulic platform, a hose-layer and two emergency tenders. Later, a unit of the London Salvage Corps arrived, having made the long journey from the capital to the coast. Fortunately, all persons in the building escaped uninjured, including four who had tried to fight the fire with an internal hose-reel, before the arrival of the Brigade. The fire was eventually put out with 16 water jets, but most of the hotel and the flats above, including the roof, were severely damaged by fire and water.

Ambulances had to be called to Sevenoaks School for Girls on March 5th 1982, when 12 girls were suffering from shock following a fire which badly damaged a wing of the school. While the girls were taken to hospital, firemen from five stations fought the blaze which destroyed six classrooms and caused water damage to five others. A major alert was in operation on May 3rd 1982, when a train full of disabled people on a day trip, ran into the buffers at Folkestone East railway station. When firemen arrived at the scene, they found the passengers and their helpers still in the damaged train, and assisted with the evacuation of some of the injured. Assistance from Dover and headquarters was dispatched, and a fleet of ambulances ordered on. Because of the position of the train, which was in a deep cutting, ambulances had to be stationed in a marshalling yard, half a mile away, and firemen had to carry the injured over the half a mile of rough ground. Other passengers, suffering from cuts and shock, were given first aid on the spot.

A call from Margate police to the Brigade on July 15th 1982, informing them of a broken liquid gas cylinder at Tivoli Park, resulted in a dangerous and complicated chemical incident which involved five fire stations, the London Fire Brigade, the Environmental Health Officer, and the ICI Plant Protection Company at Yalding. The first officer to arrive at Tivoli Park was told that the broken cylinder was marked "harmful fumes" and that several people were feeling unwell. Unable to determine the exact nature of the insecticide (Metasystox 55), he asked Control for information. They, in turn, contacted the London Fire Brigade and the ICI Plant Protection Services at Yalding. As information was beginning to arrive at Headquarters, messages were flashed by radio to Margate, first ordering the men to use breathing apparatus and gloves at all times, and later to use only foam in the affected area, and to wear full protective clothing.

Meanwhile, 11 children, five firemen and two police officers, had been overcome by toxic fumes and were taken to hospital in a fleet of ambulances. By now, senior officers from headquarters had arrived at the incident and Assistant Chief Officer Ives ordered all personnel to withdraw from the area which was completely cordoned off.

An emergency team from the Department of the Environment Health Office was alerted, and the Southern Water Drainage Authority warned that the chemical spillage could enter waterways. At the same time, an expert from the Plant Protection Services at Yalding was racing to Margate with a police escort. It was four hours after the first call before the chemical emergency team confirmed that the contamination was localised, and two hours later, the all-clear was given. Appliances and men began returning to their stations, but all had to undergo a complete check for possible contamination.

Special first attendances are pre-planned for hospitals, theatres, cinemas and other public buildings, even if the precise nature of the incident is not known. It is assumed that many lives may be endangered and that extra manpower would be required to carry out rescues and to help with evacuation. Such a situation arose, when in the evening of November 17th 1982, a large timber building, used as a hospital ward, was engulfed in flames at Pembury Hospital, Pembury. The special first attendance of three pumps and a turntable ladder from Tunbridge Wells and Tonbridge were immediately mobilised, and when the first officer arrived on the scene, he was confronted by a serious fire, with patients being evacuated by hospital staff and neighbouring wards being threatened by the flames. He immediately increased the pumps to four and later, with continuing fire-spread, to seven. Following this major alarm, men and machines from seven Kent fire stations began to arrive at the hospital, and ambulances over a wide area were put on stand-by to deal with casualties. Meanwhile, the evacuation of patients continued from threatened wards and a total of 125 bedridden men and women had to be taken to safety. With fire stations in the immediate area depleted of men and machines, appliances from Sevenoaks, Maidstone and Paddock Wood had to be moved to Tunbridge Wells and Tonbridge to cover those stations. The brigade managed to confine the blaze to the one ward, but despite the use of 10 jets, it was practically destroyed. None of the patients were injured.

A frequent, and usually difficult and dangerous task of the Kent Fire Brigade has always been ship fires, especially when they occur miles out at sea. Shortly before midnight on May 24th 1983, a call was received from Dover Coastguards to a German freighter on fire, which required senior officers, firemen and equipment to be air-lifted to the scene by helicopter, and fire-fighting operations lasted for 15 hours. The vessel, MV *Roma*, had radioed a distress signal reporting a serious fire in the engine room and giving her position as four miles off Dungeness Point. Folkestone and Lydd fire stations were mobilised and crews in the charge of a divisional officer were sent to Dungeness Lifeboat Station, a possible embarkation point. Meanwhile, an Assistant Chief Officer left for the embarking point, but on receiving a message from Dover Coastguards that due to a worsening fire situation on the vessel, the Dungeness Lifeboat had been launched to stand-by, should the crew have to be taken off; the officer requested further appliances from Dover, Deal and Folkestone to rendezvous at Lydd Airport.

At 0025 hours on May 25th, the helicopter arrived at Lydd, and brigade equipment packed in specially designed helicopter loading bags, was put on board. Twenty minutes later, the helicopter with the Divisional Officer on board, left for the burning ship. With the arrival of reinforcing crews, more equipment was prepared for airlift, and at 0058 hours, the Assistant Chief Officer with more equipment, flew to the scene. The two officers found a serious fire situation in the forward hold and 500 tonnes of timber stacked on the steel deck was alight through radiated heat. This fire had already been attacked by the ship's crew with two jets from the vessel's fire main. At this stage, a message was relayed to the shore for two fire-fighting crews to be lifted by helicopter to the ship to try and contain fire-spread. The extra firemen arrived at 0147 hours, fought the fire in the timber stacks and cooled down the red-hot deck plates. However, the fire in the hold, which had been "battened

Fig. 25. Firemen, wearing lifejackets, cooling down the deck of MV *Roma*.

down" because the timber on deck prevented entry, was still spreading, and it became obvious that fire-fighting would have to be carried out in a harbour. But when requested, neither Folkestone (the nearest harbour) nor Dover Harbour boards would accept the vessel. After assurances were given that there was no immediate danger of the vessel sinking, permission was received for the ship to proceed to the outer part of Dover Harbour.

Arrangements were made for a crane to be available to off-load the deck cargo, and appliances and men were sent to the port to extinguish the hold fire. The vessel, with its firemen still on board keeping the flames under control, finally docked at 0351 hours, and four hours later, the top cargo of timber was removed. Pumps were increased, and at 1000 hours, the hatch covers were removed. Faced with a severe fire in the forward hold, the crews had to remove blazing fibreboard and timber and extinguish it on the quayside. It took nearly another five hours before the tired men could return to their stations after what was one of the most difficult ship fires for years.

Despite the efforts of fire-fighters from ten Kent Fire Stations, the old Tudor House Hotel at Bearsted was nearly destroyed in a fire during the early morning of July 16th 1983. When the first crews arrived at the scene, the range of one and two-storey buildings was well alight. Radio messages for assistance quickly followed each other, until ten appliances, including turntable ladders, a hose-laying lorry and an emergency tender, had arrived on the scene from as far away as Medway and Strood. A request was sent to the Water Board to increase the pressure of water in the area, but because of the long dry spell, all valves were already fully open. With thousands of gallons of water being poured every minute into the blazing building, extra supplies were required and the hose-layer was used to lay lines to a pond over a quarter of a mile away. The fire was brought under control after two hours, with ten jets and one monitor, but over 75% of the hotel was destroyed in the blaze.

Seven members of an Asian family died in a fire and explosion in the early hours of November 6th 1983, in Arthur Street, Gravesend, when equipment and solvents in an illicit shoe-making business below their flat, blew up. The first of many calls was received by Brigade Control at 0040 hours, and the first attendance with a sub-officer in charge arrived at the scene three minutes later. They were confronted by an appalling sight. The two-storey terraced building was well alight, with flames billowing from every opening and through the roof. Following the explosion, part of the building had already collapsed, and five other houses were damaged by heat and fire or by the force of the explosion. Immediately in front of the property was a blazing minibus with a man, who had earlier jumped, on fire, from a window, trapped underneath. More pumps were immediately ordered on by radio and further reinforcements brought a total of eight appliances to the scene. The first crews were deployed to try to release the man under the minibus, and breathing apparatus crews searched adjoining properties to ensure they were clear of residents and to prevent fire-spread.

Although it was known that people were trapped in the inferno, it was not possible to enter the house immediately due to the intense heat and flames. Jets had to be stationed at the front and rear to contain the fire. Meanwhile, considerable difficulty was experienced in releasing the man under the minibus as the tyres had burst in the heat, throwing the whole weight of the vehicle on him. With the help of bystanders, the minibus was eventually physically lifted from the casualty, who was then taken by ambulance to hospital where he died. Three firemen who had assisted in the rescue themselves received burns, and had to be taken to hospital for treatment. Despite the extremely dangerous state of the building, with rear walls and several floors collapsed, firemen began a search of the debris when it was established that at least six persons were still missing.

On the arrival of the Deputy Chief Officer, a turntable ladder was requested, and arrangements were made for a heavy crane to attend to assist with rendering dangerous parts of the building safe. Gas and Electricity Board teams were also alerted, as was the Borough Building Surveyor. Shortly afterwards, the County Chief Officer arrived to take overall command. Despite the hazardous conditions, crews continued to search for victims and at 0215 hours four bodies were found under the debris at ground floor level (onto which the first floor had collapsed) and at 0320 hours a further body was uncovered in the same area. Search for further victims continued throughout the night and the last body was found shortly before 0800 hours. The victims, one man, three women and three small children, all of the same family, were living in a first-floor flat above the workshop.

The property was previously used as a Licensed Public House but had recently been used at basement/ground floor level (without planning permission) for the manufacture of shoes involving, amongst other things, the use of flammable adhesives and solvents.

On August 23rd 1983, the property was inspected by the Fire Brigade following notification from the Planning Authority that the premises had not been given formal consent for the use to which it was then being put. After discussions with the occupier of the workshop, it was agreed by him that only one day's supply of adhesives would be kept in the basement, and oral advice was given to him regarding the general risks inherent in the undertaking. A further inspection was made on August 25th 1983 by the Brigade, in company with the District Petroleum Officer and an inspector from the Health and Safety Executive.

The Spring of 1984 saw another period of very warm and dry weather, and Kent fire-fighters had to deal with the usual crop of grass and woodland fires. Calls increased, and in some areas of the County, the

Brigade was fully stretched. Then, during the morning of May 11th, Control received a call from Bowaters Kemsley Mill near Sittingbourne, asking for immediate assistance, as their works' brigade was fighting a serious fire amongst bales of waste paper. When the first attendance of four pumps, a hose-layer, and a hydraulic platform arrived at the 30-hectares site, large stacks of paper were burning fiercely and a strong wind was carrying flaming brands to adjacent stocks. Thick smoke, kept to ground level by the wind, blanketed the whole area, and the extent of the ground made an assessment of the fire situation very difficult.

The first officer to arrive on the scene immediately sent back a message to "make pumps six". Jets were brought into operation; the hose-layer provided the first water relay; and the hydraulic platform was extended to its full height to allow for a better assessment of the fire situation. With the flames rapidly spreading across the whole of the waste paper area, pumps were increased to ten, and shortly afterwards, the Divisional Commander further increased appliances to 15 pumps, and asked for another two hose-layers to be sent to the Mill.

Thick smoke drifted over a wide area, seeped into houses and forced residents to close doors and windows. Burning paper, scattered by the wind, set fire to undergrowth, and men and pumps had to be diverted to cover the flanks of the fire. Officers were concerned that a shift in the direction of the wind could further spread the flames, but a specially-requested weather report relayed to the fire ground, indicated that the easterly wind, with a strength of up to 40 knots, was unlikely to change. At the height of the blaze, 14 jets, six hose-reel jets and two water-relays were in use, but it took 20 hours of difficult fire-fighting before the flames were finally put out during the morning of May 12th. Even then, turning over and damping down the smouldering paper stacks took another 24 hours before the Brigade could leave the Mill. Approximately 1,500 tonnes of baled waste paper were destroyed in the blaze.

Since 1963, when the Federation of British Fire Organisations was formed to promote international and national conferences and exhibitions, members of the Kent Fire Brigade played a prominent part in its development and success. The first chairman of the Federation was Lt.-Comdr. J. H. Fordham, County Fire Officer from 1948 to 1966, and for many years, Chief Officer Doyle acted first as General Secretary and then as a member of the Management Committee. In 1965, the Federation organised its first international conference and exhibition at Olympia, in London, when speakers and delegates from 43 countries took part. Visits to conferences and events in Europe and overseas followed, and once again, Kent, with its proximity to the Continent, often played host to representatives from France, Belgium, Holland and Germany. Kent Brigade members in turn travelled widely to visit their colleagues in Europe. The Federation's second international conference was held in 1975, again at Olympia. This was also the venue of the Symposium of the C.T.I.F. (an international fire organisation comprising nearly 40 countries in Europe and Overseas) which the U.K. had joined.

Membership of the E.E.C., new developments in fire-fighting techniques and equipment, and mounting fire losses throughout the world, made international co-operation and exchange of ideas more and more important and as a result, the Federation began to organise their next conference and exhibition.

Held at the National Exhibition Centre, Birmingham, it proved to be the Federation's biggest success yet. Speakers from Europe, North and Central America, Asia, and even China, covered a wide area of subjects on fire technology from research and safety in buildings to the fire service role in changing world conditions. One of the highlights of the many social events during the Conference was a luncheon given by the Chief and Assistant Chief Fire Officers Association, at which H.R.H. Princess Anne was the principal guest. She was received and entertained by Kent's Chief Fire Officer, Mr R. Doyle, who was the Chiefs' Association's President during the year 1983/84. The Exhibition, where many manufacturers from home and abroad showed the latest fire-fighting and fire-protection equipment, was also opened by Princess Anne, and together with Chief Officer Doyle, she visited the stand of the Kent Fire Brigade which showed to the world Kent's achievements in the fight against fire.

Chief Officer Reginald Doyle, who had been in command of the Kent Fire Brigade since 1977, retired in June 1984. His place was taken by Mr Garry Whitworth F.I.Fire.E., F.B.I.M., who had been Deputy Chief Officer since January 1979. Chief Officer Whitworth joined the Fire Service in 1958 in Cambridgeshire, and from 1965–1969 held an appointment as Station Officer with Cambridgeshire and Isle of Ely Fire Brigade. He quickly rose through the ranks and during five years service with the West Sussex Fire Brigade he was promoted to Senior Divisional Officer. From 1975, until his appointment as Deputy Chief Officer of Kent, he was an Assistant Chief Officer with the Surrey Fire Brigade. Before joining the Fire Service, he spent three years in the Army, serving in Korea, Japan, Singapore and Malaya. Chief Officer Whitworth is the Vice President of the British Fire Services Association, a National Council Member of the Institution of Fire Engineers and Chairman of the local Fire Services Examinations Board.

'Semper Paratus'

Fire-fighters in Kent have come a long way from the early days when fires were fought by volunteers with hand syringes, buckets and manual pumps. The era of the small proud parish and Insurance Brigades has passed, and the steamers and early motor pumps with their solid tyres have found their way to the Museum. Gone are the bucket brigades, the colourful uniforms, the brass helmets and the hand-wheeled escape ladders. No doubt, however, even today's magnificent all-purpose fire pumps will be the laughing stock in future generations when computer controlled automated firemen have been developed.

But before this happens, let us take a look at the present-day Kent Fire Brigade which has all the latest equipment designed to deal effectively with rescues, fires and other emergencies of all descriptions. From the fires which occur in a nuclear powered station or submarine, to attending a distressed ship on fire in the English Channel, the fireman needs to know "a thousand and one" things.

The fully qualified fireman of today is a skilled technician, occupied in using the most modern equipment, methods and techniques to undertake the full range of fire-fighting, rescue, road accidents, other emergencies and fire prevention work with which the Fire Service is called upon to deal. His working life and training is geared to responding at top speed to emergency calls, regardless of weather conditions or the time of day or night. Each time the fireman is called to an emergency he must be prepared to deploy each and every skill in which he has been trained. When he arrives at an incident as part of a team under the command of a Sub-Officer or Leading Fireman, he may have to absorb a great deal of information rapidly and apply the skills he has learnt in conditions which will often be extremely dangerous and confusing. Despite his preparation for such incidents by his training, he will, from time to time, be faced with new situations where only he can provide the answer, using his previous experience as a guide. A fireman wearing breathing apparatus feeling his way in a smoke-filled building with toxic hazards, in order to effect a rescue, cannot ask for instructions. In order for him to function effectively in emergencies, a fireman's pre-eminent characteristics must be those of courage; general physical strength and the capacity for rapid, intense and sustained effort; an unquestioning acceptance of orders at emergencies combined with the capacity of initiative when on his own; the skilled technician's complete and automatic familiarity with the equipment he uses (which may range up to major items of plant such as turntable ladders); the practical understanding of the basics of a wider range of subjects which will enable him to anticipate or overcome hazards; and sympathy towards the victims of emergencies, combined with the ability to carry on in what may occasionally be emotionally harrowing circumstances. Outside his

236

attendances at emergencies, the fireman has an important role in the prevention of fire both through the inspection of premises, in accordance with legislation, and through inspection of equipment external to the fire station, e.g. hydrants, open water supplies, dry and wet risers, fireman's lifts which may be used in an emergency situation.

To enter the Fire Service today, both whole-time and part-time applicants must pass tests designed to indicate levels of literacy, numeracy and general intelligence. Furthermore, the applicant must meet laid down physical requirements for his height, chest and strength, and satisfy a medical practitioner as to his general good health and his potential to maintain minimum fitness standards for a period of 30 years. All applicants are assessed by personal interview and by testimonials, for the necessary characteristics of honesty, reliability, courage, initiative and practical application, and as to whether he has the capability to learn and go on learning new and technical subjects, and achieve acceptable performance levels.

The whole-time fireman is required to attend for a period of 14 weeks a Residential Recruit Training Course which in Kent is carried out at the Brigade Training Centre. Discipline standards are deliberately high to ensure that those who qualify will respond to instructions in later (emergency) situations without question. The Fire Service is a uniformed discipline service and "discipline regulations" ensure that appropriate standards are maintained. Part-time retained applicants to the Service undergo an initial Recruit Course consisting of 6 hours instruction on his own station and 2 days instruction at another station. After satisfactorily taking a "ride to fires" test, the retained fireman continues his training at station level, attending for an average of 2 hours each week for drills, exercises and continuation training. All firemen are on probation for a period of 2 years and during this time must satisfactorily pass three tests including qualifying as a breathing apparatus wearer before their appointments are confirmed.

Probationary firemen are expected to spend their own time in studying the Manuals of Firemanship and other technical literature in order to advance their knowledge on a wide range of subjects, including building construction, electricity, chemicals, hydraulics, practical firemanship, communications, fire service pumps and other equipment, and many more. Whole-time firemen are not deemed fully 'qualified' until they have served a total of four years and successfully completed a prescribed training module for each of those years. The modules, in addition to providing the fireman with a comprehensive technical knowledge, ensure that he acquires certain skills and practical qualifications, including pump operation, driving (HGV in some cases), special appliance operation, breathing apparatus wearing, first aid and fire prevention.

A whole-time fireman spends part of every normal working shift on training; participating in practical drills involving ladders and hose;

237

practising skills with equipment and lines; and listening to lectures on the various operational procedures. In addition, he practises techniques and procedures for dealing with special types of incident e.g. in sewers, lifts or motorways, involving spillages or gas escapes, radioactive substances, etc. From time to time he will attend a certain amount of time on programme learning and other private studies. The United Kingdom Fire Service is based on a single-tier entry system, thus, all Officers, including Chief Fire Officers, must at some time start their career in the rank of whole-time fireman.

During the modern fireman's career he may be required to attend major fires in factories, oil storage and large commercial premises, as well as fires which present specific and unusual hazards such as dangerous substances, toxic gases and even radiation. The greater proportion of his turn-outs, however, will be to smaller fires in dwelling houses.

The modern fireman, with his specialist training and equipment for all kinds of emergency, inevitably plays a much more important major role today at numerous types of incident which do not involve fire. These incidents which are referred to by firemen as "special services" range from major disasters like the Moorgate Tube Crash, down through motorway pile-ups, persons trapped in machinery, lifts, wells, etc., and in fact, any incident where anyone is either trapped or at risk. In road accident cases, for instance, which often happen in extreme conditions of weather, the fireman must arrive at the incident as speedily as possible in the same adverse conditions. He can be expected to use modern cutting gear including cold cutting equipment, hydraulic rescue equipment, winches, pulleys, jacks and a variety of other rescue tools including power-saws and specialist lighting equipment. Where tankers carrying chemicals are concerned he must be capable of identifying the nature of the chemical and use the correct materials to contain or dilute the load. He must be capable of donning special chemical protective gas-tight suits and be able to decontaminate himself and other persons who might have been in contact with a very dangerous substance. All of this can happen in rain, snow or fog whilst other transport may still be using the road close by.

Dealing with operational situations is an urgent business and quite often physically demanding, and exhaustion and minor injuries such as burns and lacerations are considered as 'routine'. More serious injuries are occasionally caused by collapsing structures or by firemen falling through holes and openings in smoke-logged situations. Mental stress can result from a constant subconscious knowledge that the primary purpose of being on duty is to respond instantly to emergency calls which can occur without warning at any moment.

The modern Kent Fire Brigade is one of the largest in the country, consisting of 65 Fire Stations (12 Whole-Time Shift Manned; 10 Day-

Manned Stations and 43 Part-Time Retained Stations), the current establishment of the Brigade provides for 891 whole-time men and 874 part-time retained members. The Brigade is organised into five Divisions ('A' to 'E') each commanded by a Divisional Commander.

At Brigade level, under the direction of the Chief Fire Officer are three Operational Principal Officers and one Administrative Principal Officer. The Deputy Chief Officer assumes the full responsibilities of the Chief Fire Officer in his absence, but additionally is responsible for all personnel matters (e.g. recruitment, training, promotion, discipline, commendations and awards) and Brigade standards. The Assistant Chief Officer (Operations) deals with all matters relating to operations including equipment, transport (workshops), health and safety, water supplies and Brigade Fire Control. The Assistant Chief Officer (Technical) is responsible for all premises matters, fire prevention and fire investigation reports and press relations. The Principal Administrative Officer has responsibility for all administrative and technical support services and for ensuring reports are prepared for the Fire and Public Protection Committee. At Brigade Headquarters there are four uniformed specialist sections including Fire Staff, Fire Prevention, Training and Brigade Fire Control and Communications.

The Brigade Headquarters Fire Prevention Section co-ordinates inspection policy and prepares advice on major projects maintaining liaison with other County Council Departments, Local Authorities, Justices' Clerks, Officers of the Health and Safety Executive and similar organisations necessary in connection with the fire prevention responsibilities of the Brigade.

The Brigade Fire Control in Kent is being completely re-equipped and re-housed to provide the most modern facilities in the country. Work on the construction of the New Command and Control Centre is now complete and changeover from the old Fire Control to the new Control took place in September 1984. The new Command and Control Centre will employ the very latest technology and will provide a fully integrated computer-based communications and mobilising system.

The new computer-based system will cut seconds off the receipt and handling of calls and the response of stations to emergency incidents will be even faster. The new Control will incorporate a fully automated display map designed by the Brigade. The map will display electronically information held in the computer showing the total resources of the Brigade and also indicate the availability of all officers and their locations. The data bank programmed into the new Control computer includes details of all known addresses in the whole of Kent County, known special risks, the nearest water supplies and hydrants together with the nearest location of pumping appliances and specialist vehicles to each address given. In future it will also be possible for all operational statistics to be produced automatically by the computer.

239

KENT FIRE BRIGADE
ROLL OF HONOUR

MEMBERS COMMENDED BY HM THE QUEEN FOR GALLANTRY	MEMBERS RECEIVING THE QUEEN'S HONOURS	MEMBERS WHO GAVE THEIR LIVES IN THE EXECUTION OF DUTY
1953 Stn O F. A. F. Chambers, Gravesend	1950 Sub O R. Parsons, B.E.M., Ramsgate	5.9.49 Ret Fm A. C. Young, St Margarets
Sub O C. W. Horton, Herne Bay	1951 Ret Stn O C. Petley, Q.F.S.M., Wingham	29.11.57 ADO L. A. Pearce, "C" Div H.Q.
Ret Sub O J. W. Witherden, Cliffe	1952 DO F. L. Murrell, M.B.E.	Ret Fm A. E. Farrow, Loose
1962 LFm M. Young, Dover	1953 Stn O L. G. Wicham, B.E.M., Sheerness	Ret Fm J. A. Hawkes, Loose
1965 Fm J. A. B. Brain, Medway	1955 DCO T. B. Goodman, M.B.E., Headquarters	11.5.65 Ret LFm R. Deveson, Eastry
1968 Fm H. Myers, Strood	Sub O W. L. E. Tunstall, B.E.M., Erith	2.9.70 Ret Fm M. Farrow, Maidstone
Fm R. F. Boulstridge, Strood	LFm W. J. Way, B.E.M., Erith	14.5.72 Ret Sub O C. S. Homeward, Maidstone
1978 LFm J. Sharp, Dover	Fm T. A. Graves, B.E.M., Erith	9.1.73 Fm N. McCulloch, Medway
Fm J. W. Hogben, Dover	1958 DCO L. G. Bridgman, Q.F.S.M., Headquarters	8.11.74 Fm R. J. Bell, Medway
Fm K. J. Fairchild, Dover	1964 DCO L. G. Bridgman, M.B.E., (Q.F.S.M.), Headquarters	Fm D. J. Holley, Medway
Fm D. Dadd, Dover	1965 Aux DO J. B. Forster, M.B.E.	24.3.76 Ret Fm W. H. C. Rayfield, Cliffe
	1966 Fm B. J. Shoveller, B.E.M., Sittingbourne	27.3.77 LFm J. Sharp, Dover
	1967 CO J. H. Fordham, (C.B.E.), Q.F.S.M., Headquarters	6.8.80 LFm R. Chapman, Tonbridge
	AGO N. I. Bratchell, B.E.M., Headquarters	
	1969 CO W. Babington, Q.F.S.M., Headquarters	
	1972 CO W. Babington, C.B.E., (Q.F.S.M.), Headquarters	
	1980 CO R. D. H. Doyle, C.B.E., Headquarters	
	1981 FCO S. Wain, M.B.E., Headquarters	
	1982 Sub O P. New, B.E.M., Dartford	

NOTE

Fm = Fireman
Ret. Fm = Retained fireman
LFm = Leading fireman
Sub O = Sub Officer
Ret. Sub O = Retained Sub Officer

Stn O = Station Officer
Ret. Stn O = Retained Station Officer
ADO = Assistant Divisional Officer
DO = Divisional Officer
DCO = Deputy Chief Officer

CO = Chief Officer
AGO = Assistant Group Officer
FCO = Fire Control Officer

240

Breakdown of Calls Received

Year	Fires	Chimney	FAGI[1]	FAM[2]	Special Services	Total
1948/49	2,414	1,892	441	283	462	5,492
1949/50	7,252	2,400	551	239	282	10,724
1950/51	5,020	2,658	424	236	260	8,598
1951/52	5,260	2,771	516	303	334	9,184
1952/53	7,875	3,643	673	321	439	12,951
1953/54	6,431	3,314	530	280	337	10,892
1954/55	6,529	3,405	586	307	359	11,186
1955/56	7,882	3,321	705	235	472	12,615
1956/57	6,306	2,716	556	273	384	10,235
1957/58	8,517	3,524	690	289	335	13,355
1958/59	6,570	3,263	631	346	460	11,270
1959/60	12,303	3,018	932	453	294	17,000
1960/61	6,902	3,184	683	506	655	11,930
1961/62	9,253	3,679	970	611	463	14,976
1962/63	9,342	4,420	909	824	629	16,124
1963/64	7,966	3,903	974	766	575	14,184
1964/65	9,746	3,388	1,283	1,127	703	16,247
1965/66	5,965	2,553	834	766	703	10,821
1966/67	6,122	2,519	985	739	704	11,069
1967/68	7,304	2,896	1,151	946	769	13,066
1968/69	6,565	2,774	1,232	1,104	2,276	13,951
1969/70	5,034	2,525	1,411	1,077	718	10,765
1970/71	5,781	2,357	1,303	1,188	894	11,523
1971/72	5,454	2,365	1,543	1,361	1,056	11,779
1972/73	6,476	2,278	1,636	1,546	1,190	13,126
1973/74	6,683	1,746	1,789	1,359	2,074	13,651
1974/75	5,632	1,783	1,739	1,369	1,265	11,788
1975/76	3,706	1,844	1,283	799	926	8,558
1976/77	9,102	1,720	2,647	1,447	1,441	16,356
1977/78	5,191	1,788	2,280	1,523	1,250	12,032
1978/79	6,022	1,768	2,673	1,404	1,713	13,580
1979/80	6,142	1,529	2,833	1,426	1,688	13,618
1980/81	5,478	1,339	2,530	1,322	1,246	11,915
1981/82	5,589	1,539	2,811	1,385	1,444	12,768
1982/83	6,016	1,467	3,080	1,325	1,600	13,488
1983/84	6,939	1,458	3,464	1,736	1,669	15,266

NOTE

Calls received are recorded from April 1st to March 31st the following year.

FAGI[1] – false alarms good intent.

FAM[2] – false alarms malicious.

241

Today's Appliances

A water tender/ladder showing some of the equipment carried on the appliance.

A Magirus 100-foot turntable ladder.

A display of modern fire appliances at Maidstone Fire Station.

A series of special appliances including foam tender, hose layer and emergency tender.

An EPL "Firecracker" 75-foot hydraulic platform.

246

KENT FIRE BRIGADE
Industrial & Commercial Training

Basic Fire Awareness   Breathing Apparatus   Fire Legislation

Whatever your fire training needs the KFB has the facilities and resources to meet them.

The Brigade offers both standard courses or a course tailored to meet your own specific needs.

Telephone Maidstone (0622) 54311 Ext 292 for details.

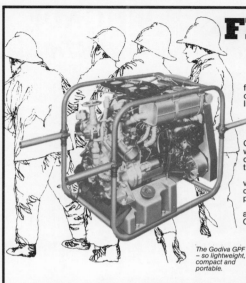

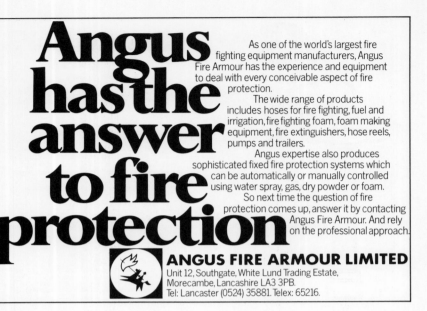

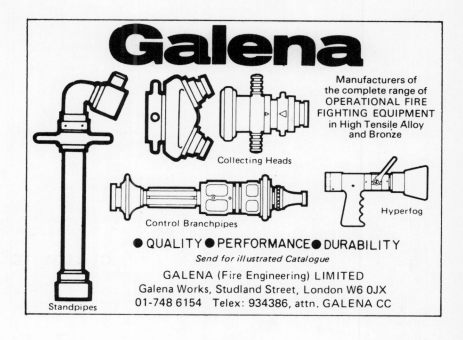
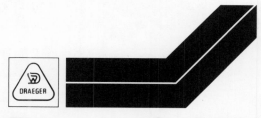
251

254